ROCK CLIMBS

of

THE SIERRA EAST SIDE

ROCK CLIMBS of THE SIERRA EAST SIDE

ALAN BARTLETT
ERRETT ALLEN

CHOCKSTONE PRESS

Denver, Colorado
1988

Published and distributed by:
Chockstone Press, Inc.
526 Franklin Street
Denver, Colorado 80218
(303) 377-1970

ISBN 0-934641-11-0

Cover photo:
Tom Herbert on Expresso Crack
by Chris Falkenstein

All uncredited photos by the authors.

TABLE OF CONTENTS

The Owens Valley didn't strike me right away as a climbing area. It looked, rather, like a desert. Wall-to-wall sage relieved only by a ragged line of willows down along the river.

At first, I passed right on through. Headed for the Palisades trailhead, Mt. Mendel, or the Whitney Group. Get on to the high country; no crag climbing around here.

But then it was also hard to see, at first, that I was at the bottom of the deepest valley in the country. Sheridan Anderson, the brilliant alpine cartoonist who I'd met in Yosemite, persuaded me to slow down and look. Got me a job hoeing thistles behind a truckstop out at the Y in Bishop. In July. I soon raised enough blisters on my hands to stop and lean on my hoe and take a look around.

There was snow on the peaks up there, ten thousand feet above. There were glaciers swimming in the heat rising off sage. High country; I'd been up there.

Then I looked below the skyline. North of town were tiers of rock walls. A band of grey granite towers, then a row of salmon-colored granite, and below that white. The outcrops of the Wheeler Crest looked modest enough – until the scale of that 7,000-foot hillside began to sink in. Galen Rowell and I had to be turned away from the Smokestack in mountain boots before the difficulty registered, too. Routes have been averaging grade IV, 5.10, and there's plenty of rock left.

Lower yet and out to the west were foothills so lumpy with granite outcrops that they looked like curdled buttermilk (no, that's not where the name came from . . .). Sheridan soon introduced me to the local cragmaster Smoke Blanchard, who ran us ragged through labyrinths of chimneys and over dozens of summits. You won't find Smoke's Rock Course in here because he's still the only one who can find all of it.

Sixty miles south the rainbow colors give way to solid white, but the cliffbands are still stacked up, from the Alabama Hills all the way to the base of Mt. Whitney. It took Fred Beckey's eye to get climbing started there. Sixty miles north there isn't even granite, but superb volcanic outcrops lie hidden in the Ponderosa forest.

In that whole expanse, that entire cliff-edged Deepest Valley, there lived at the time only one crag climber, Smoke Blanchard. That was twenty years ago. Today . . . well, here's the new guide book – see for yourself.

DOUG ROBINSON

PREFACE

The idea of a guidebook to Eastern Sierra rock climbs first occurred to me soon after I moved to Bishop in 1976. This was obviously an ego-inspired thought, since it was the first time in my climbing career that I had begun to do first ascents on a regular basis. But even then I thought that it was best to wait because I knew that there were (and still are) many fine routes to do in this region due to the vast amount of unclimbed rock. The idea was shelved indefinitely when I left the area for a few years in the early 80s, but resurfaced soon after I got back. Initially I had only intended to cover the crags with which I was most familiar, namely those close to Bishop, but during my absence a lot had gone on. New crags and routes were being discovered all around the Mammoth Lakes region (partially due to the increasing popularity of Tuolumne Meadows as a summertime hang). It seemed obvious that these areas would have to be covered since they had already become more popular than other cliffs I was intending to cover in the guidebook. Gary Slate agreed to co-author the guide book and provide the information on areas with which I was unfamiliar. Early into the project, however, work commitments forced Gary to bow out and Errett Allen agreed to pick up where Gary left off.

One of the initial decisions we had to make was exactly what to include in the guide. There was early talk about including some of the more popular backcountry areas, the Whitney region, the Palisades, and Tuttle Creek. Finally, though, we opted to limit it to those areas closest to roads, that is, areas not requiring a backpacking-type approach which would necessitate bivouac gear; with only a few exceptions, all the routes listed within this book can be easily done car-to-car in a day. Another reason for choosing not to include those backcountry areas was that they have already been covered in previous guides, however incomplete they may be now. It was not our intention to update Steve Roper's *Climber's Guide to the High Sierra* but more to open up newer crags that had never before received publicity.

The Eastern Sierra truly is a delightful place for crag climbing. Variety of rock, environment and terrain, as well as an incredibly beautiful setting, all contribute to the pleasures found here. But for me, the feeling of solitude has always been the most special attraction. There was always a feeling that this area was "ours" – the locals, that is – not so much out of a feeling of protectionism, but mainly because there were so few visits by outside climbers. Since there are no real world- class "known" routes here, no one bothered too much to make the Eastern Sierra crags a high priority on their climbing itinerary, and that was fine with us. This guide will certainly change that, but to what degree remains to be seen. It is safe to assume that a number of these crags will not see a marked increase in traffic due to their general obscurity. But the better areas will undoubtedly see more climbers, and it is hoped that those people brought to the area because of this guide will treat the area as they would their own. Remember, the degree to which the environment suffers as a result of increased use is entirely up to all of us.

The following product has been a labor of love – a lot of work at times – but great fun also. I can only hope that this guide book can help others experience, as I have, the joys that climbing in the Eastern Sierra has to offer.

Of course, this guide book would not have been possible without the help of many people. In particular, we would like to thank:

Richard Hunt, for reproduction of the photographs.

Dennis Jensen, for his map of the Peabody Boulders (no complaints about the ratings, please!)

Gary Slate, whose early work on the guide laid the groundwork for certain areas and made him a constant reference source in the final stages.

Kathy Stewart, for her two fine area overview maps.

Mike Strassman, for graciously providing topos and descriptions to areas with which we were both unfamiliar.

Katie Wilkinson, for her drawing of the Buttermilk Outcrops, as well as assistance with a variety of things, including photography, transportation, and reproduction of the text.

James Wilson, for his ecological comments.

In addition to these, the following people provided information or in some other way helped to make this a better book. John Aughinbaugh, Pat Brennan, Richard Cilley, Vern Clevenger, Scott Cole, Bob Harrington, Tom Herbert, Grant Hiskes, Dean Hobbs, Jay Jensen, Randy Jewett, David Krueger, Kevin Leary, Doug Nidever, Ron Overholtz, Kevin Powell, Tony Puppo, Alan Roberts, Doug Robinson, Joe Rousek, Galen Rowell, Bill St. Jean, Alex Schmauss, Jim Stimson, Rick Wheeler, Gordon Wiltsie, and Ken Yager.

ALAN BARTLETT

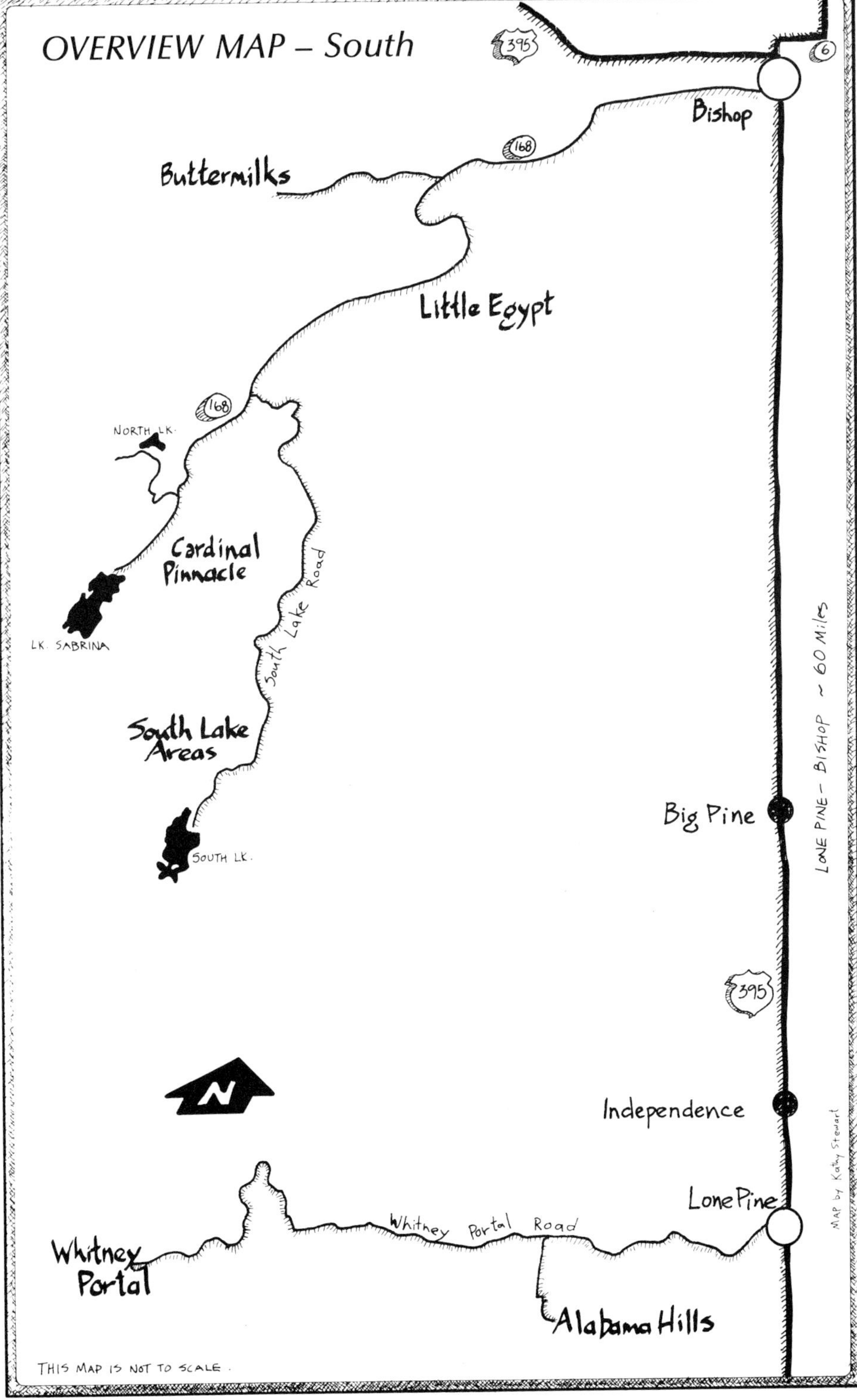
OVERVIEW MAP – South
395
6
Bishop
168
Buttermilks
Little Egypt
168
NORTH LK.
Cardinal Pinnacle
LK. SABRINA
South Lake Road
South Lake Areas
SOUTH LK.
Big Pine
LONE PINE – BISHOP ~ 60 Miles
395
N
Independence
Lone Pine
MAP by Kathy Stewart
Whitney Portal Road
Whitney Portal
Alabama Hills
THIS MAP IS NOT TO SCALE.

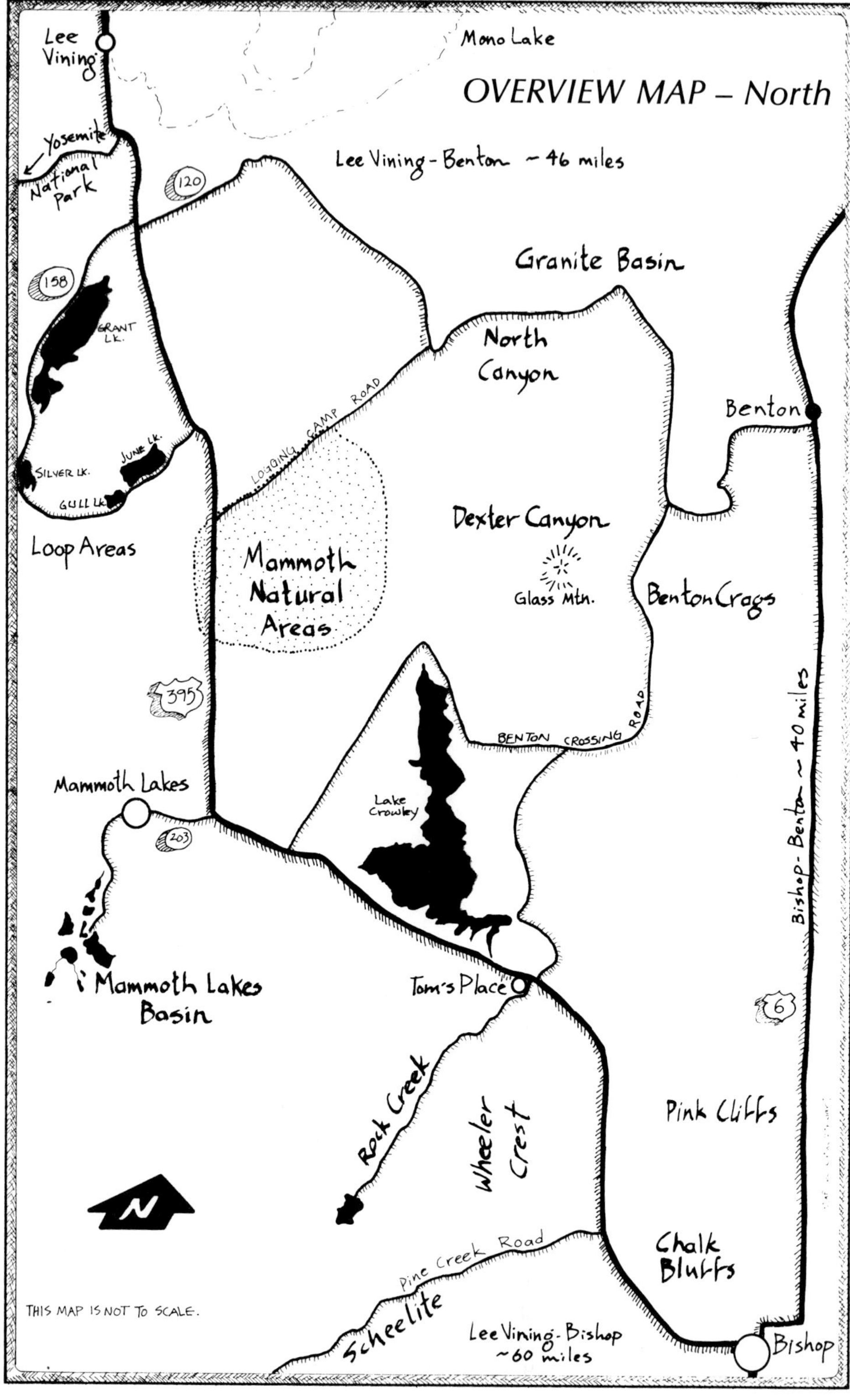

OVERVIEW MAP – North
Lee Vining
Mono Lake
Yosemite National Park
120
Lee Vining - Benton ~ 46 miles
Granite Basin
158
GRANT LK.
North Canyon
LOGGING CAMP ROAD
Benton
JUNE LK.
SILVER LK.
GULL LK.
Dexter Canyon
Loop Areas
Mammoth Natural Areas
Glass Mtn.
Benton Crags
395
BENTON CROSSING ROAD
Bishop - Benton ~ 40 miles
Mammoth Lakes
Lake Crowley
203
Mammoth Lakes Basin
Tom's Place
6
Rock Creek
Wheeler Crest
Pink Cliffs
N
Chalk Bluffs
Pine Creek Road
Scheelite
THIS MAP IS NOT TO SCALE.
Lee Vining - Bishop ~60 miles
Bishop

INTRODUCTION

Situated within view of the beautiful High Sierra, the resort towns of Inyo and Mono counties – the East Side of the Sierra – have increasingly become the home of mountaineers and climbers. This has led to the development of many climbs on short, steep rock faces that are easily approached by car. A 130-mile stretch of U.S. Highway 395 provides access to all areas covered in this book: in general, the climbing from just south of Lee Vining, east of Tioga Pass and Yosemite National Park, south to the crags west of the town of Lone Pine, at the foot of Mt. Whitney. This book does not cover mountaineering routes in the High Sierra. For information on these refer to *The Climber's Guide to the High Sierra,* a Sierra Club book by Steve Roper. The areas covered in this guide book offer a wide variety of climate and geology as well as an interesting diversity of rock groups and types of climbing. Try the slab face climbs of Whitney Portal or a steep crack in Dexter Canyon. Areas range from an elevation of 4000 feet to over 10,000 feet. One may climb in the high alpine setting of South Lake Tower, or the high desert climate of Granite Basin. Many of the lower elevation areas offer year-round sport, although this varies widely from year to year, depending on current weather conditions, winter severity and depth of snow-pack. All areas are usually accessible from May until the first heavy snowfall of winter. Generally, the areas that exist in the High Sierra offer glacially sculpted smooth granite of high quality, reminiscent of Yosemite. Whitney Portal and Cardinal Pinnacle are good examples. Several areas offer more ancient granitic rock that is very weathered and "grainy". Alabama Hills, The Buttermilks, The Benton Crags, and Granite Basin fit this catagory. Many of the areas east of Mammoth Lakes and June Lake are composed of a volcanically deposited tuff that offers excellent high angle face and crack climbing. Deadmans, The Stumps, and Dexter Canyon are typical. Almost all the routes described here have never been covered by any previous publication. Indeed, some areas are quite obscure and known only to a few locals. As many as 25 percent of the routes have never been repeated.

To reach the East Side areas, one can travel south on U.S. 395 from Reno, Nevada or north from the Los Angeles metropolitan area. From the west, take U.S. Highway 50 east from Sacramento or State Highway 88 east from Stockton and turn south on U.S. 395. Alternatively, one can take State Highway 178 east from Bakersfield and turn north on U.S. 395. Three other roads provide access from the west in summer but are closed by winter snows. These are State Highway 4 from Stockton, State Highway 108 from Modesto, and State Highway 120 from Manteca/ Yosemite. One turns south on U.S. 395 from these three roads.

All visitor services, grocery stores, and gas stations will be found in the towns of Lone Pine, Independence, Big Pine, Bishop, Mammoth Lakes, June Lake, and Lee Vining, situated along U.S. 395. The U.S. Forest Service maintains many campgrounds in this region and no climbing area is very far from one. Although some campgrounds are free, most require a fee and have self- registration forms availible at the bulletin boards near campground entrances. Please observe all posted Forest Service rules regarding use of these areas. It is also possible to camp almost anywhere within a National Forest outside of developed campgrounds; however, a wilderness permit and/or a fire permit may be required. These may be obtained at any Forest Service Visitor Center. Three U.S. Forest Service Visitors Centers exist along the East Side, one each in Lone Pine, Bishop, and Mammoth Lakes. These are very useful as sources of maps, local condition and camping information. A Forest Service map of Inyo National Forest is recommended as a useful adjunct to this guidebook. Various United States Geological Survey (USGS) maps are also availible. A list of campgrounds near the climbing areas will be found in the appendix.

CLIMBING HISTORY

Climbing has gone on in the Eastern Sierra for about as long as anywhere in the country. The trials and tribulations of Clarence King in trying to become the first person atop Mt. Whitney in the 1870s are well documented in many mountaineering histories. It is also generally accepted fact that the first use of a rope and "modern" belay techniques were practiced by Robert Underhill and a Sierra Club group on the flanks of Laurel Mountain, above Convict Lake about 1931. Soon after that, the Eastern Sierra produced one of America's most prolific climbers ever: Norman Clyde. Clyde was to do hundreds of first ascents in his lifetime, usually solo and with little or no fanfare. Archetypical of the modern climbing bum, Clyde shunned steady work and the security of a regular paycheck in favor of a more spartan existence in the Sierras. Clyde was a summiteer, however, and it was not until the 1960s that climbers began to explore the various crags along the eastern slope of the Sierras. Smoke Blanchard was one of the first of these. Like Clyde, Blanchard often climbed alone and unroped on what he called "mountain scrambles." These scrambles were often up to 5.6 in difficulty and included many summits in the Wheeler Crest and above the Scheelite Crags. Smoke was probably also the first person to explore Buttermilk Country and realize its wonderful potential. With one exception, none of Smoke's routes are listed in this book, though it is probable that he may have ascended certain routes before the credited first ascent party.

In 1967 noted first ascentionist Fred Beckey visited Whitney Portal for the first time and promptly climbed Whitney Portal Buttress, the most attractive feature there. "I couldn't believe it!" Fred later said. "Robbins, Wilts, Powell, Harding, all those guys had walked right by it on their way to Whitney or Keeler . . . they'd all seen it and no one had climbed it! A thousand foot wall a half hour from the car! I just couldn't believe it!" Within two years Fred had returned and climbed an even longer route, Bastille Buttress on Lone Pine Peak, which is the only Grade V route listed in this guide. Fred also climbed two smaller features, Premiere and El Segundo Buttresses. Characteristic of his style, he put one route on each of four features which attracted him the most, then turned his attention elsewhere, having done his climbs. It would be almost twenty years before modern climbers would "rediscover" the vast potential for quality climbing at Whitney Portal.

In the early 1960s, a climbing school was established in the Palisade region of the Sierras, attracting guides and clients alike to the Eastern Sierra. A loose-knit band of local climbers had gathered in Bishop by the end of the decade, mainly composed of guides for the Palisades School of Mountaineering. Calling themselves the "Armadillos", the core of this group was John Fischer, Jay Jensen, Doug Robinson and Gordon Wiltsie. Younger, and more espoused to the 60s ideals than their predecessors, the Armadillos and their fellow guides were the first to seek out difficult free climbs on the crags surrounding Bishop. Although their standards were slightly behind those in the more well-known rock climbing areas (standards of difficulty in the Eastern Sierra have consistently remained a few years behind the top standards of the sport), the Armadillos were the first to crack the 5.10 barrier with such classics as **Sheila, Cucumbers,** and **Crack of No Hope.** The Armadillos were not hard-core rock climbers, though, but all-around general mountaineers, and they never pursued a policy of trying to develop crags. Like Fred Beckey, they did the few most obvious lines and were content to leave it at that. It is interesting to note that two "outsiders" figured heavily in the two most famous climbs of this era: Chuck Pratt on **Pratt's Crack** and Galen Rowell on **The Smokestack.**

By the late 1970s, new groups of climbers had begun to settle in the Eastern Sierra, mostly transplants from larger urban areas who had learned to climb in a more popular and populous environment. Two distinct groups of locals formed in Bishop and Mammoth Lakes, and the pace of new routes picked up. The Bishop contingent was mainly composed of Alan Bartlett, Paul Brown, Will Crljenko, Robb Dellinger, Bob Harrington, Ron Overholtz, Allan Pietrasanta, Tony Puppo, Bill St. Jean, Kim Walker, Rick Wheeler, and James Wilson. The most active climbers centered around Mammoth were Vern Clevenger, Kevin Leary, Dennis Phillips, Joe Rousek, Jim Stimson, and Bill Taylor. This period of time saw increased activity in Bishop Creek, Pine Creek, Wheeler Crest, Rock Creek, and at Deadman Summit. Although friends, the two groups didn't intermingle a whole lot, and each group pretty much stuck to their home areas. The exception to this was Kevin Leary, one of the best free climbers in the area at the time. A thin crack specialist, Kevin firmly introduced 5.11 to Bishop with leads of **Wild Rose** (5.11A), **Artichoke Crack** (5.11B), **Cannibal** (5.11C), and the first top rope ascent of **Expresso Crack** (5.12A). Kevin also showed form in wide cracks with his ascent of **The Gong Show** (5.11C), an off-width out a large roof in Rock Creek.

In the early 80s, the scene shifted more to the north, and the climbing population in Mammoth Lakes increased rapidly. Most of these new Mammoth climbers were people who had been living in Yosemite for the previous few years and were looking for a better place to winter. This group was mainly composed of Erret Allen, Scott Cole, Bob Finn, Grant Hiskes, Gary Slate, and Ken Yager. Eager to explore, these climbers made a point of checking out the countless volcanic outcrops east of Highway 395. This led to development of the Stumps, Dexter Canyon, Benton Crags, and a wealth of new bouldering and top rope areas. As the new route activity increased near Mammoth, it dwindled in the Bishop area to such a point that it was the Mammoth climbers who were developing new routes in Buttermilk Country, the closest area to Bishop. Quietly, though, Dean Hobbs and a variety of partners were filling in lines between lines at Little Egypt, Cardinal Pinnacle and in Pine Creek and Rock Creek. Dean, unlike the other locals, had grown up in Bishop and learned to climb there. His penchant for exploration led to many fine new routes in areas other locals had either ignored or thought climbed out. Many of Dean's finest efforts came on Cardinal Pinnacle with such classics as **Wild Kingdom** (5.10C), **Romancing the Stone** (5.11C), and **Redline** (5.11D).

More climbers visted the area in the early 80s and the standards rose. Dale Bard was the best of these, and claimed the area's first 5.12 lead by freeing the third pitch of **The Prow** on Cardinal Pinnacle (the second pitch still requires aid). Dale also spent lots of time in Buttermilk Country and is responsible for most of the hardest problems in the Peabody Boulders.

As the popularity of soft-rock climbing grew in other areas of the country, so did the popularity of the Indiana Summit Natural Areas. Many climbers began to view this area as an ideal training ground for the desperate routes found at Oregon's Smith Rock and in Southern France, due to its incredible overhanging face climbs which follow holes and pockets.

In 1985, southern California climbers Kevin Powell and Darrel Hensel visited Whitney Portal. Honed on the face climbs of Joshua Tree and Suicide Rock, the pair bagged two difficult bolt- protected routes, **El Gaucho** and **No Pie Ala Mode.** Word of these leaked out to the locals who quickly went to see what the fuss was about. Instantly realizing the area's potential, the race for new routes was underway. During the mild winter of 1986-87 and into the spring, over 60 new routes went in, mostly bolted slab climbs. Chief architects of these climbs were John Aughinbaugh, Erret Allen, Alan Bartlett, Dennis Jensen, Steve Plunkett, and Gary Slate.

What of the future? Well, there are many more new routes to be done in lots of the areas. New areas will undoubtedly be found, most likely in Mono County, east of Highway 395. Lately, Mike Strassman has been exploring a lot in this region and has been instrumental in developing Granite Basin, a large but long- overlooked crag off Highway 120. In the Bishop vicinity, John Aughinbaugh and Tom Herbert have shown the most interest in seeking out new lines. One thing is sure, though; the Eastern Sierra will remain a great place to climb due to its offbeat adventuresome nature and its incredible variety.

HOW TO USE THIS BOOK

The areas are arranged in a south to north order until one reaches the June Lake area and Highway 120; then the areas are arranged from west to east along Highway 120. Generally, the routes and crags in each area are listed from left to right. Individual climbs are depicted in at least one of three formats: topos, photos, or written descriptions. A topo is a hand drawn diagram of a cliff or route that shows individual features of the routes using internationally accepted symbols. Photos of the rock formations are often included, with lines drawn in to show the routes. In instances where topos and photos are inadequate or don't exist, a written description of the route is included. Following is a key explaining the symbols used in the topos.

Key to the Topos

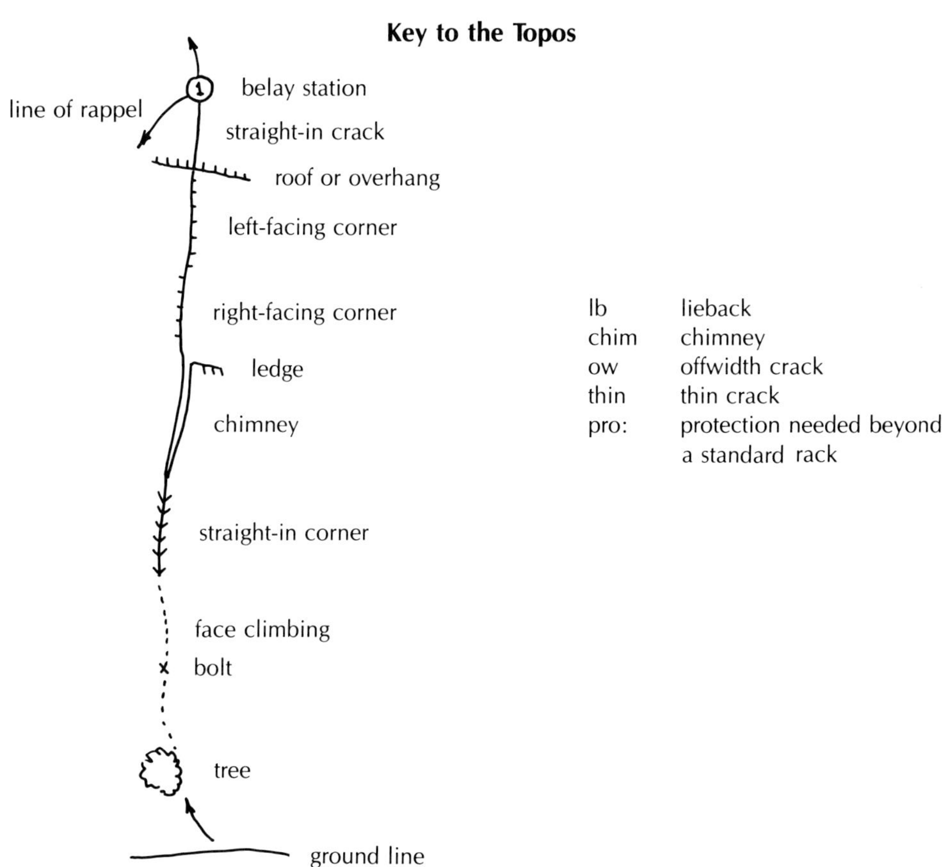

lb	lieback
chim	chimney
ow	offwidth crack
thin	thin crack
pro:	protection needed beyond a standard rack

EQUIPMENT

The hardware needed for climbing will vary widely with the individual climb. Often, if a climb requires many pieces in a particular size range, some mention of size will be made in the route description or topo. For many areas and routes, no information is given and the climber must use personal judgement. On routes that follow crack systems of unknown size, an "all purpose" rack that includes a wide variety of stopper and Friend sizes should be taken. What to take on a face climb may be more obscure. Many of the face climbs in the East Sierra have all "fixed protection". Fixed pitons and ¼-inch bolts are widely used. Both these devices should be used with caution. They may have been in place for years and the processes of natural erosion often weaken the placements, causing them to pull out without warning. A fixed piton should be tested with a few light hammer blows to determine if the placement is solid or loose. Hammer home a loose piton before relying on it! On the other hand, bolts should NEVER be hit with a hammer as this will only weaken the placement. The majority of face climbs have a mixture of "fixed" and "removable" protection and unless you know in advance that a climb has all fixed protection, it is wise to carry a selection of gear on any face climb. Many of the routes have been established in the last five years, since the advent of "modern" protection devices such as RPs, tiny Friends, and three-cam units, often called TCUs. Doing these routes without such devices may make the climber feel the protection is inadaquate. In addition, a selection of standard size stoppers and Friends should also be carried, as well as some 9⁄16-inch special slings for tying off knobs and horns. A good variety of standard slings, quick-draw slings, free carabiners and a belay seat will prove useful. Modern kernmantle ropes of 165-foot length should be considered mandatory.

RATINGS

The rating system used in this book is the open-ended Decimal system commonly used to rate free climbs in Yosemite and most other climbing areas in America today. This system long ago ceased to be a strictly "decimal" system with the advent of climbs rated 5.10 and above. The hardest routes in existence today are rated 5.14; the hardest routes in this guidebook are rated 5.12, however. Much exploration remains to be done. Also, a "Grade" rating is used, reflecting the amount of time a competent party of climbers may take to do a route. Grade ratings of I to III (½ day or less), have been omitted; any routes listed in this guide without a grade rating is Grade III or less. Grade IV will take most or all day, Grade V will take 2 days and require spending the night on the climb, and a climb with two or more bivouacs is Grade VI. Only one Grade V is listed in this book; there are no Grade VI routes. Although the East Sierra does not attract the "big wall" climber, a few routes using direct aid will be found in the book and these will also have an aid rating of A1 through A5. With aid climbing the climber uses hardware and/or the rope to support his weight, as opposed to "free" climbing, where the gear is only used as a safety system to catch a falling climber. Generally, A1 is easy to place and completely bombproof. A2 is harder to place but still very secure. A3 are placements that will only hold short falls. A4 placements will only hold body weight and A5 involves long sections of A4 placements where the climber risks taking falls of 60 feet or more. No A4 or A5 routes are known to exist along the Eastern Sierra. In addition, a simple "star" rating system is used to indicate the relative quality of a route in relation to the other routes at that area. One star indicates a recommended route. Two stars indicates a highly recommended route. Because rock quality varies widely, a two-star route at one area may rate no stars at another area.

ETHICS

A widespread and often heated debate has raged in the climbing community for many years over the varieties of style in which a route may be climbed. This is particularly true where first ascents are concerned. On one extreme are the strict traditionalists who feel that a route must always be started from the bottom and climbed completely free, using a minimum of fixed protection which detracts from the natural setting and the adventure and enjoyment of those who follow. On the other extreme are the "new wave" climbers who feel that any tactics are justified to ensure eventual success on a route. These tactics include rappelling the route first, either to preview the moves or to pre-place the protection, and top roping a shorter route many times to rehearse the moves before attempting to lead it. The use of direct aid may also be employed to place protection and fixed pieces may be placed often. Portable electric drills for quick bolt placements are becoming popular.

Without diving into this morass, the authors would like to simply state that the vast majority of routes in the East Sierra were done in the traditional style. We feel that if a route is short enough to be bolted on rappel, then it is short enough to remain as a top rope problem. We know of only two routes that were bolted on rappel and one of these was quickly removed by an indignant local. Two other routes were led using an electric drill, and one of these was also "chopped". What this 50 percent "chop rate" portends for the future of new wave tactics in the Sierra we can't predict. The one ethic almost univerally accepted is that an established lead should remain "as is", without the addition of more bolts.

CAUTION

This book is not intended as an instruction guide to the safety techniques of modern climbing. Existing in the mountain environment, rock climbing is an inherently dangerous sport. Bad weather, falling rock and other hazards exist and may be expected at any time of year. Proper precautions will minimize the impact of these hazards on the climber. Although helmets are not widely used by day-tripping rock climbers in the East Sierra, loose rock abounds at many areas and the use of a helmet may, in fact, save you from injury. Anyone using this book should be familiar with the proper use of the rope and mountaineering anchoring devices. Lacking this knowledge, prospective climbers are urged to seek competent instruction from highly experienced climbers or professional guides. The authors have attempted to make the topos and route descriptions as accurate as possible; however, inaccuracies undoubtedly exist and this should be kept in mind. Route finding is a skill that develops with experience and this guide book is no substitute for personal judgement. Route descriptions generally show the line of first ascent or the line that most climbers would go, but possible variations or escapes exist on many routes.

ENVIRONMENTAL COMMENTS

Offroad driving by climbers in search of a closer approach to the crags has begun to be seen for what it is, unnecessarily stressful on the delicate backcountry. It is easy to drive a vehicle off the existing roads in many parts of the Eastern Sierra, particularly in the Buttermilk and Deadman areas. Please drive only on established roads and park in existing spots. Local climbers are working with the Forest Service to close many of the illegal roads in these areas. Please respect road closure signs.

Besides protecting the land itself, climbers have a duty to respect the wildlife with which they, uniquely, come in contact. Predatory birds – hawks, eagles, owls, and falcons – build their nests on cliffs, sometimes the same cliffs on which we climb. Especially in spring, birds nesting on the cliffs should not be disturbed. If these birds seem alarmed, circling and crying or perhaps swooping at you, leave the area! You can do the route in the fall. If you disturb birds with young, they may abandon their nests. Besides being protected by federal law, the homes of these birds have sat sometimes for thousands of years on these cliffs and they deserve to be respected.

ALABAMA HILLS

The Alabama Hills are a vast expanse of desert granite outcrops west of the town of Lone Pine. Sort of a "poor man's Joshua Tree", there is a great deal of rock in the area; unfortunately, most of it is poor to mediocre quality. Some good rock exists, but it tends to be the exception rather than the rule. Climbing has gone on in all areas of the Alabama Hills, although there is generally little evidence of it. It seems safe to assume that most of the small pinnacles which abound throughout the area have been ascended, mostly via solo technique; potential first ascentionists should take this into consideration before breaking out the bolt kit. The routes listed here are all in one small area of the Alabama Hills known as Gunga Din. This is due to lack of information and the wish to preserve the pristine nature of the region.

To reach Gunga Din, drive west on the Whitney Portal road from the town of Lone Pine. This leaves Highway 395 at the only traffic signal in town. After about five miles, turn left on the Horseshoe Meadows road. Turn left again after about ¾ mile on a dirt road which leads slightly downhill between rock formations to a circular parking area. Five of the routes will be found on the north and east facing crags on the right. The other five routes are on the north faces of the outcrops off to the left and can be approached from here or from the Horseshoe Meadows road about ⅛ miles north of the dirt road. Other potential climbing can be found along the Tuttle Creek road or along Movie Road, and potential bouldering is everywhere. In general, the north-facing rock tends to be the best. It often forms solid plates which offer protection via slings and stoppers on faces that would otherwise require some bolting.

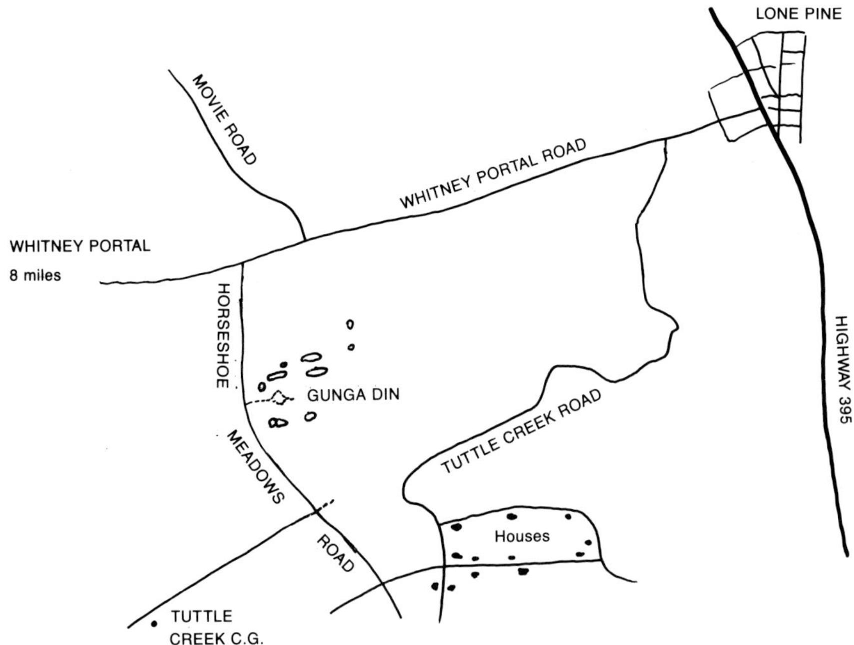

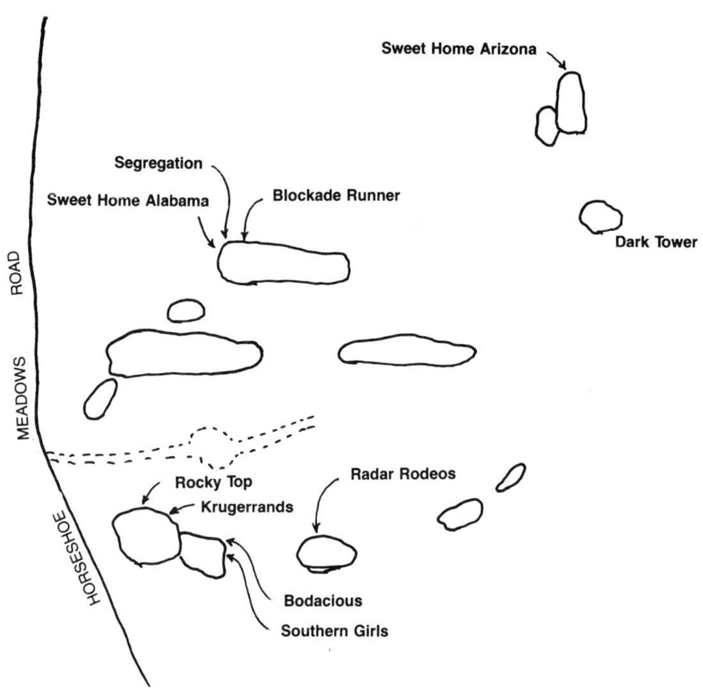

ROUTES

Krugerrands 5.8 On the highest wall to the right of the circular parking area, climb a short vertical crack to a horizontal crack. Continue up the face past a bolt to the top. The bolt was added after the first ascent.

Rocky Top 5.8 Climb the face about 30′ right of Krugerrands. No bolts; take some thin nuts and slings for tying off flakes.

Bodacious 5.9 ★ This is a 2-bolt face climb on a face down and left from the preceding routes.

Southern Girls 5.10C This climbs a thin crack about 20′ left of Bodacious. The two routes meet after 50′.

Radar Rodeos 5.8 Discontinuous thin cracks on the north face of the next formation east of the preceding four climbs.

Blockade Runner 5.10C ★★ This free climbs a bolt ladder on the north face of a formation several hundred feet north of the circular parking area.

Segregation 5.11A TR ★ The face about 20′ right of Blockade Runner and left of an outside corner.

Sweet Home Alabama 5.9 ★ Around the corner to the right of the preceding routes is this hand crack. It is the left of two cracks forming a "V".

Dark Tower 5.10A This is 2-bolt climb on the north side of a tower several hundred feet east of the previous routes. Bolts may not be good.

Sweet Home Arizona 5.8 ★★ Another 2-bolt climb on the north side of the tower north of Dark Tower. Excellent rock.

WHITNEY PORTAL

Many of the best routes in the East Sierra will be found at Whitney Portal. The longest route and only Grade V in the guide is here, as well as many enjoyable two to ten-pitch face climbs. An occasional classic clean crack and beautiful views of Mount Whitney and the Owens Valley round out the menu. Although rotten rock exists, the climbing is generally on good quality white granite intermingled with smooth brown glacial polish reminiscent of Tuolumne's golden rock. Surrealistic swirls of high quality black rock, fields of large black knobs, and fields of white feldspar crystal knobs are also encountered. Camping and limited supplies are available near the road end at Whitney Portal. One may also camp at Lone Pine Campground, 5 miles east of the road end or in the Alabama Hills, 10 miles east, where no fees are required, but bring your own water. All services are available 13 miles east of the road end in Lone Pine, on Route 395. Most of the climbs are south facing, making them climbable year-round, but winter snows often block the road and the approaches.

To reach this area, follow Highway 395 to Lone Pine and turn west at the stop light onto the Whitney Portal Road. All approaches except the Bastille are made from the last 1½ mile section of the road.

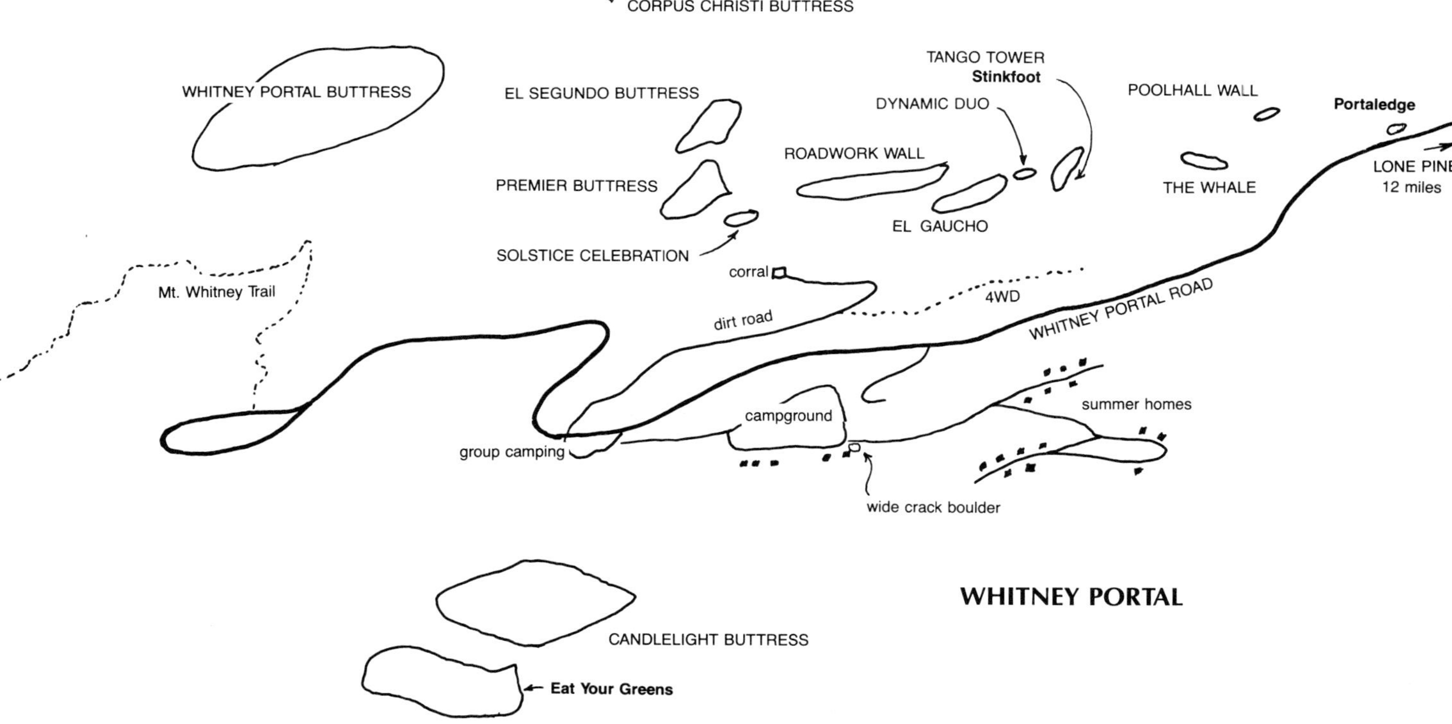
MOONSTONE BUTTRESS
CORPUS CHRISTI BUTTRESS
WHITNEY PORTAL BUTTRESS
EL SEGUNDO BUTTRESS
TANGO TOWER
Stinkfoot
DYNAMIC DUO
POOLHALL WALL
Portaledge
ROADWORK WALL
PREMIER BUTTRESS
THE WHALE
LONE PINE
12 miles
EL GAUCHO
SOLSTICE CELEBRATION
corral
Mt. Whitney Trail
4WD
dirt road
WHITNEY PORTAL ROAD
summer homes
campground
group camping
wide crack boulder
WHITNEY PORTAL
CANDLELIGHT BUTTRESS
Eat Your Greens

BASTILLE BUTTRESS

As you drive up Whitney Portal Road above the Alabama Hills, this large white buttress is easily seen to the left of the main canyon of Lone Pine Creek and Whitney Portal. About 8 miles west of Highway 395, turn left on the Lone Pine Campground road. In ½ mile, don't turn right to the campground, but go straight and follow this road until it deadends near the start of steeper ground. Follow the obvious Inyo Creek drainage above to the start of the buttress. Alternately, one may drive farther up Whitney Portal Road and park at the Meysan Lakes Trail parking. Hike left through the campground across Lone Pine Creek, turn left at a huge boulder and pass several summer homes to the Meysan Lakes Trailhead. Follow the trail for approximately ½ mile, past the ridge above the summer homes, then exit left and contour/traverse across the Meysan Creek canyon and around a long ridge of Lone Pine Peak and descend to the base of the buttress. Allow two hours for either approach.

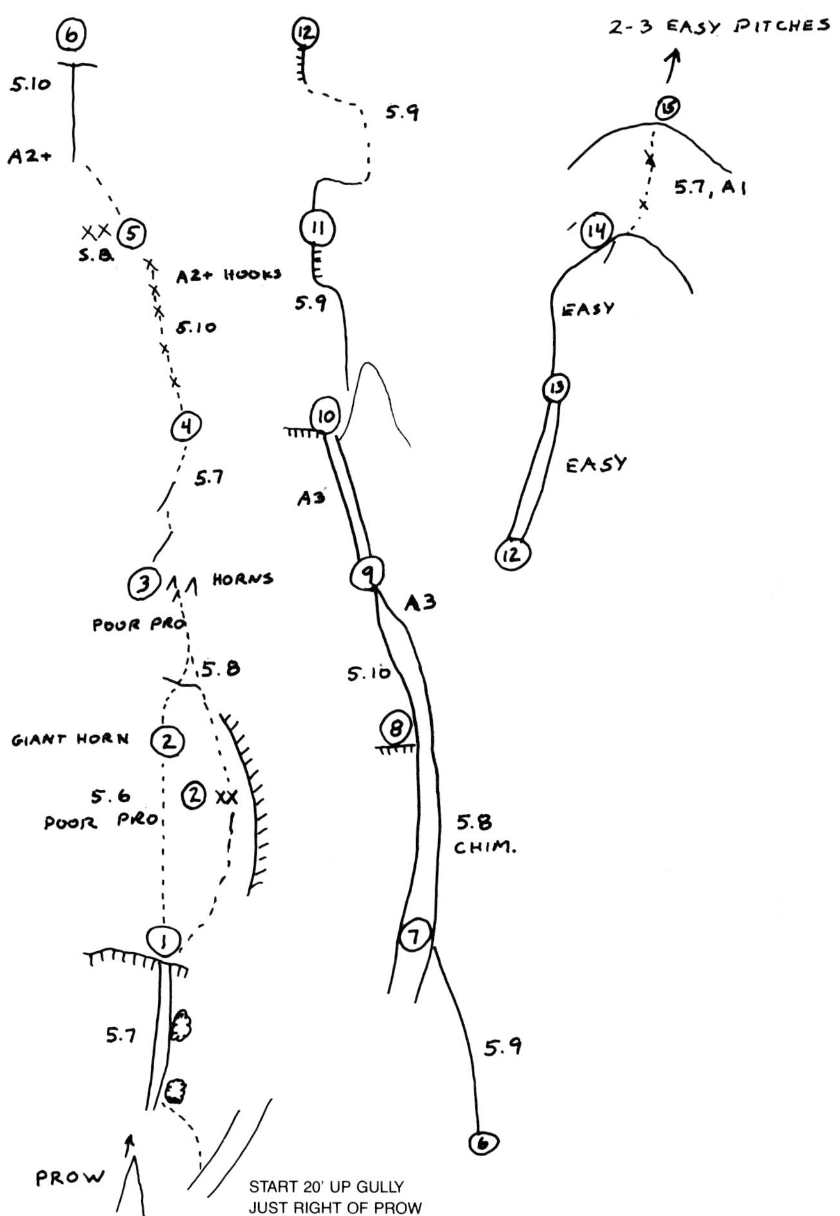

Bastille Buttress V 5.10 A3 ★
Pro: 2 KB, 2 LA, 2 each ½" to 1", Friends to #4, 2 bathooks.
Descent: Gullies ¼ mile left of the buttress.

CANDLELIGHT BUTTRESS

1 Pro Bowler's Tour **3 Bobo's Bonanza**
2 Two-Lane Blacktop **4 Moe's Liquors**

After the Whitney Portal Road enters the main Lone Pine Creek gorge, above a single long switchback, this smooth triangular buttress is seen straight ahead on the south side of the canyon, above and behind the summer homes. Follow the Meysan Lakes Trail for 100 yards until it veers to the left. Go straight up a long gully to the base of the buttress. Another large buttress exists above Candlelight. Two distinct crack systems can be seen.

Eat Your Greens (5.9), a four pitch route, begins in the right crack system, then follows a diagonal crack leading to the left crack system. Step left into a chimney on the fourth pitch. To descend, traverse 100 yards across sandy ledges directly behind Eat Your Greens and do two long rappels off trees into the approach gully.

Mr. Green Jeans 5.10B ★ This route is on the northeast face of Candlelight Peak, below and right of Candlelight Buttress, and climbs discontinuous left-slanting cracks in a round shield-shaped slab. The first pitch is short and passes a bolt to a belay at a tree. The second pitch follows the cracks past four fixed pitons. Rappel 165′ from bolts at the top.

Dinty Moore 5.8 This and the following route lie many hundreds of feet right of the preceding route on the north face of Candlelight Peak. They are on a clean, slabby section of rock and are approached via right-slanting tree-covered ramps. They can be seen clearly from the vicinity of the small store at Whitney Portal. This climb is right-facing corner bordering the left side of a smooth slab; one long pitch. Rappel with two ropes.

Mulligan Stew 5.10C ★ To the right of Dinty Moore, this is a 2-pitch bolted face climb. The first pitch is 180′ long and requires simul-climbing. Rappel with two ropes.

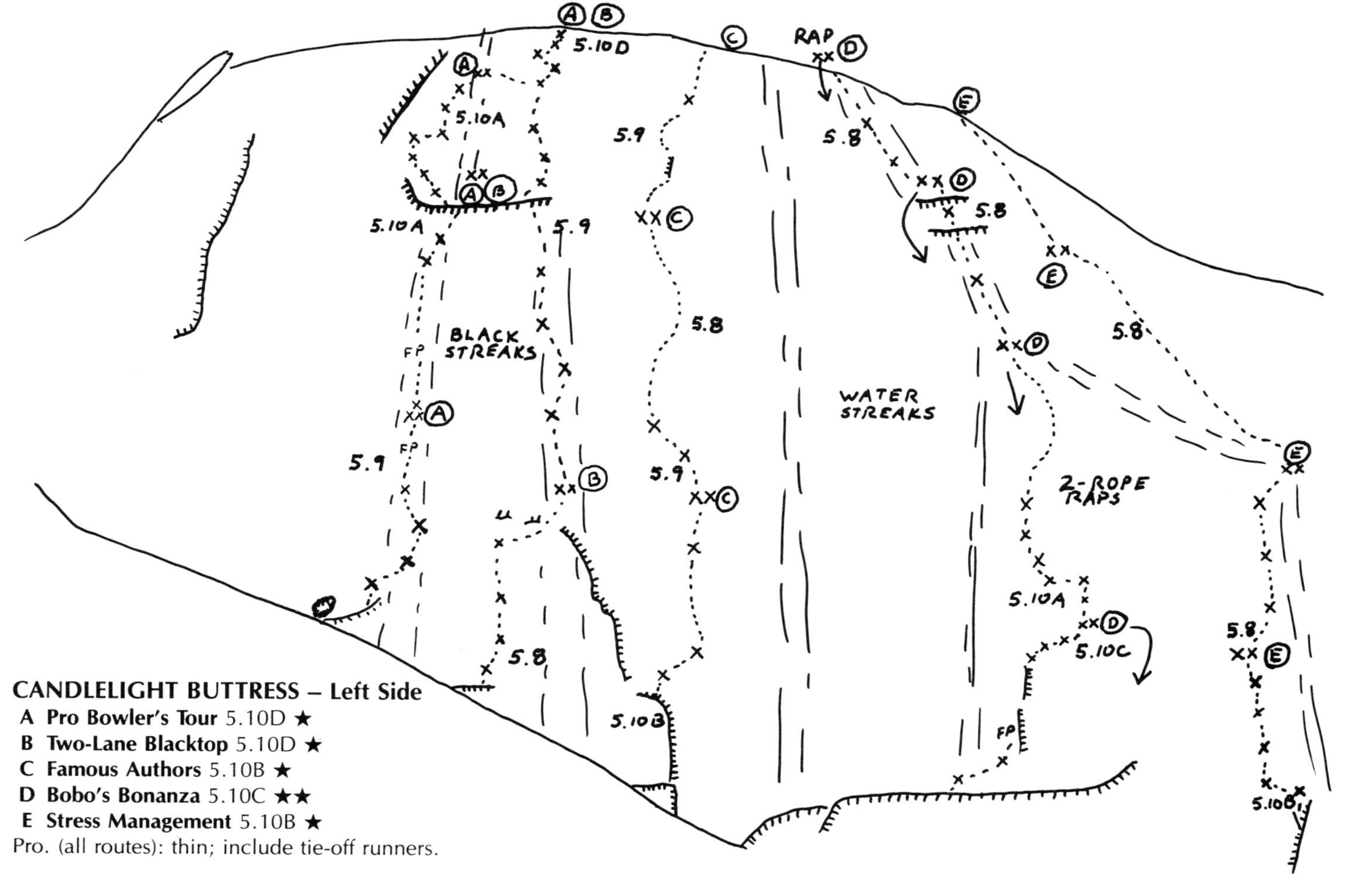

CANDLELIGHT BUTTRESS – Left Side

- **A Pro Bowler's Tour** 5.10D ★
- **B Two-Lane Blacktop** 5.10D ★
- **C Famous Authors** 5.10B ★
- **D Bobo's Bonanza** 5.10C ★★
- **E Stress Management** 5.10B ★

Pro. (all routes): thin; include tie-off runners.

CANDLELIGHT BUTTRESS – Right Side

A **Bobo's Bonanza** 5.10C ★★
B **Stress Management** 5.10B ★
C **No Pie a la Mode** 5.10D ★
D **Nervous Habits** 5.10D ★
E **Moe's Liquors** 5.9 ★ pro: to 3½″
Pro. (all routes): thin, incl. 9/16″ runners.

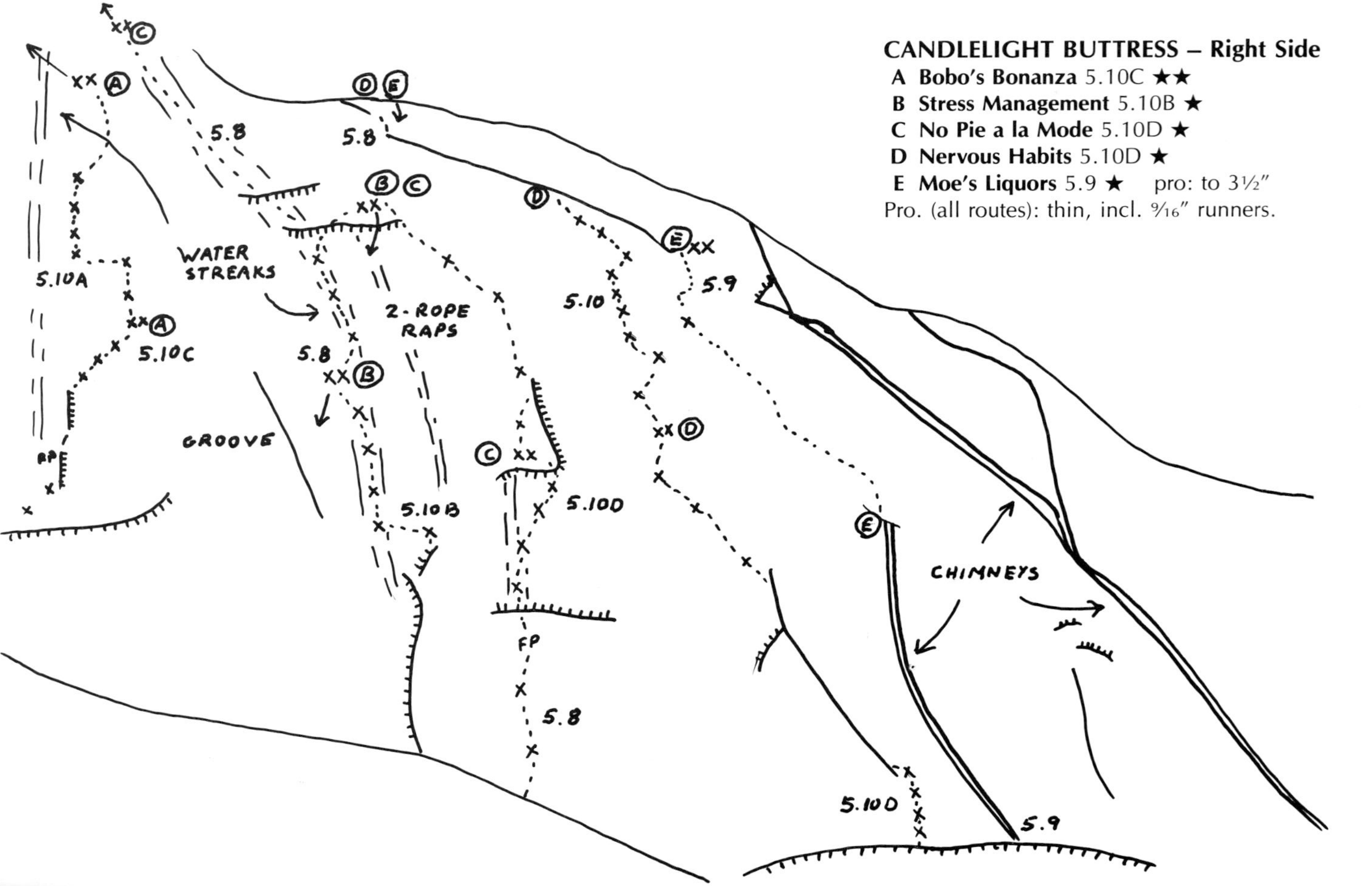

WHITNEY PORTAL BUTTRESS

1 upper part of **Beckey- Callis**
2 Sartoris
3 Wonderwall
4 Clouds

Hike up the Mount Whitney Trail about ¼ mile until it makes a sharp switchback to the left. Ascend through talus and trees directly above this switchback to the base of the wall. Nimbus is 100 yards to the right; all other routes lie to the left.

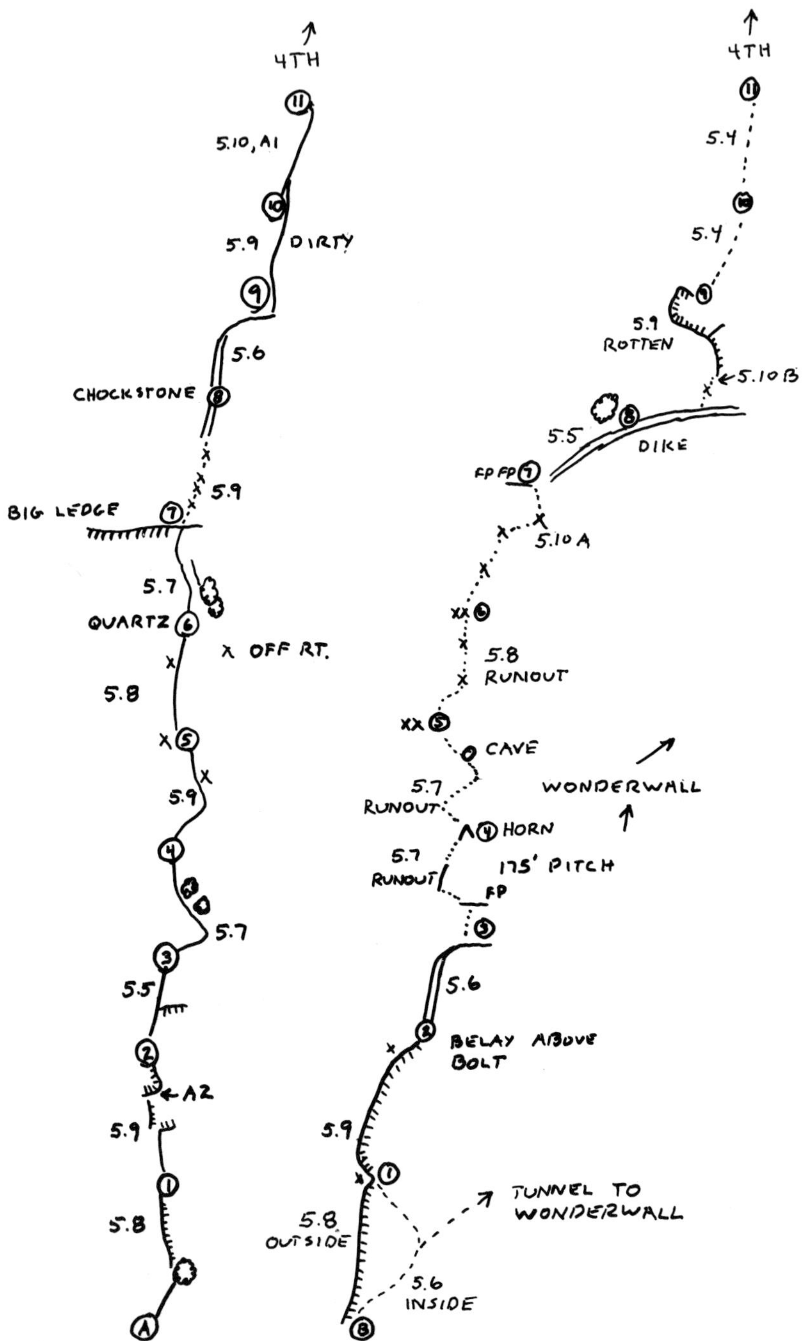

WHITNEY PORTAL BUTTRESS – Left

A **Beckey-Callis Route** IV 5.10 A2 ★ pro: to 3″; 1 KB, 3 LA, 1 each baby angle.

B **Sartoris** IV 5.10B ★★ pro: to #4 Friend; double runners.

Descent: down the farthest north gully on the right side via class 4 and 5.

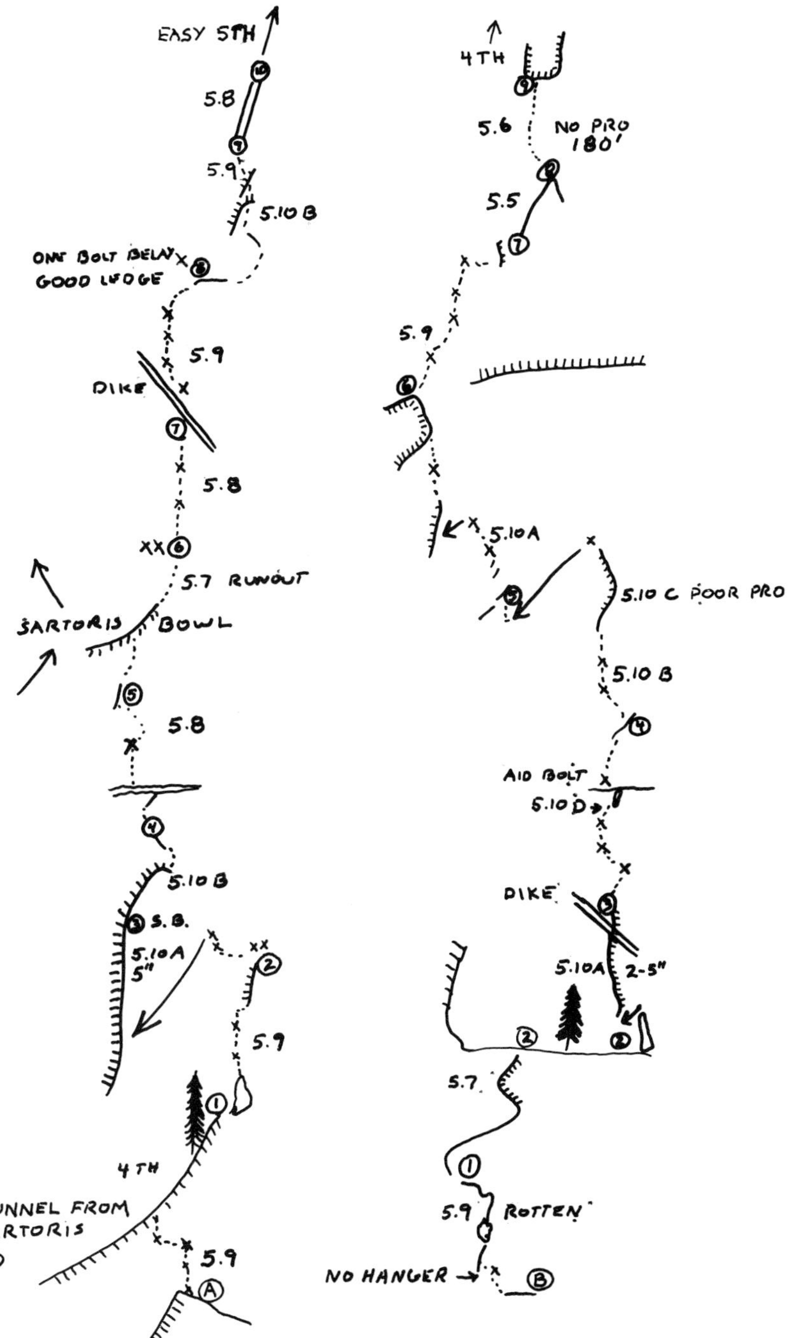

WHITNEY PORTAL BUTTRESS – Right

A Wonderwall IV 5.10B A1 ★★ pro: to 5"; 3 KB, 2 LA

B Clouds IV 5.10D A1 ★★ pro: up to and incl. 2 #4 Friends, double runners; 2KB, 4 LA

Nimbus 5.10C ★★ pro: extra ½″ to ¾″; double Friends to #4; tiny RPs, TCUs

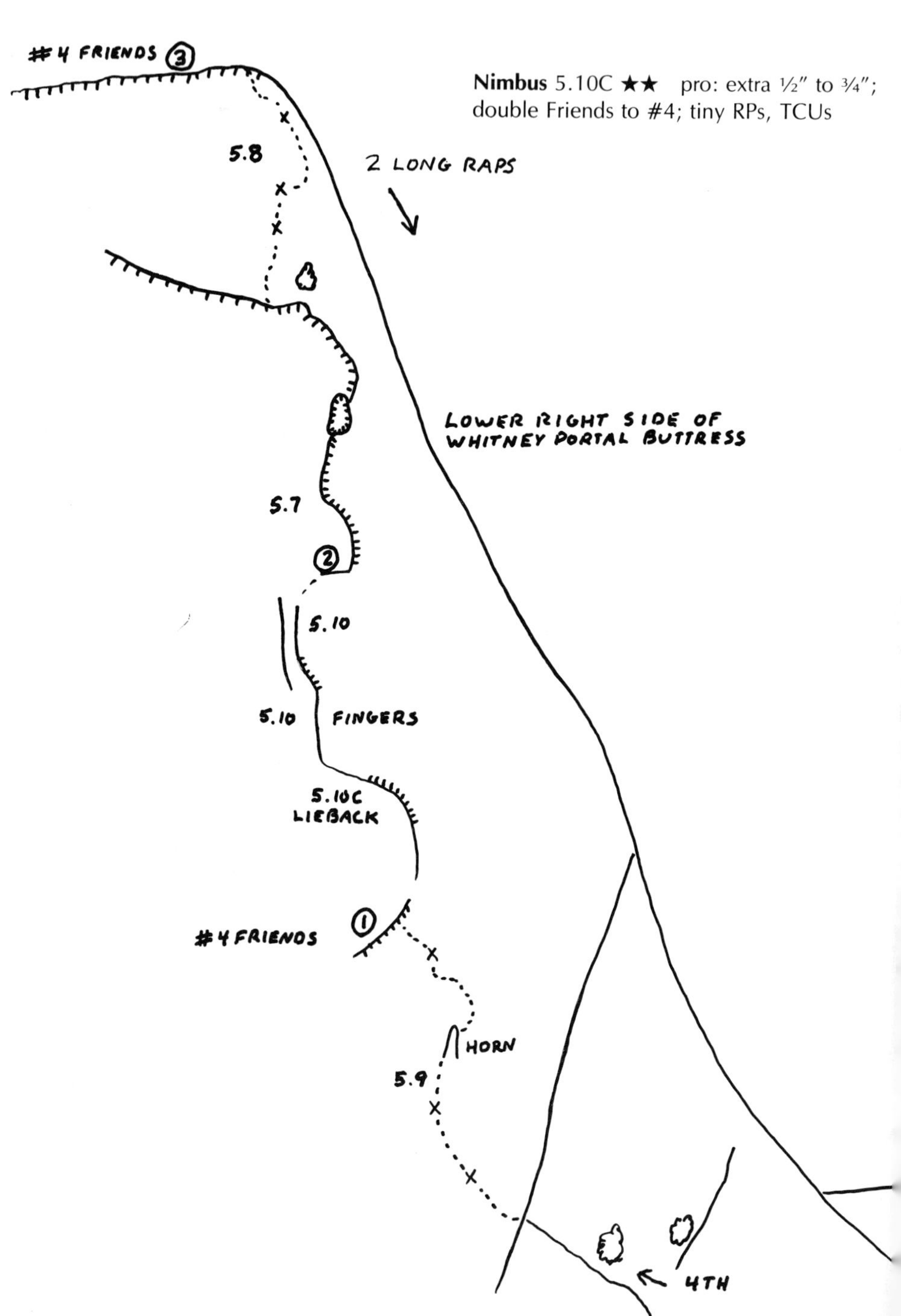

MOONSTONE BUTTRESS AREA

1 Tycho
2 Pleiades
3 Corpus Christi Buttress

Follow the Whitney Portal Buttress approach to Nimbus. Traverse up and right across talus to the base of a long, narrow, sand-filled gully. Follow this gully for 600 feet, third classing out left at one point to avoid rotten rock. Then traverse right across brush gullies and third class rock to the base of Moonstone.

MOONSTONE BUTTRESS

A **Moonchild** 5.11A A1 ★★
B **Tycho** 5.10C ★
C **Venus** 5.11D ★★
D **Pleiades** 5.11A ★★

Pro. (all routes): to 4″, esp. thin. Include tie-off runners.
Descent: down right side of buttress (4th class), or rap Venus (2 ropes).

Corpus Christi Buttress 5.9 This climb ascends a rounded, brushy buttress on the left side of the wall right of and above Moonstone Buttress. The descent from Moonstone Buttress passes by the base of this climb. Two pitches (5.9 and 5.7) lead up the right side of a pillar. Climb thin cracks above (KB protection) and pass 2 bolts. Two more pitches go up a chimney system. Rappel the route.

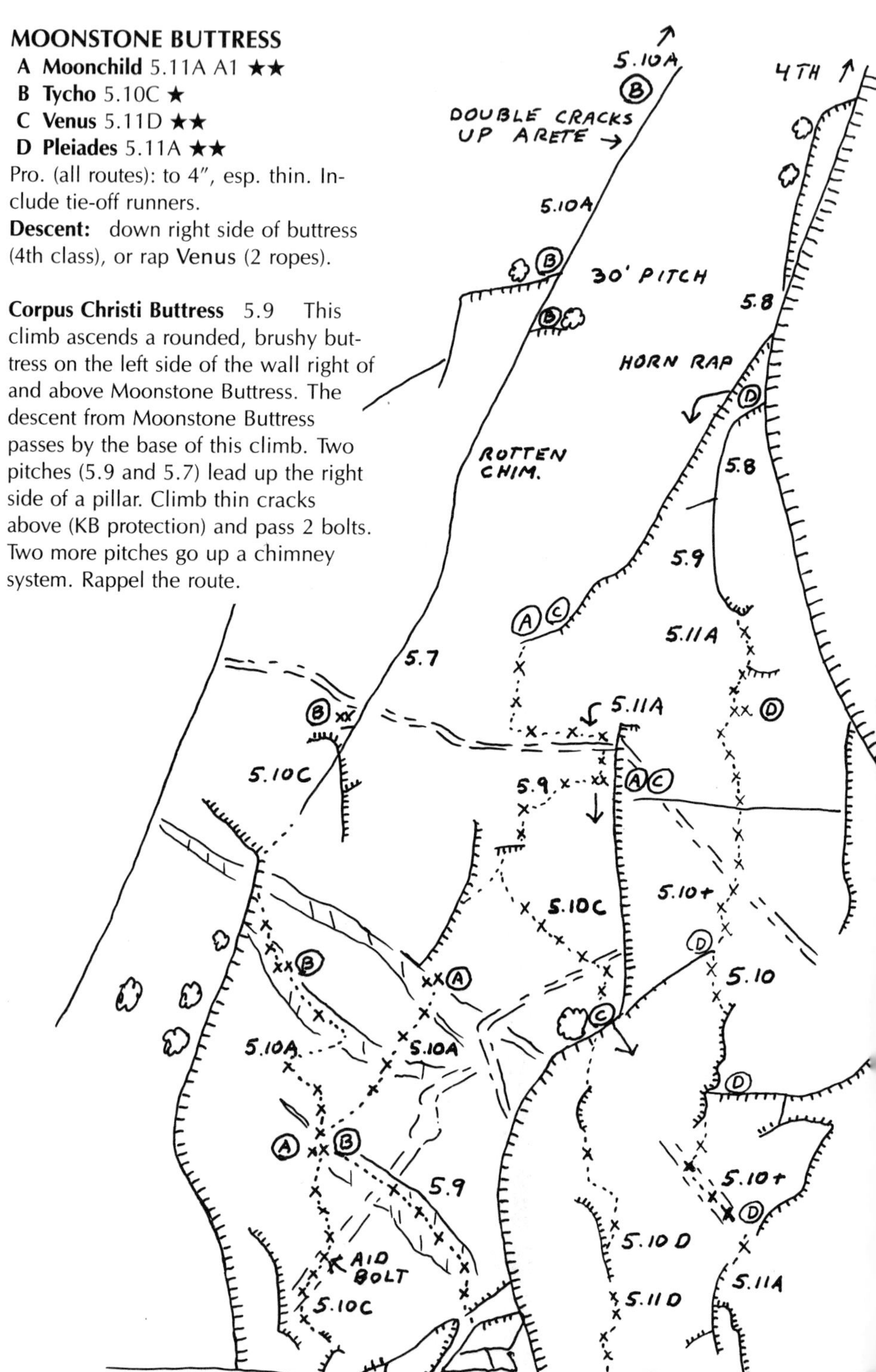

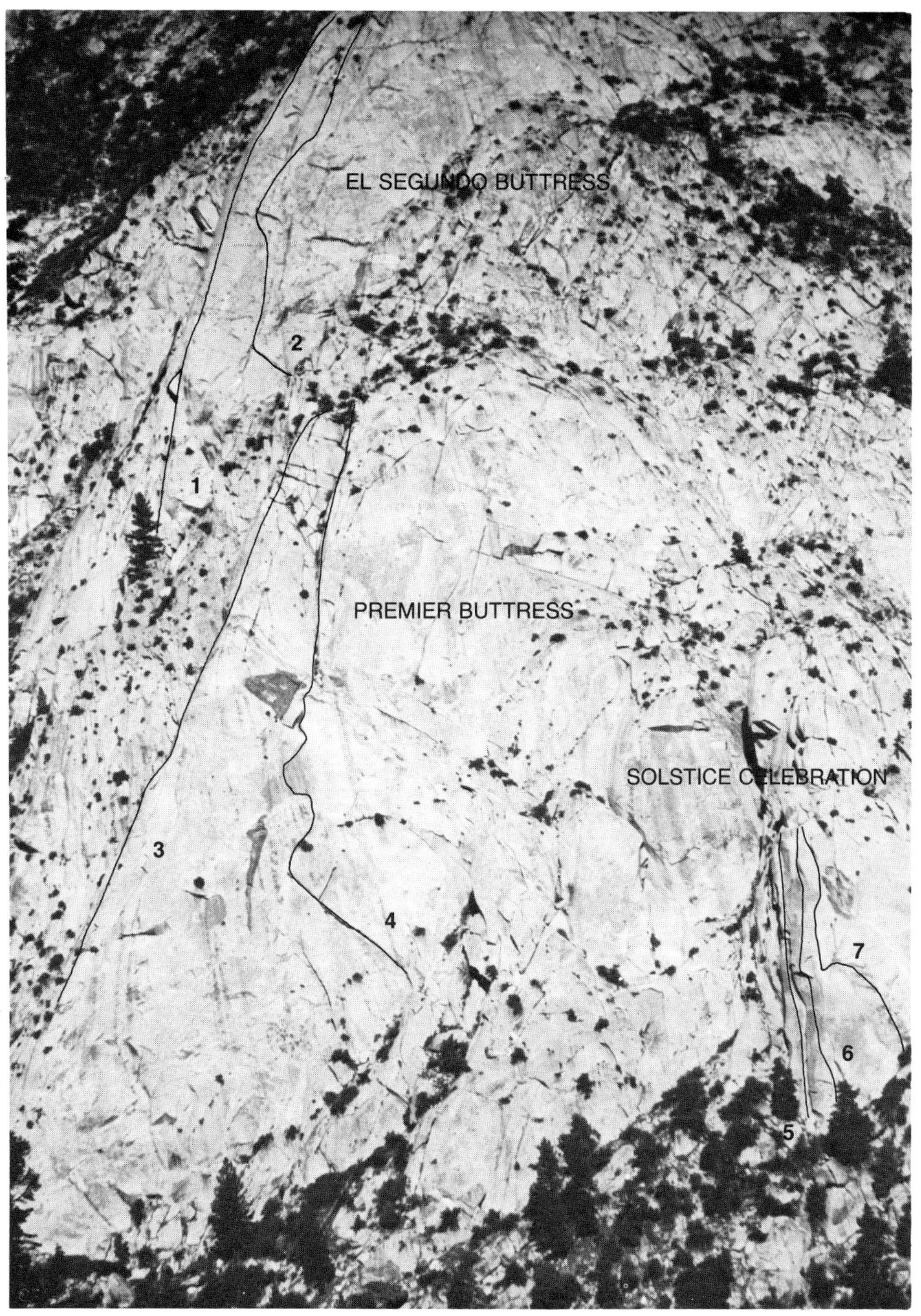

EL SEGUNDO AND PREMIER BUTTRESSES

1 Beckey Route
2 Brainstorm
3 Premier Route
4 The Phoenix
5 Tooth Decay
6 Barn Dance
7 Solstice Celebration

SOLSTICE CELEBRATION WALL
1 Tooth Decay
2 Barn Dance
3 Solstice Celebration

The following eight crags, Solstice Celebration, Premier Buttress, El Segundo Buttress, Roadwork Wall, El Gaucho, Dynamic Duo, Tango Tower, and the Whale, are all approached from a dirt road that branches off Whitney Portal Road to the north about ½ mile below the road end and directly below an obvious switchback. There is a small "no parking" sign here. The first 100 feet of the road is paved and a locked metal gate will be found in 100 yards. Beyond the gate this dirt road continues past a switchback and ends at a square fenced corral. El Segundo Buttress, Premier Buttress, and Solstice Celebration are approached from here. Roadwork Wall, and El Gaucho are approached from the switchback. Dynamic Duo, Tango Tower, and the Whale are approached from a fainter road that branches to the right 100 feet below the switchback. Alternately, El Segundo and Premier Buttresses can be approached from the obvious switchback of the paved road. See the map on page 15.

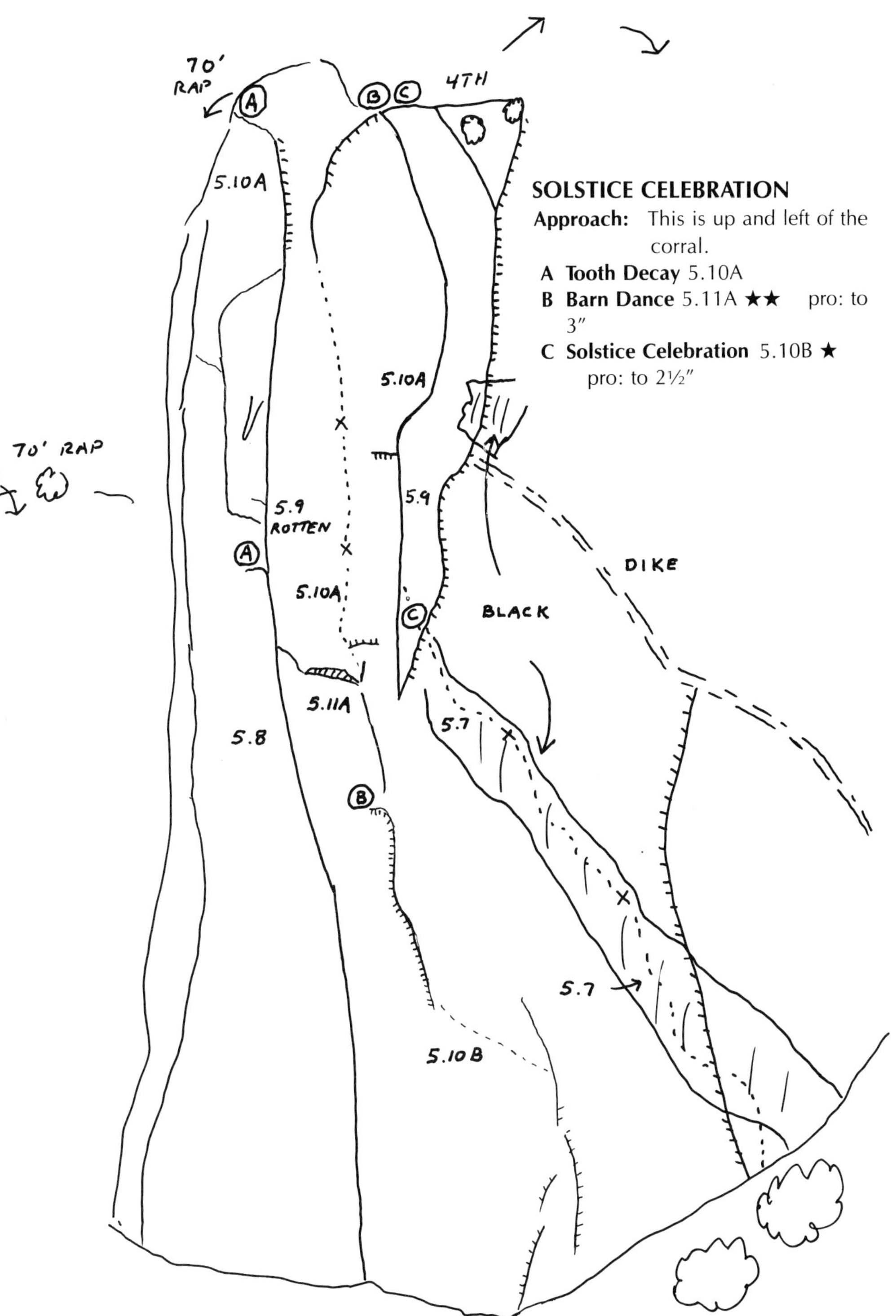

SOLSTICE CELEBRATION

Approach: This is up and left of the corral.

A **Tooth Decay** 5.10A

B **Barn Dance** 5.11A ★★ pro: to 3″

C **Solstice Celebration** 5.10B ★ pro: to 2½″

PREMIER BUTTRESS

A Premier Route 5.8 A1 or 5.10C ★

B The Phoenix 5.9 A2
pro: to 3″; 2-3 pitons ¼″-½″

Approach: This crag is left and up a gully from Solstice Celebration.
Descend: a gully left of the buttress.

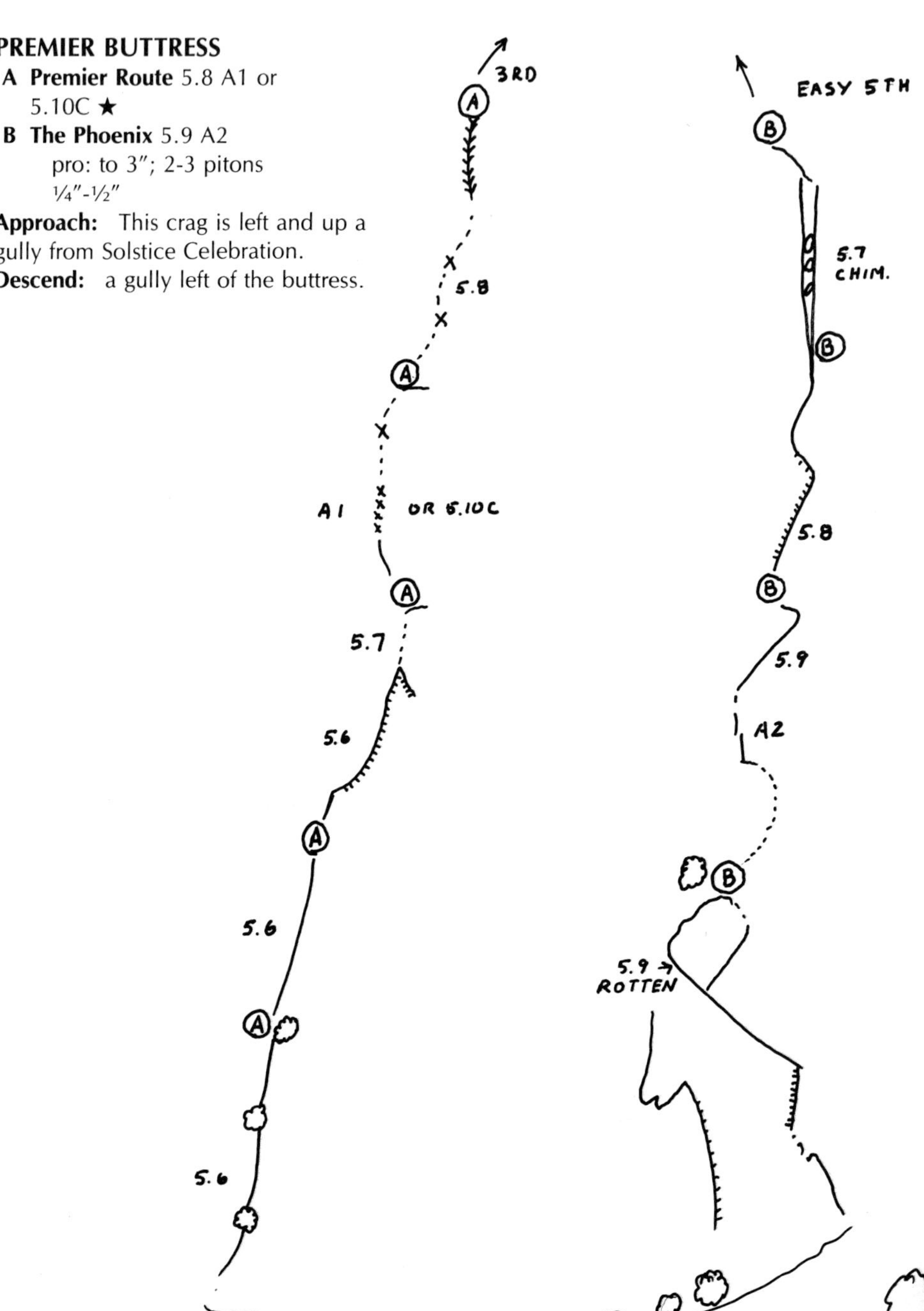

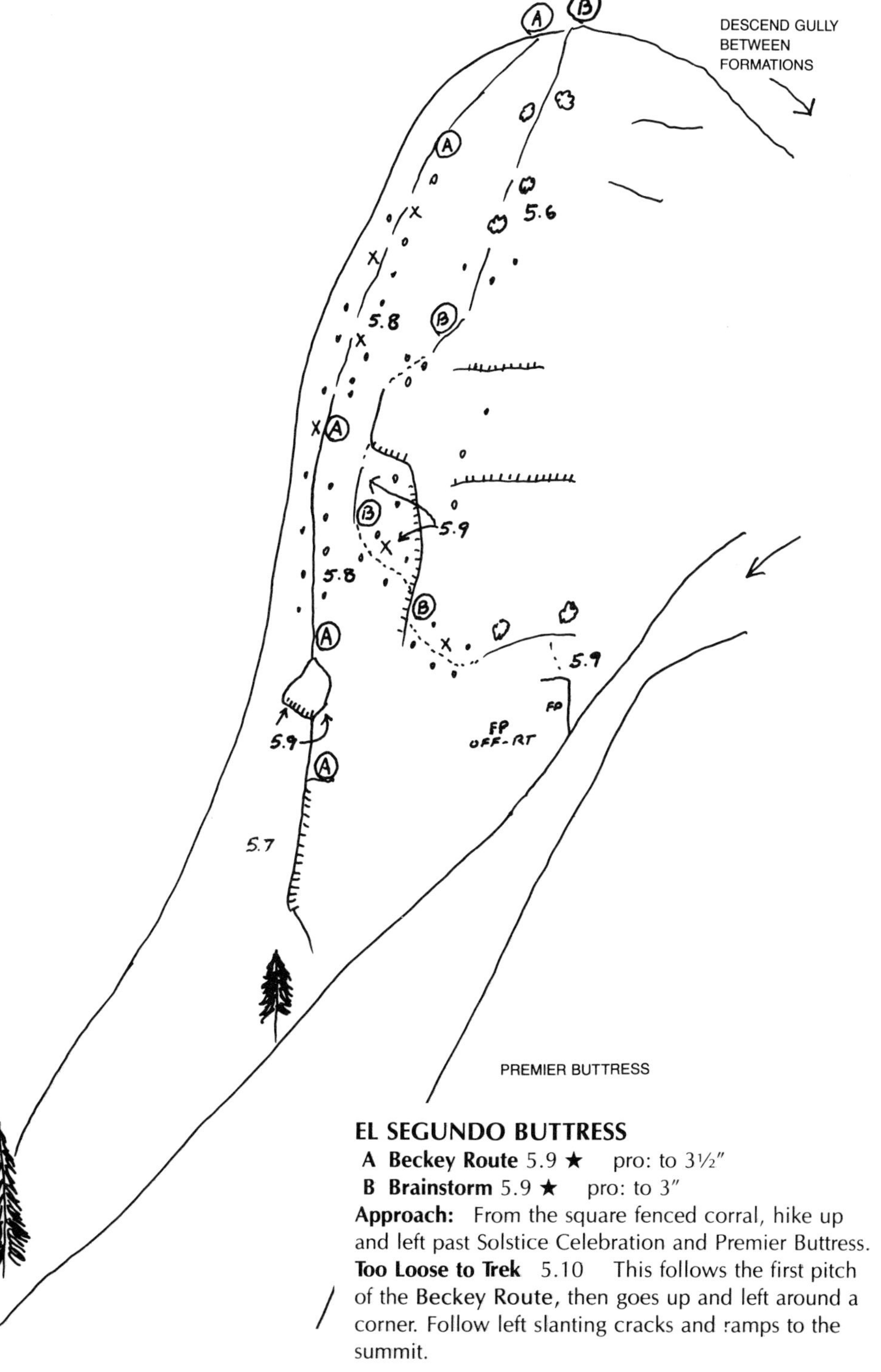

EL SEGUNDO BUTTRESS

A Beckey Route 5.9 ★ pro: to 3½″

B Brainstorm 5.9 ★ pro: to 3″

Approach: From the square fenced corral, hike up and left past Solstice Celebration and Premier Buttress.

Too Loose to Trek 5.10 This follows the first pitch of the Beckey Route, then goes up and left around a corner. Follow left slanting cracks and ramps to the summit.

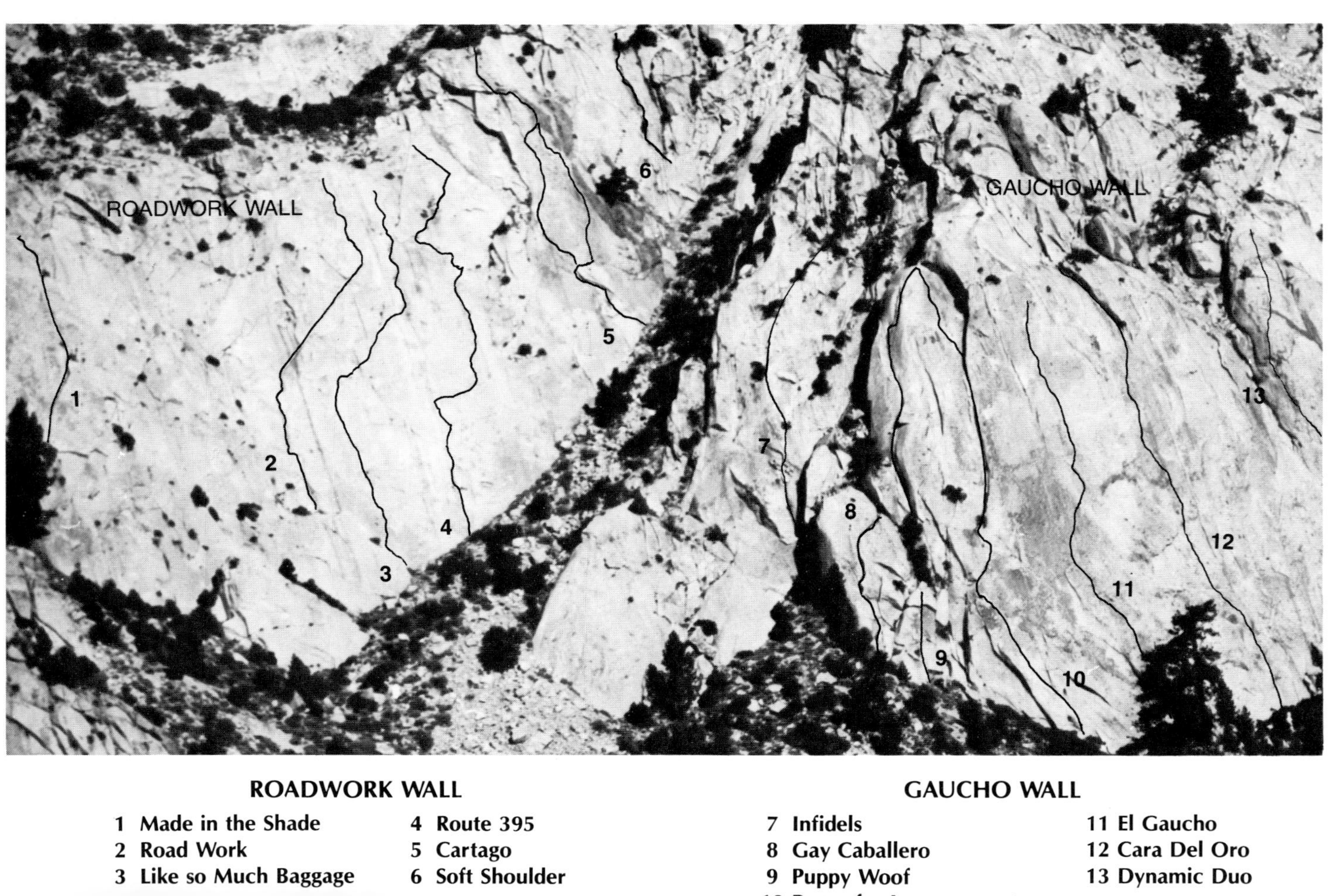

ROADWORK WALL

1 Made in the Shade
2 Road Work
3 Like so Much Baggage
4 Route 395
5 Cartago
6 Soft Shoulder

GAUCHO WALL

7 Infidels
8 Gay Caballero
9 Puppy Woof
11 El Gaucho
12 Cara Del Oro
13 Dynamic Duo

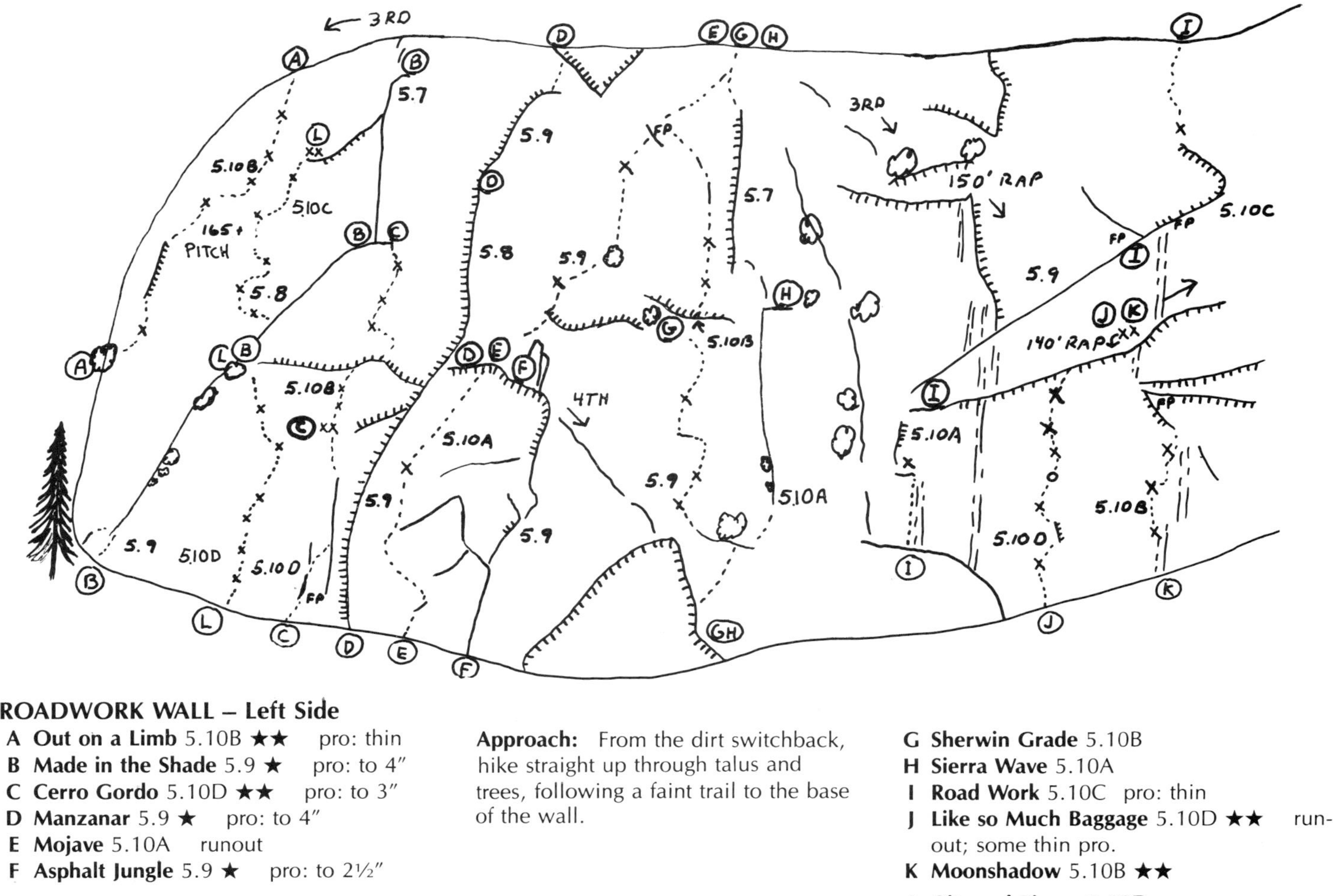

ROADWORK WALL – Left Side

- **A Out on a Limb** 5.10B ★★ pro: thin
- **B Made in the Shade** 5.9 ★ pro: to 4″
- **C Cerro Gordo** 5.10D ★★ pro: to 3″
- **D Manzanar** 5.9 ★ pro: to 4″
- **E Mojave** 5.10A runout
- **F Asphalt Jungle** 5.9 ★ pro: to 2½″

Approach: From the dirt switchback, hike straight up through talus and trees, following a faint trail to the base of the wall.

- **G Sherwin Grade** 5.10B
- **H Sierra Wave** 5.10A
- **I Road Work** 5.10C pro: thin
- **J Like so Much Baggage** 5.10D ★★ run-out; some thin pro.
- **K Moonshadow** 5.10B ★★
- **L Bits and Pieces** 5.10D

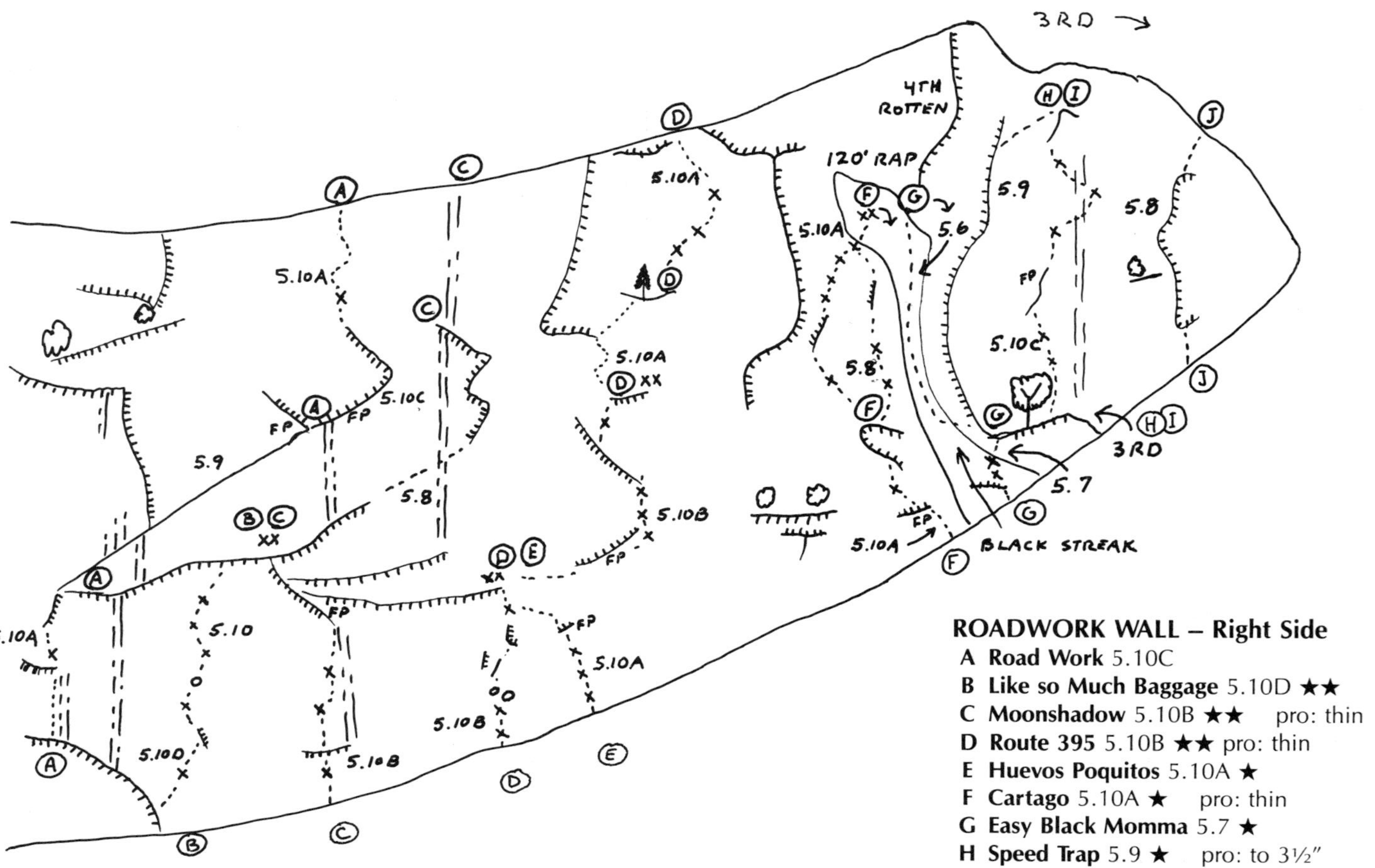

ROADWORK WALL – Right Side

- A **Road Work** 5.10C
- B **Like so Much Baggage** 5.10D ★★
- C **Moonshadow** 5.10B ★★ pro: thin
- D **Route 395** 5.10B ★★ pro: thin
- E **Huevos Poquitos** 5.10A ★
- F **Cartago** 5.10A ★ pro: thin
- G **Easy Black Momma** 5.7 ★
- H **Speed Trap** 5.9 ★ pro: to 3½″
- I **Skid Mark** 5.10C ★★ pro: thin
- J **Soft Shoulder** 5.8 ★ pro: to 3″

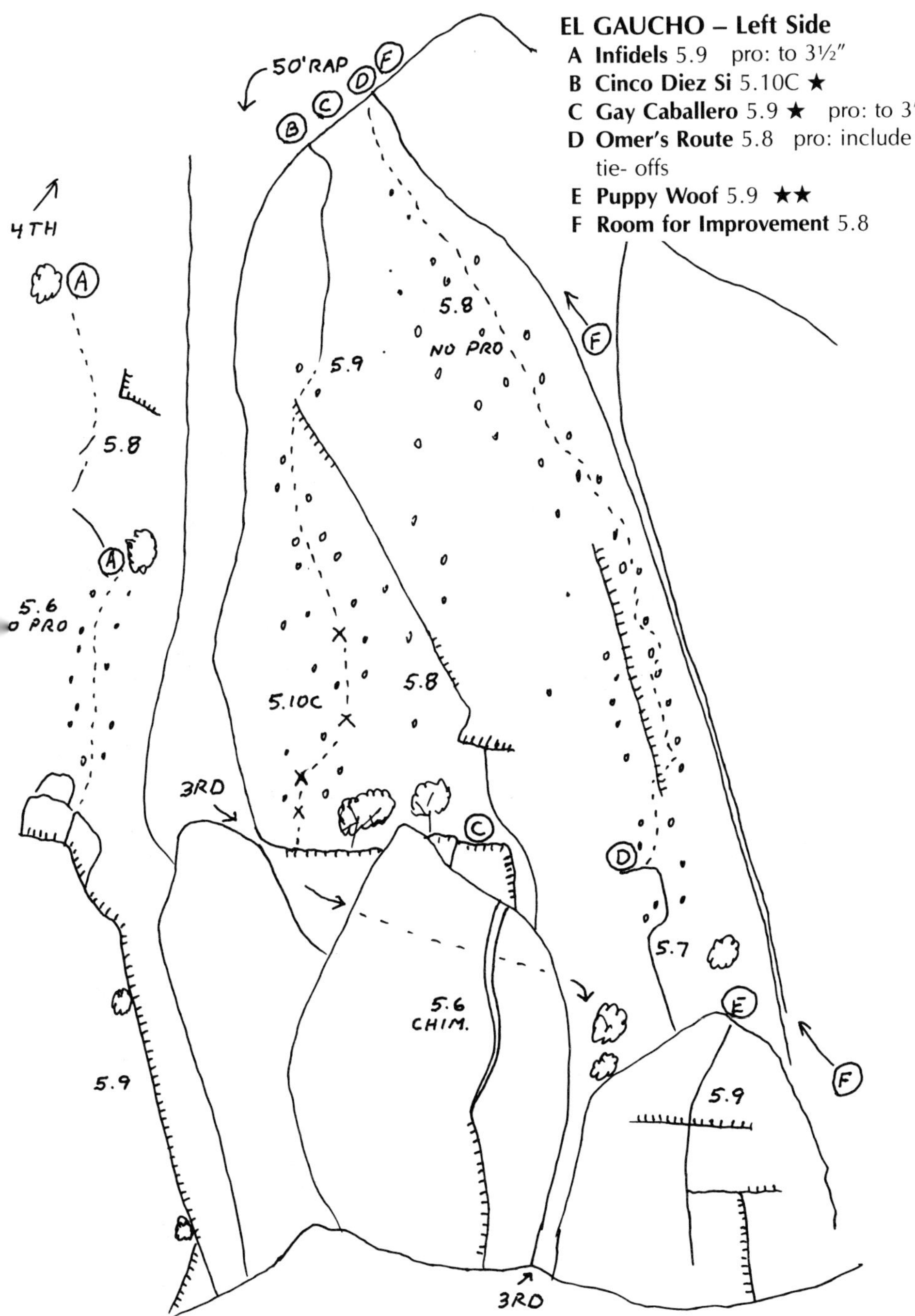

EL GAUCHO – Left Side

- **A Infidels** 5.9 pro: to 3½"
- **B Cinco Diez Si** 5.10C ★
- **C Gay Caballero** 5.9 ★ pro: to 3"
- **D Omer's Route** 5.8 pro: include tie- offs
- **E Puppy Woof** 5.9 ★★
- **F Room for Improvement** 5.8

Approach: From the switchback, follow ⅔ of the Roadwork approach. Then traverse up and right over a brushy shoulder to the base of Room for Improvement. One may also walk right to Dynamic Duo from here.

EL GAUCHO – Center

- **A** **Puppy Woof** 5.9 ★★
- **B** **Omer's Route** 5.8
- **C** **Room for Improvement** 5.8
- **D** **El Diablo** 5.10C ★ pro: include tie-offs
- **E** **El Gaucho** 5.10C ★★ pro: include a double length runner
- **F** **El Bolo** 5.10B ★ pro: include TCUs

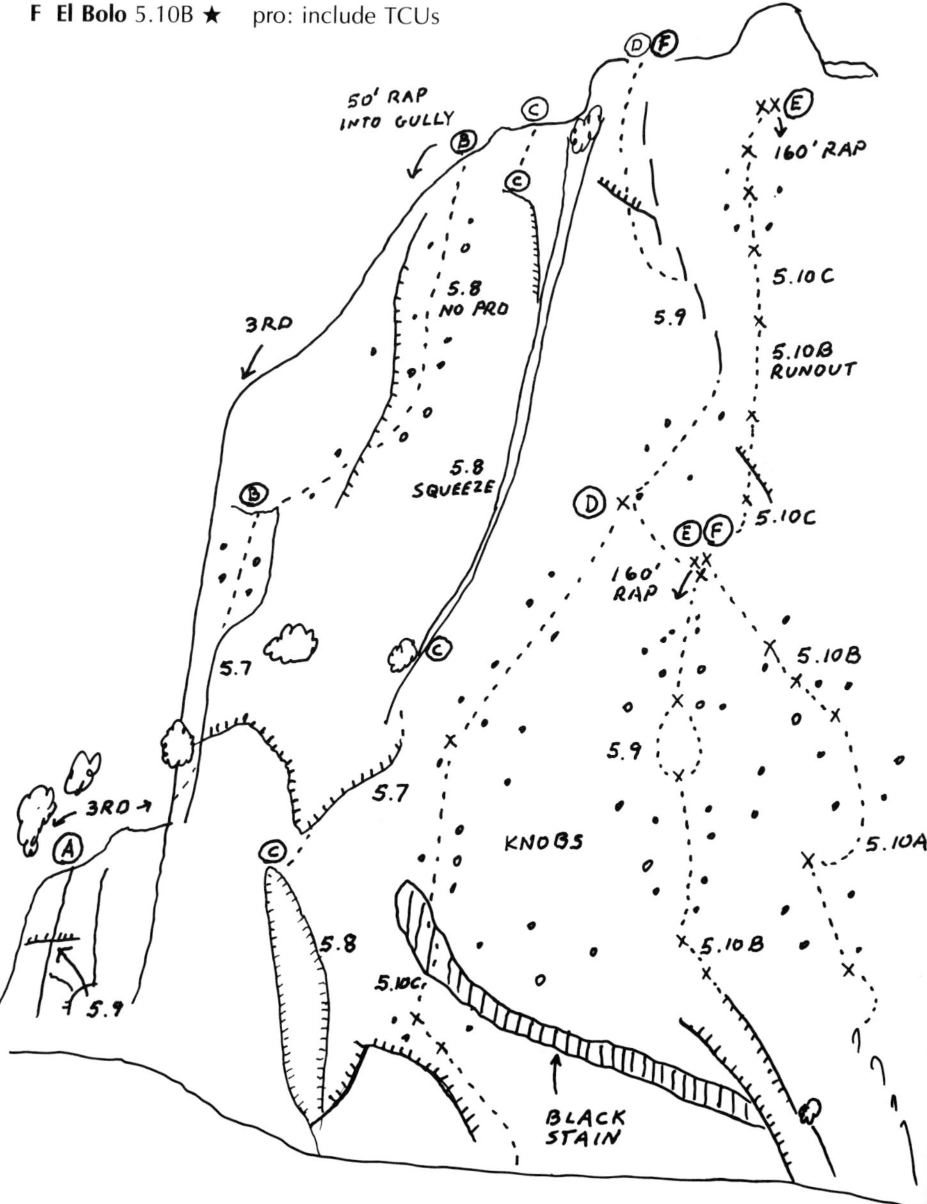

GAUCHO WALL – Right

F El Bolo 5.10B ★

G Cuban Slide 5.10C pro: to 3½"; incl. tie-offs

H Cara Del Oro 5.10D ★★ pro: to 3½"

I Frigidaire 5.10D ★★ pro: to 3"; incl. tie-offs

J Delerious 5.11B ★★ pro: to 3½"

K Way Bent 5.11B ★ pro: to 3½"

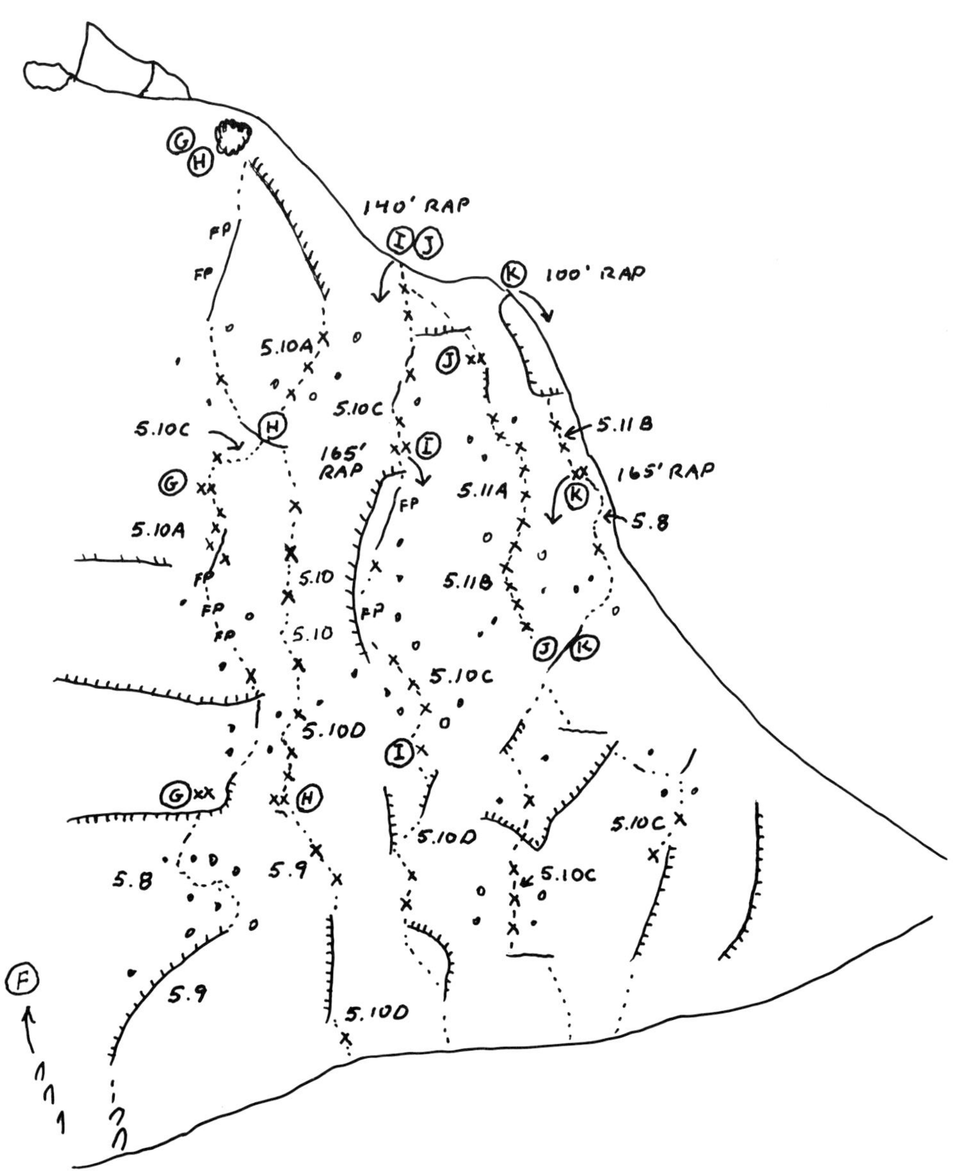

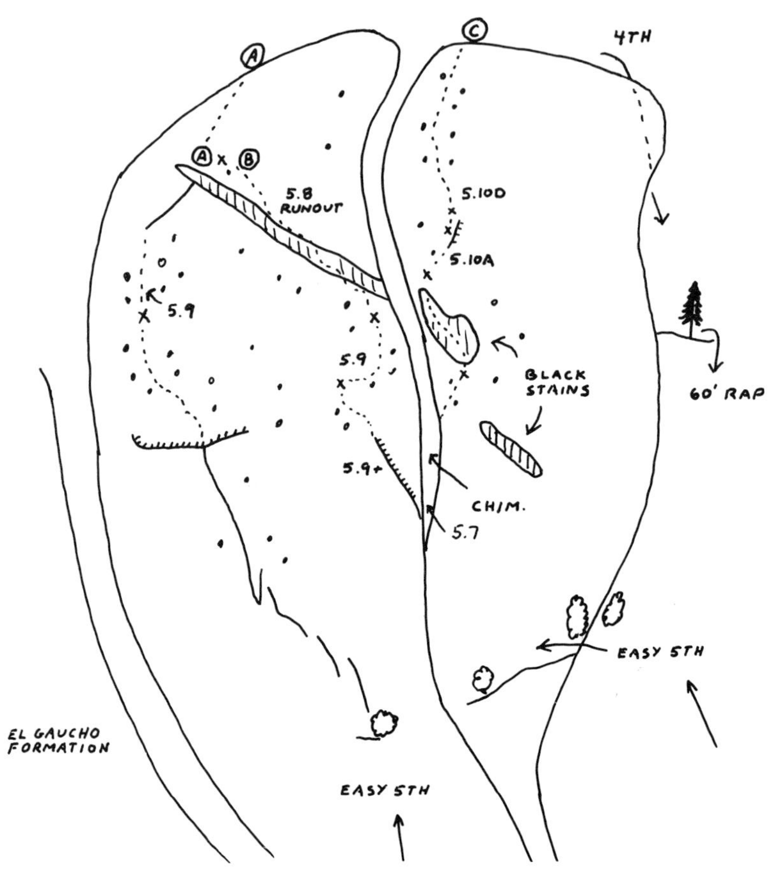

DYNAMIC DUO

Approach: Follow the faint road to its end and hike up a talus slope above to the base of the right side of El Gaucho. Dynamic Duo is a smaller formation to the right, separated by a narrow gully.

A Dynamic Duo 5.9 ★★

B Stage Fright 5.9 ★★

C Steel Drivin' Man 5.10D ★★

Pro. (all routes): thin; include 9⁄16" runners

Stinkfoot 5.9 ★ This and the following route are on a small outcrop right of the Dynamic Duo formation and separated by a gully. Stinkfoot follows a dogleg crack with a tree 1⁄3 of the way up.

Steel Drivin' Blues 5.10B ★ This is a 4-bolt face climb just right of Stinkfoot.

Calypso 5.10D ★ This climb is on Trango Tower, a pointed formation above Stinkfoot. The route more or less ascends the southwest arete. Ascend the class 4-5 gully left of Stinkfoot for several hundred feet. A rotten 5.4 pitch leads out of the gully, passing an evil bush right at the start. Work into an obvious crack in a corner leading to a large ledge. Climb a wide crack leading to the top of a block, then ascend a headwall, passing several bolts. From the last bolt, climb down and right around a corner, then up lower-angle and runout face to the left. Descend left with one or two rappels. Pro: to 4".

THE WHALE
1 Bony Fingers
2 Aplomb
3 Dancing on the Edge

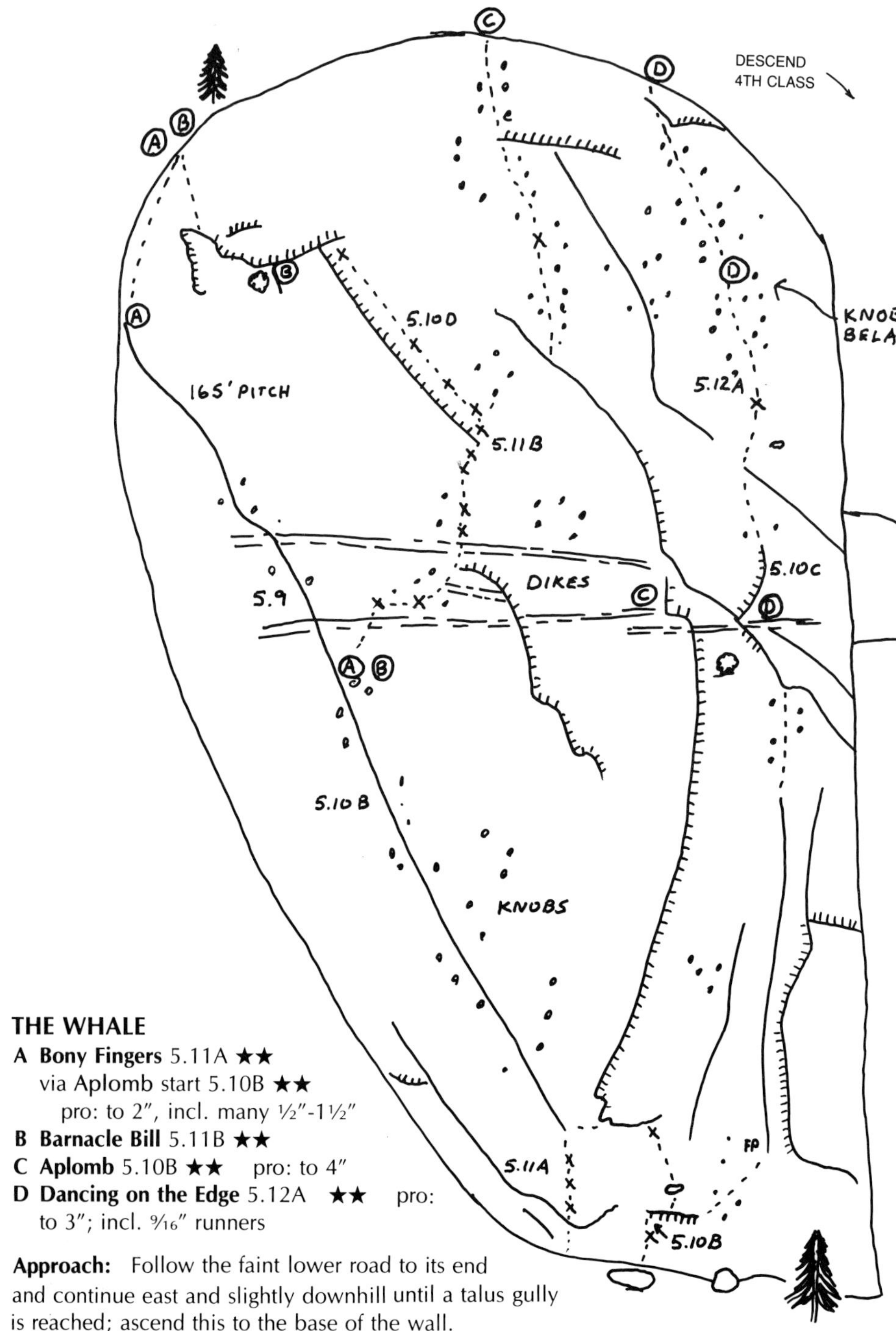

THE WHALE

A Bony Fingers 5.11A ★★
via Aplomb start 5.10B ★★
pro: to 2", incl. many ½"-1½"

B Barnacle Bill 5.11B ★★

C Aplomb 5.10B ★★ pro: to 4"

D Dancing on the Edge 5.12A ★★ pro: to 3"; incl. 9/16" runners

Approach: Follow the faint lower road to its end and continue east and slightly downhill until a talus gully is reached; ascend this to the base of the wall.

Famous Potatoes 5.9 ★ To the right of the Whale is a rocky ridge. This 2-pitch climb ascends a curving handcrack in the biggest formation on the ridge. The climb starts off a detached flake shaped like the state of Idaho.

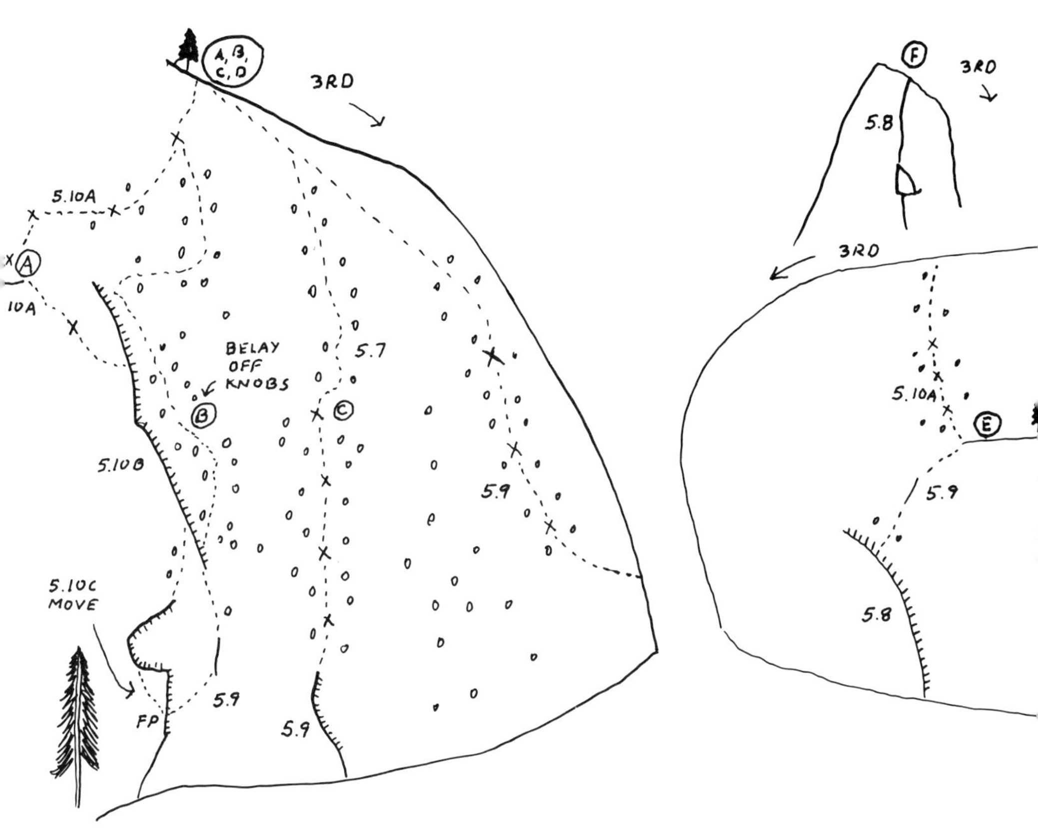

POOLHALL WALL

A Corner Pocket 5.10C ★ pro: to 3″

B Blackballed 5.9 ★ pro: to 2″; incl. many runners

C Blue Balls 5.9 ★ pro: to 1½″; incl. many runners

D Snooker 5.9 ★

E Marvin Gardens 5.10A ★ pro: to 3½″

F Crack Addict 5.8 ★ pro: to 2½″

Approach: This wall is to the right of the Famous Potatoes ridge. It can be reached by following the Whale approach and continuing east about ⅓ mile until a brush and talus gully is reached leading to the wall. In ascending the gully, stay to its right side or fifth class climbing will be encountered. A shorter (but more uphill) approach can be made directly from the Whitney Portal Road about ¾ mile before the dirt road approach, at a point where the road jogs slightly left and there is a large dirt pullout on the south side of the road. The Poolhall Wall can be seen from the dirt pullout.

Portaledge 5.10A ★ Just after entering the main Whitney Portal Canyon, a rib of rock comes almost down to the road. There is a short section of dynamited rock at its base. Portaledge ascends this rib in 2 pitches, passing some bolts and fixed pins.

UPPER BISHOP CREEK

The Upper Bishop Creek areas are reached by driving west from the town of Bishop on Highway 168 (Line Street). This road intersects Highway 395 at the southernmost traffic signal in Bishop. After about 20 miles, there is a left turn leading to South Lake; three of the areas, Billy's Pillar, Wild Rose Buttress, and the Bridge Crags, are found along this road. The fourth area, Cardinal Pinnacle, is reached by continuing straight on Highway 168 towards Lake Sabrina. The rock is white Sierra-type granite of usually good quality. The high elevations of these areas make them best for climbing in the summer and fall.

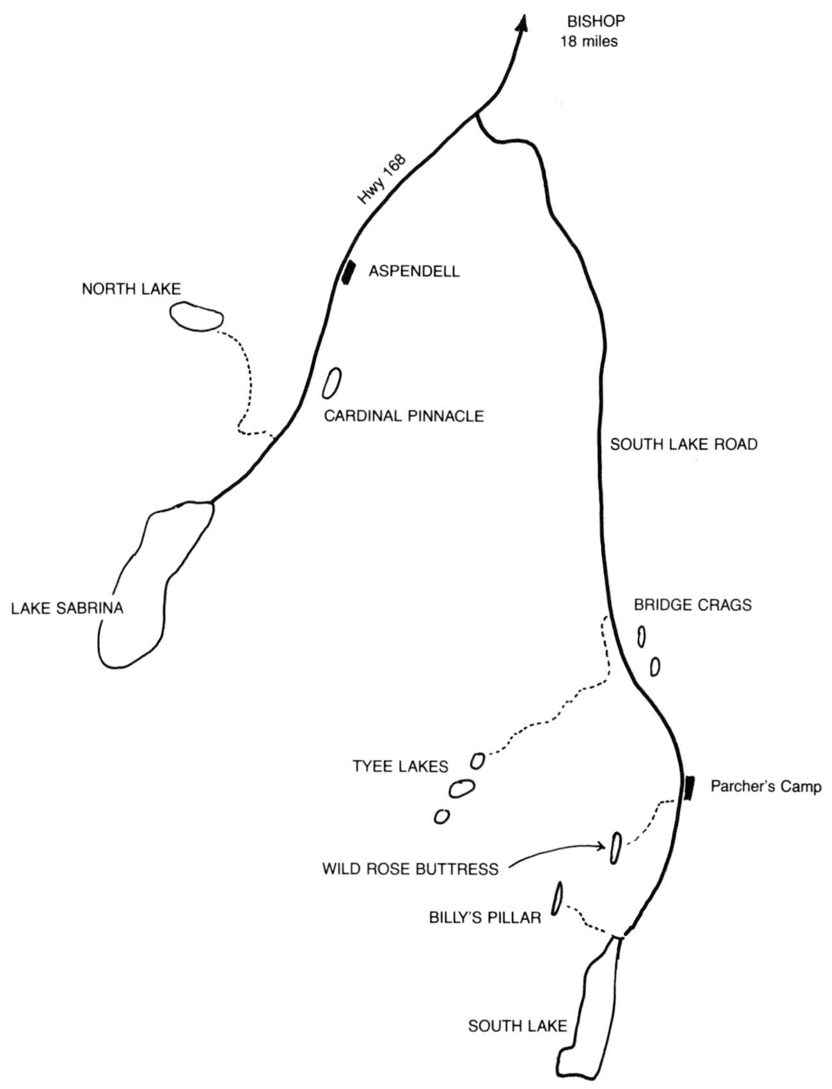

BILLY'S PILLAR AREA

Park at South Lake. Billy's Pillar will be seen high on the slopes across the lake as an orange-white tower split by a chimney. Walk across the dam and wander up a brushy hillside and Class 3 cliffiets to reach the base of the tower. Approach time: 45 minutes to an hour. **Descent:** Work back from the summit and down toward the gully on the left side of the tower. A short rappel or medium 5th class downclimbing leads to 4th class downclimbing in the gully.

1 **Chimney Cricket** 5.4
2 **Derelict's Delight**
3 **Two Fingers**
4 **Peach Jam**
5 **British Chimney**
6 **Billy's Pillar – Left Side**

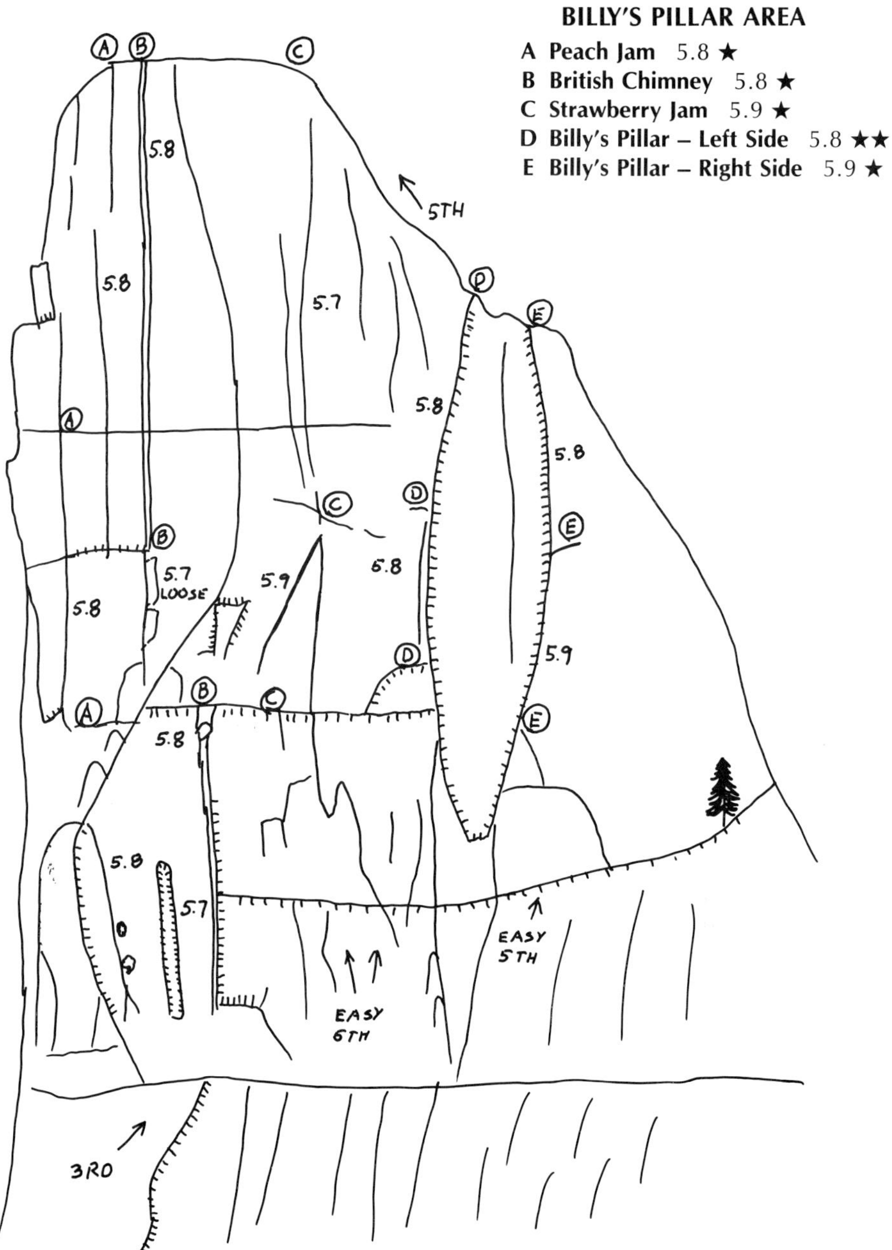

Two Fingers 5.10B ★ Work up the gully left of the main face past a class 4 section. Climb a short pitch on the right to a belay alcove. Follow a thin left-slanting crack (crux) to a semi-hanging belay. Move left and up to the top.

Derelict's Delight 5.10B ★ Continue up the gully past the descent for routes on the main tower. This is a left-slanting crack 50′ left of a large right-facing book capped by a roof.

WILD ROSE BUTTRESS

1 Thin Man
2 Wild Rose
3 Bob-Bob-a-Ramp
4 Bobcrack
5 Slot Machine

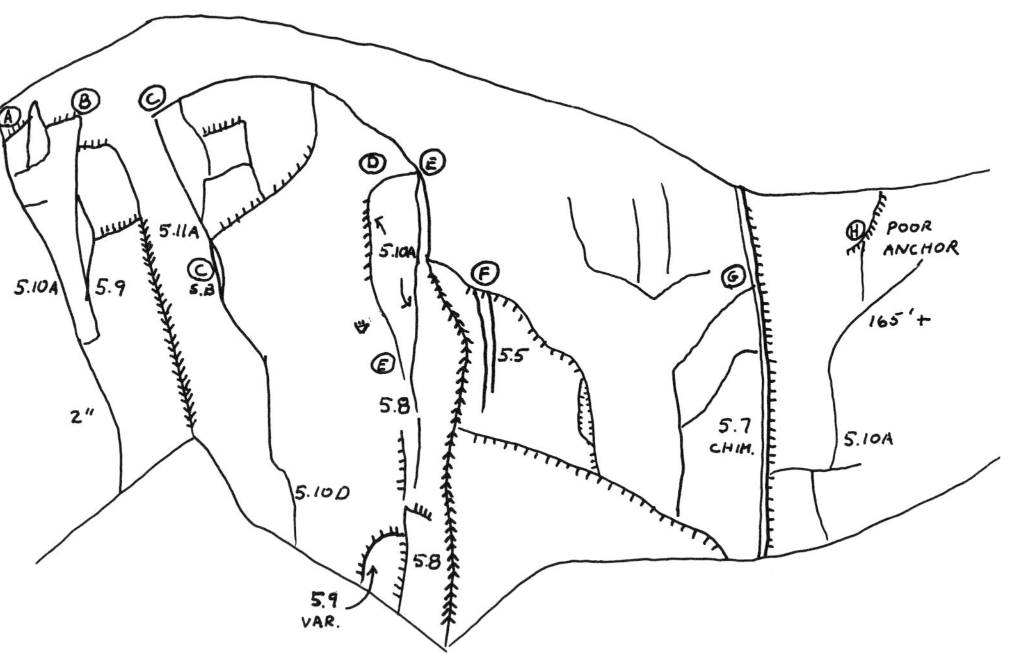

WILD ROSE BUTTRESS

Drive about six miles up the South Lake Road until one passes Parcher's Camp, a small resort on the left. Just past this, a gated road leads right across a bridge to a group of summer homes. Park near here and walk up past the homes through brush and talus to the base of the cliff. Another approach can be made by driving about ½ mile further, almost to South Lake, and walking directly to the cliff from there. This involves crossing Bishop Creek, which may be difficult until mid-summer or so. Descend the right side of the cliff.

- A **Thin Man** 5.10A ★
- B **Stems and Seeds** 5.9
- C **Wild Rose** 5.11A ★★ Pro: to 2½", many thin
- D **Bob-Bob-a-Ramp** 5.10A ★★ Pro: to 2½
- E **Bobcrack** 5.10A ★★ Pro: to 2½"
- F **Spiral Staircase** 5.5 May be used as downclimb
- G **Slot Machine** 5.7 ★
- H **Stronger Than Dirt** 5.10A

BRIDGE CRAGS

Drive up the South Lake Road for about five miles until a wooden footbridge is seen, the trailhead for Tyee Lakes. Just past this, the Bridge Crags are the two largest outcrops on the left side of the road.

A **The Shyster** 5.7 ★★ Follow a steep hidden hand crack on the right side of a flake.

B **Flaked Out** 5.9 ★★ A thin right- facing flake starting 15 feet right of The Shyster. The two routes join near the top.

C **Blockhead** 5.9 ★ Climb either side of a pillar, pass through a (crux) roof and continue up a squeeze chimney to the top.

CARDINAL PINNACLE

This is the finest crag in the Bishop area, offering many fine multi-pitch routes on superb rock. Drive past the South Lake turnoff for about two miles until Cardinal Pinnacle is seen up the talus slopes to the left. Park below the crag and walk up the talus for about ½ hour to reach the base of the rock.

Descents: From the summit there are several ways down. 1) Work off the back until one can downclimb a short, steep, improbable wall into the notch behind the pinnacle. From here, either side of the formation can be circled around. 2) Climb down along the south ridge (the right skyline when viewed from below) until one can drop into the gully on the pinnacle's right side. 3) Work down the south ridge, but rather than drop into the gully, circle around the base of the No Bozos pillar; this takes one to the base of the main west face routes. All three of these descents involve class 4 or easy class 5 climbing, and rappel anchors will probably not be found.

CARDINAL PINNACLE – West Face

1 V-8 Crack Formation
2 Crack of No Hope
3 Cardinal Sin
4 The Prow
5 Shadows in the Rain
6 Redline
7 Cucumbers
8 Red Bush
9 Regular Route
10 No Bozos
11 Heard it Through the Grapevine
12 Tan, Don't Burn

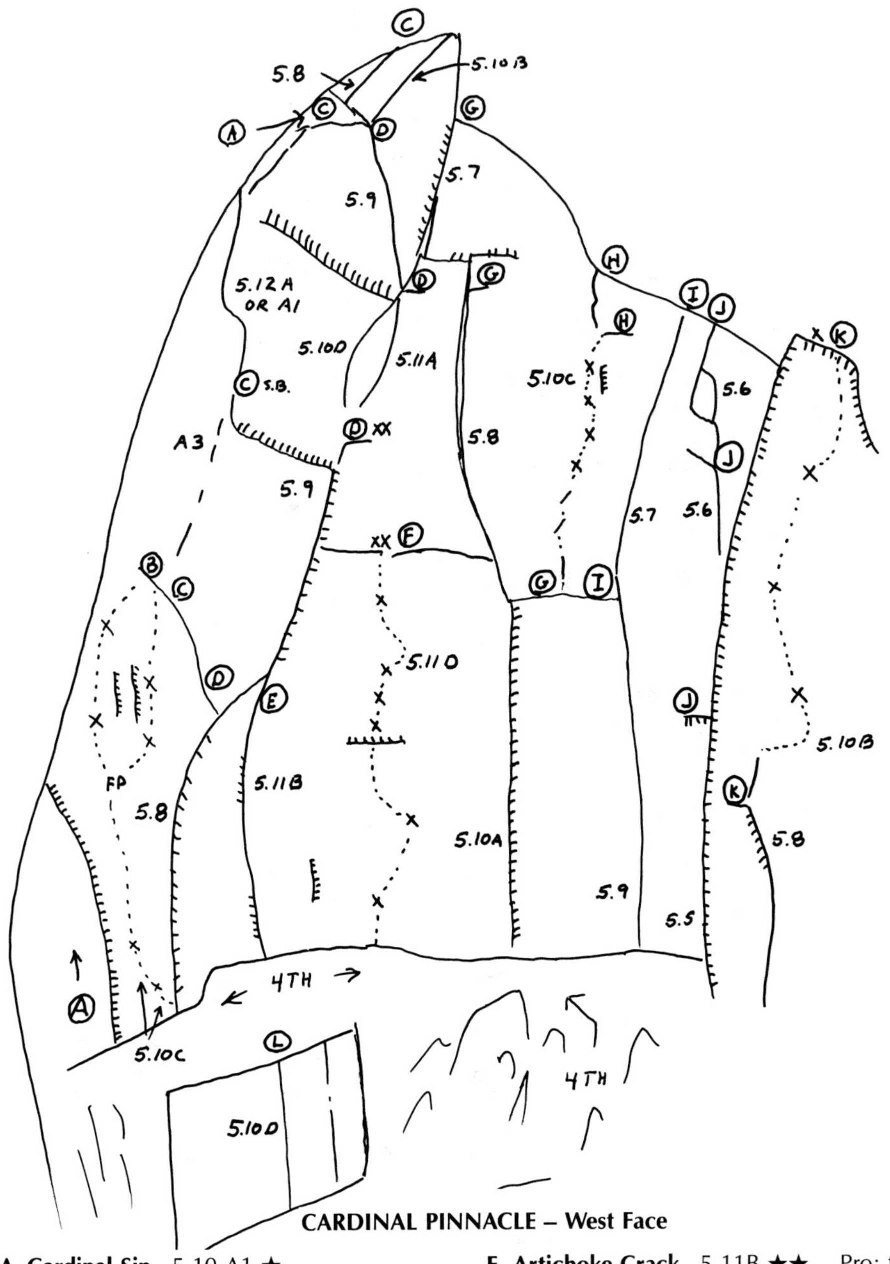

CARDINAL PINNACLE – West Face

A Cardinal Sin 5.10 A1 ★

B Reach for the Sky 5.10C ★

C The Prow 5.8 or 5.12A A3 Pro: include 4-6 pitons from KB's to a thick Arrow.

D Shadow in the Rain 5.11A ★★ Pro: to 3″, incl. many thin.

E Artichoke Crack 5.11B ★★ Pro: to

F Redline 5.11D ★★

G Cucumbers 5.10A ★★ Pro: to 3″

H Where Eagles Dare 5.10C ★★

I Red Bush 5.9 ★★ Pro: to 3″

J Regular Route 5.6 ★

K No Bozos 5.10B ★

L Tan, Don't Burn 5.10D ★

CARDINAL PINNACLE – North Face

1 Wild Kingdom
2 Crack of No Hope
3 Romancing the Stone
4 Cardinal Sin
5 Bard-Harrington Finish

CARDINAL PINNACLE – North Face

A **Wild Kingdom** 5.10C ★★ Pro: to 3½″
Marlon Perkins (var.) 5.10C ★★
B **Crack of No Hope** 5.10B ★★ Pro: to 3½″
C **Romancing the Stone** 5.11C ★★ Pro: to 2½″, many thin
D **Cardinal Sin** 5.10 A1 ★ Pro: to 5″, incl. 6-8 pitons, KB's to thick Arrows.
E **Bard-Harrington Finish** 5.10B ★★

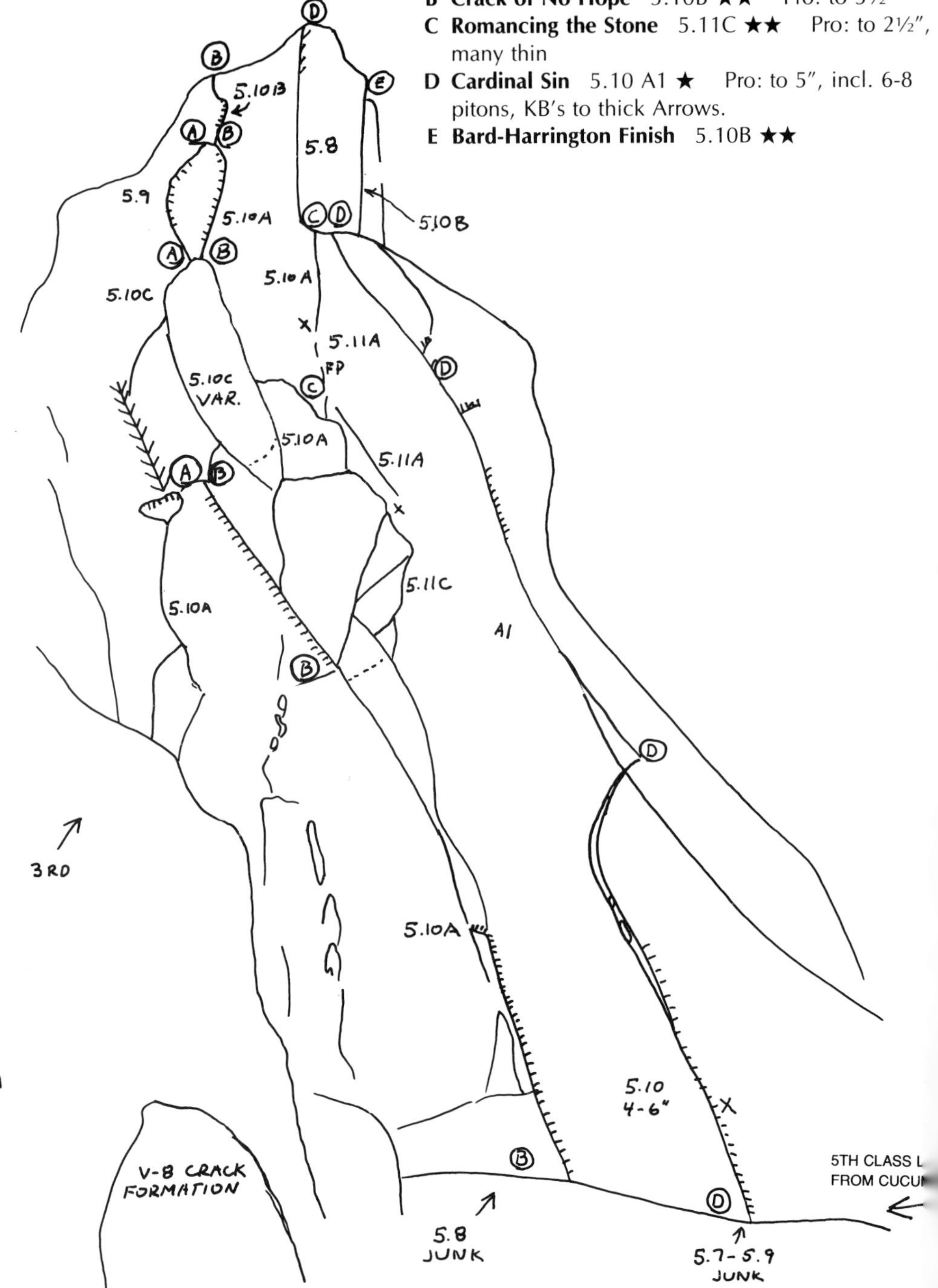

ROUTES WITHOUT TOPOS:

V-8 Crack 5.10D ★★ Pro: to 3½″ This striking crack is located on a small formation just left of the main pinnacle. It faces the main formation, more or less.

Tan, Don't Burn 5.10D ★ This is the longer of two cracks on a small copper-colored wall.

I Heard it Through the Grapevine 5.10D ★ Pro: many thin. Left around the corner from Tan, Don't Burn, climb a thin crack leading into a left-facing corner.

Dag Style 5.11A ★★ An obvious 1¼″ crack about 50′ long rising out of the north gully; descent #2 drops into the gully about 20′ left of the crack.

Agrarian Reform 5.11A ★ Across the gully from Dag Style, on a separate formation, is this long, left- facing corner.

Glass Houses 5.10B ★★ Rising almost directly out of the notch behind the pinnacle, this one-pitch climb passes by a thin "potato-chip" flake.

Stone's Throw 5.9 ★★ Just north of the notch and about 50′ right of Glass Houses is this thin crack.

LOWER BISHOP CREEK

The lower Bishop Creek areas are reached by driving west on Highway 168 (Line Street) from downtown Bishop. After 7.7 miles, Buttermilk Road will be seen on the right; this road leads to two of the areas, Buttermilk Country and Grouse Mountain. The third area, Little Egypt, is reached by continuing on Highway 168 about three miles until an unmarked paved road on the left leads down to Intake #4, one of Southern California Edison's power stations. Park at the end of the pavement.

LITTLE EGYPT

Little Egypt has some of the best hard cracks in the Bishop vicinity. The rock is coarse, high-desert type granite and tape might be desirable for many climbers. Seen from Highway 168, there appears to be three main outcrops, each behind the other and running away from the highway. The two rear ones are larger, but the rock is very poor; the quality climbing is all on the smaller, front formation. Climbing at Little Egypt is possible year-round, though the fact that the crag faces northwest makes it mainly a warm weather or late afternoon spot.

From the parking area walk across the dam. This involves climbing over a fence and down onto the dam. Continue through a patch of brush and a short distance up a hillside until a faint path leads straight left. Follow this for about ½ mile, staying low. A common mistake is to start uphill too soon, which leads to unpleasant terrain. The path will finally begin to rise and deteriorate just below the ridgecrest which has kept the crag out of view for the length of the approach. Crossing the ridge, the climber should come out near the left side of the cliff.

Coffee Bean 5.9 This is a giant boulder near the base of the left side of the cliff. One bolt protects its northeast side, the only known way up.

Route in Exile 5.8? This follows a left-facing corner near the left side of the large formation behind the main cliff. A grainy, unprotected approach slab leads to the corner. 3-4 pitches.

Exploding Crystal Galaxy 5.9 To the right of the main cliff and slightly further back, this climbs a left-curving arch. A bolt protects the final face moves out of the arch.

Death in the Afternoon 5.11D ★ Several hundred yards to the right of and behind the main cliff, this is a thin, left- curving crack which leads to a roof. Pro: Friends to #4.

Easy Way Out 5.8 A short crack immediately left of Death in the Afternoon. The routes share the final moves.

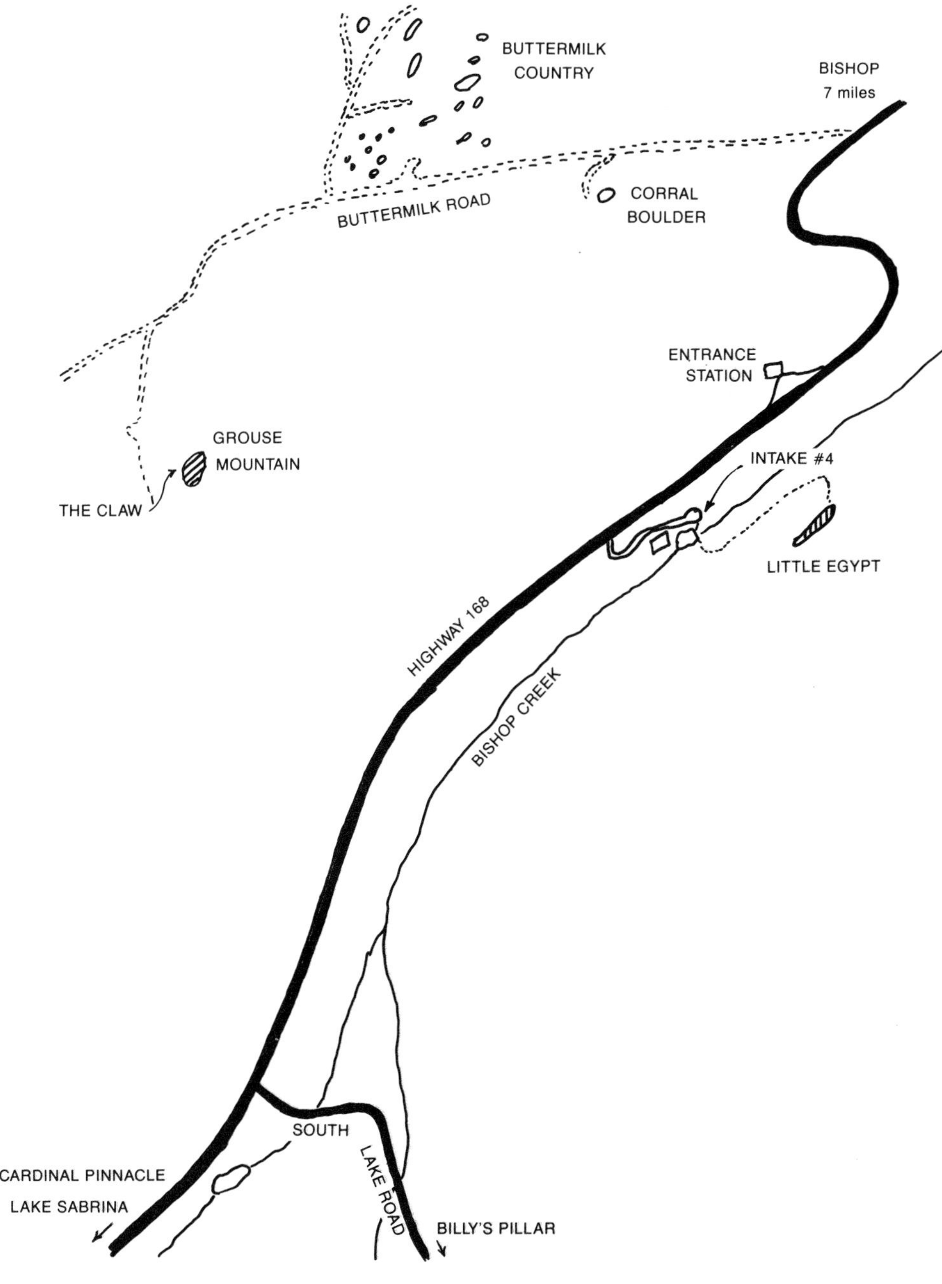
BUTTERMILK COUNTRY
BISHOP
7 miles
CORRAL BOULDER
BUTTERMILK ROAD
ENTRANCE STATION
GROUSE MOUNTAIN
THE CLAW
INTAKE #4
LITTLE EGYPT
HIGHWAY 168
BISHOP CREEK
SOUTH
LAKE ROAD
CARDINAL PINNACLE
LAKE SABRINA
BILLY'S PILLAR

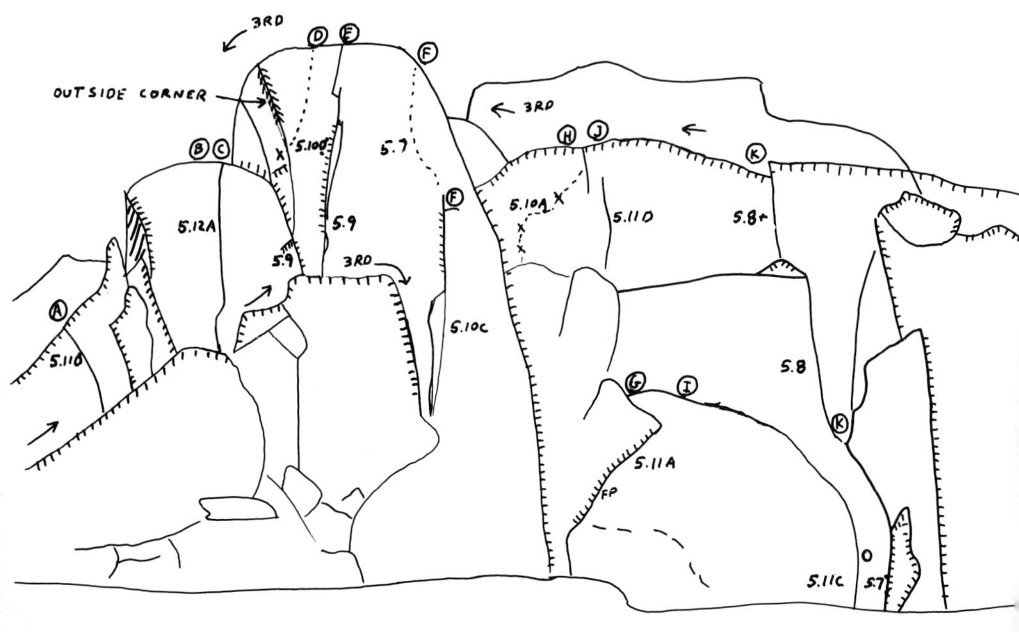

LITTLE EGYPT – Left Side

- **A Dog Day Afternoon** 5.11D ★ pro: to 2½″
- **B Expresso** 5.12A ★★ pro: to 3″, mostly ¾″ to 1¼″
- **C Hieroglyphics** 5.9 ★
- **D Flight** 5.10D ★
- **E Classic Crack** 5.9 ★★ pro: to 3½″
- **F The Gutter** 5.10C ★
- **G 4 Those About 2 Rock** 5.11A ★★ pro: to 3″
- **H Rosetta Stone** 5.10A
- **I Cannibal** 5.11C ★★ pro: to 2″
- **J Decaf** 5.11D ★★
- **K Pyramid Power** 5.8+ ★★ pro: to 2½″

LITTLE EGYPT – Left Side

1 Dog Day Afternoon
2 Expresso
3 Classic Crack
4 The Gutter
5 4 Those About 2 Rock
6 Rosetta Stone
7 Decaff

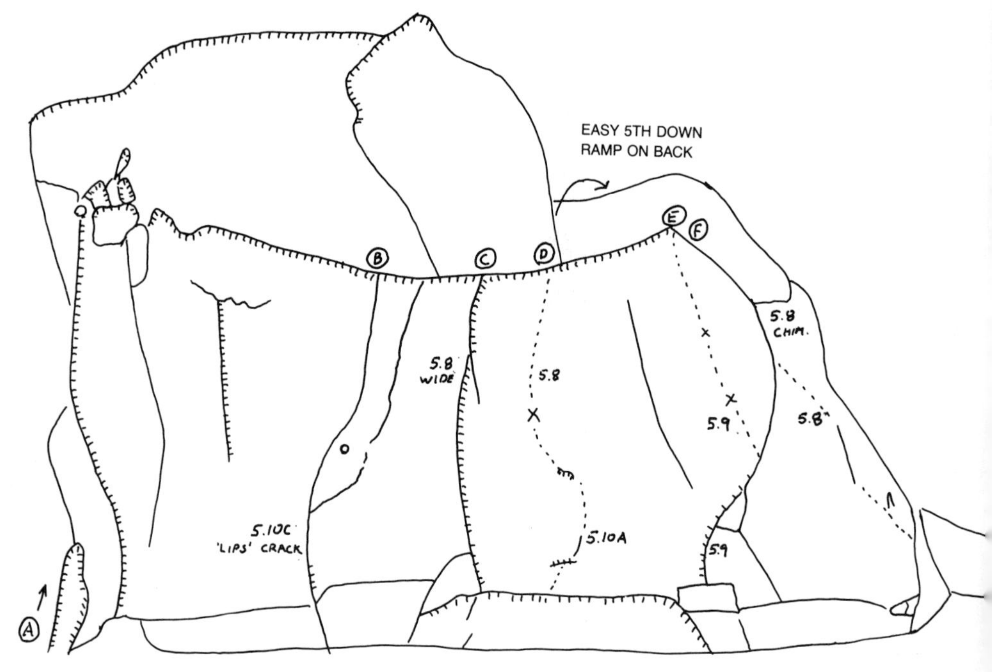

LITTLE EGYPT – Right Side

- **A Pyramid Power** 5.8+
- **B King Tut's Tomb** 5.10C ★★ pro: to 2½″
- **C Jamming with Jane** 5.8 pro: to 3½″
- **D Caravans** 5.10A ★ pro: to 2″
- **E Arabesque** 5.9 ★★ pro: to 2″
- **F Last Route** 5.8 ★ pro: to 3″

LITTLE EGYPT – Right Side

1 King Tut's Tomb
2 Caravans
3 Arabesque
4 Last Route
5 Exploding Crystal Galaxy

BUTTERMILK COUNTRY

The Buttermilk, or Peabody Boulders are probably the best-known climbing area in this guide. These large granite boulders are renowned for their many overhanging problems, some of which require a fair degree of boldness. Very few of the boulders have anchors on top, and it is advisable to check out potential descents before ascending a given boulder for the first time. Toproping is usually only done on the two largest boulders, Grandpa and Grandma Peabody; both of these boulders have bolt anchors on top. The accompanying map shows some, but certainly not all, of the best problems. Not as well known are a number of short leadable routes in the outcrops on the hillside above the boulderfield. The rock is not as consistently good here as on the boulders themselves; nonetheless, a few fine short routes exist. Generally, climbing is possible year-round in Buttermilk Country, although midsummer gets fairly hot and snow in early winter can close the area for a few days or weeks.

To reach Buttermilk Country, turn right on Buttermilk Road (dirt) from Highway 168 (Line Street). After two miles, faint dirt roads lead left by an old corral to a large round boulder about ⅛ mile from Buttermilk Road. This is the Corral Boulder. On its east face (left skyline when viewed from the turnoff) are two overhanging toprope cracks: the Corral Cracks. The left crack is the more overhanging of the two and is 5.11; a backrope is probably necessary to ensure a safe belay. The right crack is 5.12.

Continuing on Buttermilk Road, the main areas soon come into view. About 3.4 miles from Highway 168 is a large dirt parking turnout on the right. This is the best parking for most routes in the upper outcrops and will be referred to as the frontside parking area. It can also be used as parking for the Peabody Boulders, though most people park 150 yards or so farther along the road. A cattle guard will be reached 0.4 miles past the frontside parking area. A right turn here takes one to the backside of the Buttermilks. About ¼ mile past the cattle guard another road branches right, heading uphill. A short distance up this road is a small turnout on the right; this is the backside parking area, used for other crags in the upper outcrops. If one continues straight past the backside parking area turnoff, the road branches again in about ¼ mile. The left branch heads towards the Y-Boulder, an obvious large boulder with two cracks forming more of a "V" than a "Y". The right branch curves around the back of the formations, passing by a small slab on the right; this is Rump Rock. There are also a few good boulders a short distance farther along the road. This road eventually turns back east and rejoins the main Buttermilk Road, but a 4-wheel drive vehicle is probably necessary for crossing a wash. Please stay on the most established dirt roads and do not attempt to drive uphill from the frontside parking area or beyond the backside parking area.

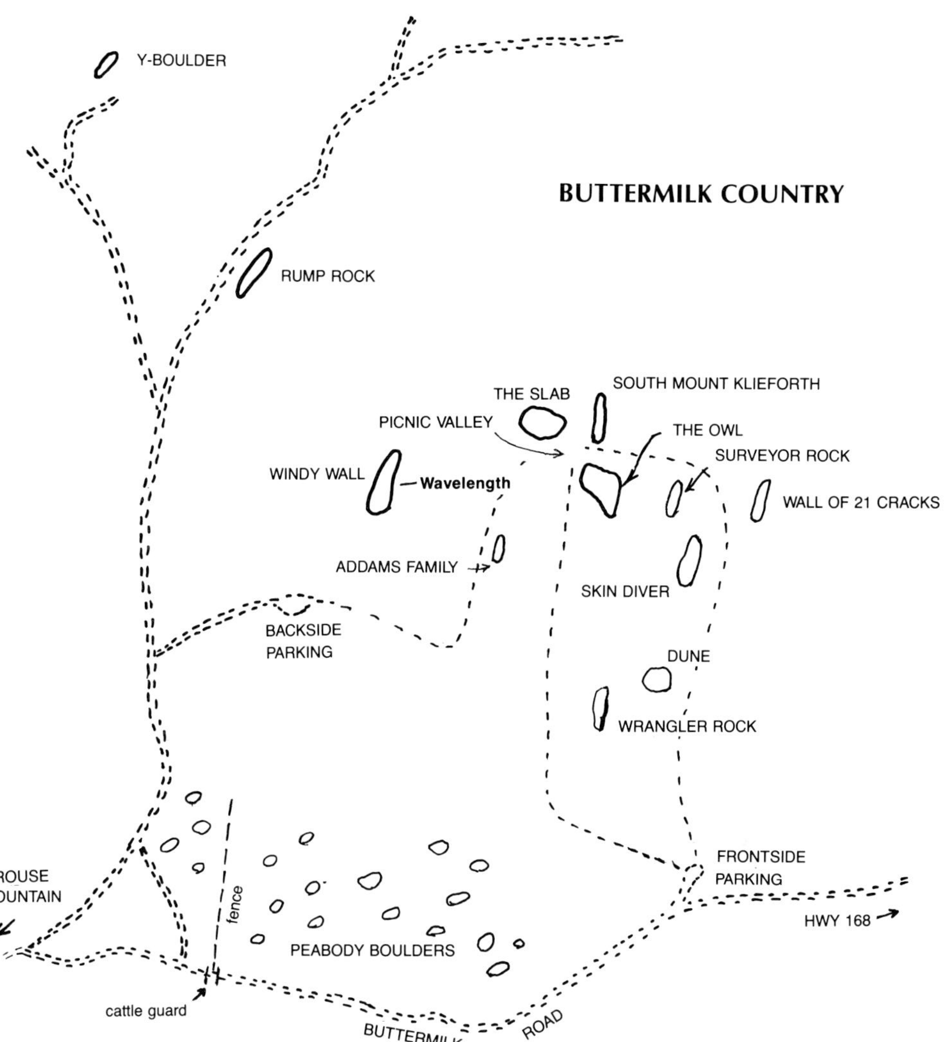
BUTTERMILK COUNTRY
Y-BOULDER
RUMP ROCK
THE SLAB
SOUTH MOUNT KLIEFORTH
PICNIC VALLEY
THE OWL
SURVEYOR ROCK
WINDY WALL
Wavelength
WALL OF 21 CRACKS
ADDAMS FAMILY
SKIN DIVER
BACKSIDE
PARKING
DUNE
WRANGLER ROCK
FRONTSIDE
PARKING
GROUSE
MOUNTAIN
fence
HWY 168
PEABODY BOULDERS
cattle guard
BUTTERMILK
ROAD

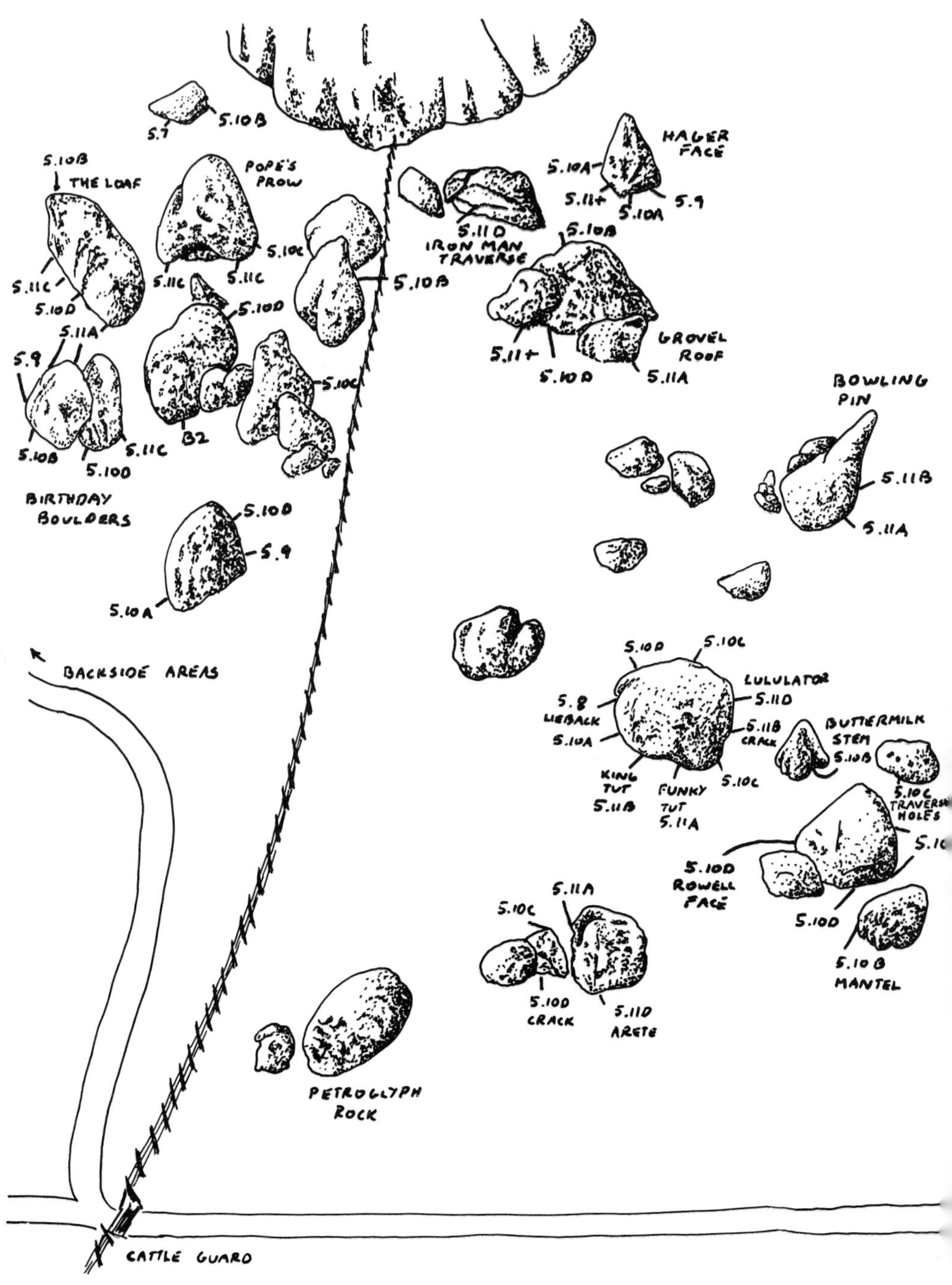
5.7
5.10B
HAGER FACE
5.10A
5.11+
5.10A
5.9
5.10B
THE LOAF
POPE'S PROW
5.10C
5.11C
5.11C
5.11C
5.10D
5.11D
IRON MAN TRAVERSE
5.10B
5.10B
5.10D
5.11A
5.9
5.10B
5.10D
5.11C
B2
5.10C
5.11+
5.10D
5.11A
GROVEL ROOF
BOWLING PIN
5.11B
5.11A
BIRTHDAY BOULDERS
5.10D
5.9
5.10A
BACKSIDE AREAS
5.10D
5.10C
LULULATOR
5.8 LIEBACK
5.11D
5.11B CRACK
5.10A
BUTTERMILK STEM 5.10B
KING TUT 5.11B
FUNKY TUT 5.11A
5.10C
5.10C TRAVERSE HOLES
5.10D ROWELL FACE
5.10D
5.10B MANTEL
5.11A
5.10C
5.10D CRACK
5.11D ARETE
PETROGLYPH ROCK
CATTLE GUARD

PEABODY BOULDERS

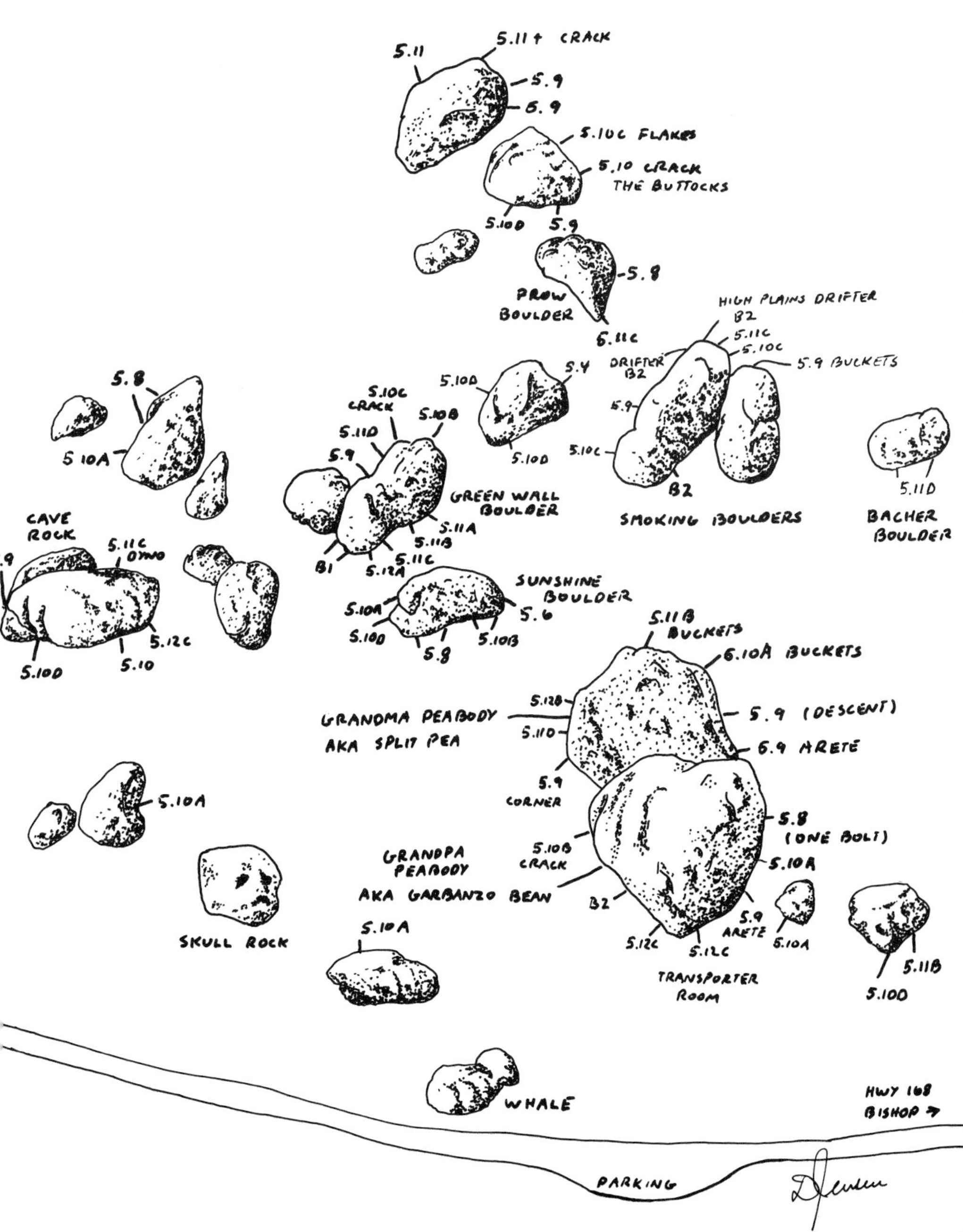

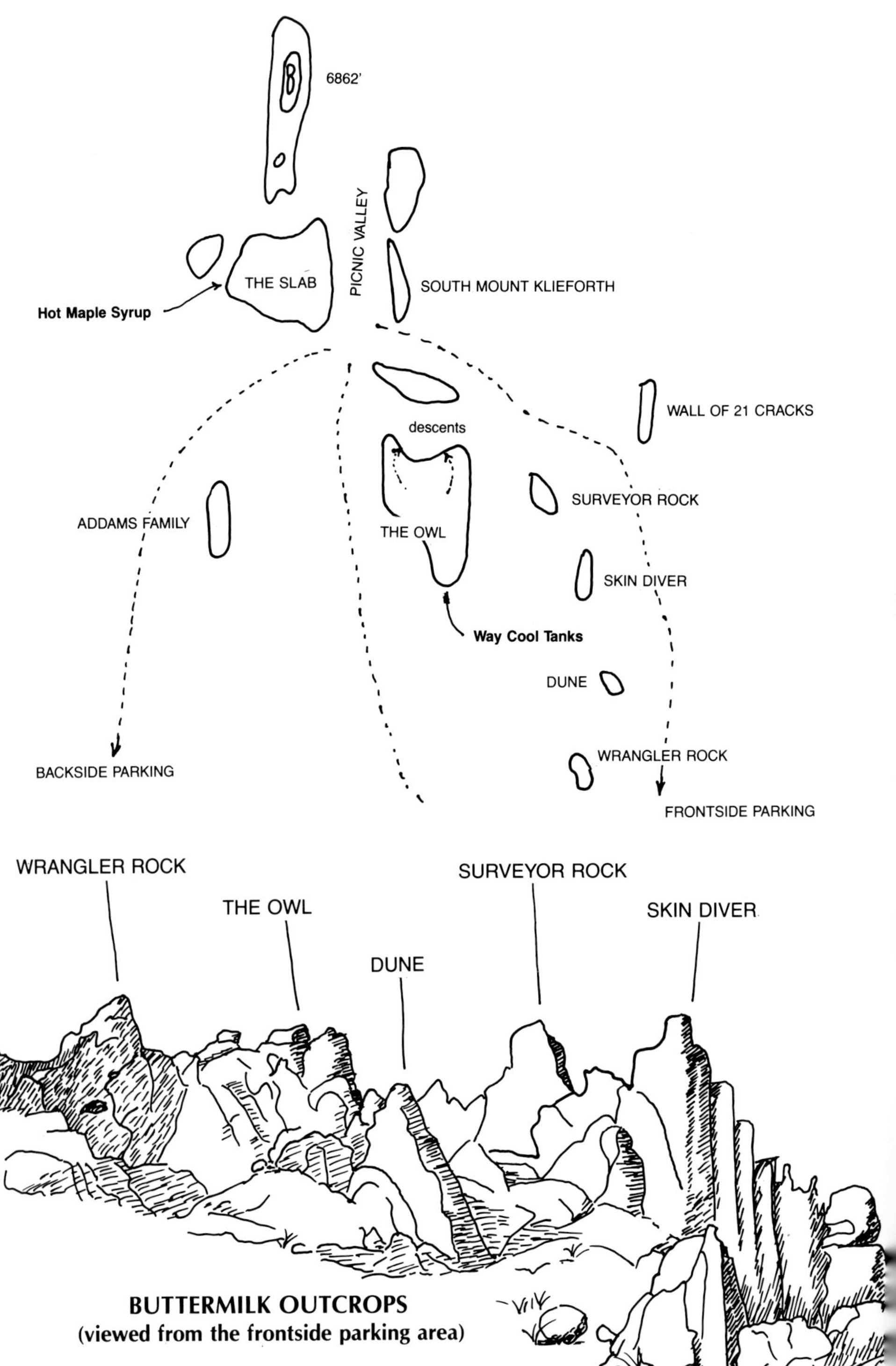

BUTTERMILK OUTCROPS
(viewed from the frontside parking area)

WRANGLER ROCK AND VICINITY

Seen from the frontside parking area, this is the leftmost (closest) of several towers to the north, a pointed tower with a dark, bucketed face.

- A **Lisa's Crack** 5.8
- B **The Spittoon** 5.6
- C **Buttermilk Pancakes** 5.9 ★ pro: to 2½"; best done as one pitch.
- D **Granola** 5.10A ★ pro: to 2"
- E **Dune** 5.9 ★

SKIN DIVER

This is the next pointed tower northeast of Wrangler Rock.

A Freedom of Choice 5.10D ★★ pro: to 2″
B My Beach, My Wave 5.10B ★★ pro: to 3″
C Weekend Warriors 5.10A
D 5.7 approach pitch

WALL OF 21 CRACKS

This wall is a short distance past Skin Diver and contains a number of cracks ranging from 4th class to 5.10, offering soloing, toproping, or leading.

SURVEYOR ROCK

This is an orange formation with several left- slanting cracks on its east face.

Miracles of Modern Science 5.10C This is the leftmost crack. The bouldering start is the crux. Pro: to 3″

Wide Berth 5.10A The rightmost crack, which doesn't quite reach the ground. Pro: to 4″

BUTTERMILK COUNTRY FROM THE BACKSIDE ROAD

PICNIC VALLEY AREA

Picnic Valley is the north-south running corridor between The Slab (on the west) and The Owl and South Mount Klieforth (on the east). It is the central region of the Buttermilk outcrops and can be approached from the previous routes by continuing past Surveyor Rock and through a narrow passage between The Owl and South Mount Klieforth. An alternate approach from the frontside parking area is to walk uphill (west), following a faint road to the top of a crest, then turning right and entering Picnic Valley from the south, passing behind Wrangler Rock. A third approach is from the backside parking area; walk up the road to its end, then turn left and pass by the Addams Family before coming to the south face of The Slab.

SOUTH MOUNT KLIEFORTH

This rock, just north of The Owl, has an overhanging west face. Two routes are known.

Daydream 5.10A? Near the left side of the west face, climb a crack with large buckets to its left. About 30′.

Dean's Dream 5.11A ★★ Left of the center of the west face, a bouldering start leads to overhanging face and crack climbing that passes a piton near the top. Pro: to 3″.

THE OWL

This is a large, jumbled formation with several summits and routes on all four faces. Descents off both the true summit and the lower west summit are made to the north, in to the narrow passage between this formation and South Mount Klieforth; both descents involve grainy downclimbing (class 4-5).

Sean's Toprope 5.11A (TR) This is on the east face of the Owl, directly behind Surveyor Rock. It follows a thin crack, with one jog to the left.

Regular Route 5.5 Climb the descent route to the lower west summit, then work up to the true summit via a right-slanting ramp that leads to a short headwall protected by an old fixed pin.

A Extreme Levine Meets Godzilla 5.10B ★ This is on the west face. Pro: regular rack, incl. (2) 4″

B Vertical Smiles 5.10C ★★ pro: to 3″

Way Cool Tanks 5.10B ★ This route is on the south face of the Owl, most easily approached from that direction. It is a knobby bucketed wall with four bolts. The crux is getting off the ground.

Armadillo Crack 5.8 ★ A hand and fist crack just right of the previous route.

THE SLAB – South Face

A No Fat Chicks 5.10A

B Great Buttermilk Crack 5.11C ★ pro: to 3½″, incl. many ⅜″ to ¾″

C Bear Fight 5.10A

Hot Maple Syrup 5.10D ★★ This route is on the west face of The Slab, left and around the corner from No Fat Chicks. Starting from a pit, climb an overhanging thin crack which leads to a steep, plated face.

THE SLAB – East Face

A The Slab – Regular Route 5.6 On the left side of the east face, climb either of two cracks (both 5.6) up and right to a belay behind a large detached block. Tunnel behind the block and belay on its top. Traverse left (Sharp's Scenic Stroll) and climb a short vertical crack to the top.

B The Slab Direct 5.9 ★

C Robbins Crack 5.10A (TR) ★

Macho Homo 5.9 Near the right side of the east face, climb a short corner to a roof. Work up and left to a bolt, then continue bearing left to top out near the top of the Robbins Crack.

THE ADDAMS FAMILY

This small rock lies a short distance south of The Slab and is best approached from the backside parking area.

Morticia 5.8 A wide crack lies on the left side of the rock.

The Tempest 5.11B (TR) Just right of Morticia face climbing leads to a thin crack.

Pugsley 5.6 This is the chimney in the center of the face.

Uncle Fester 5.10D (TR) A right-slanting crack just right of Pugsley.

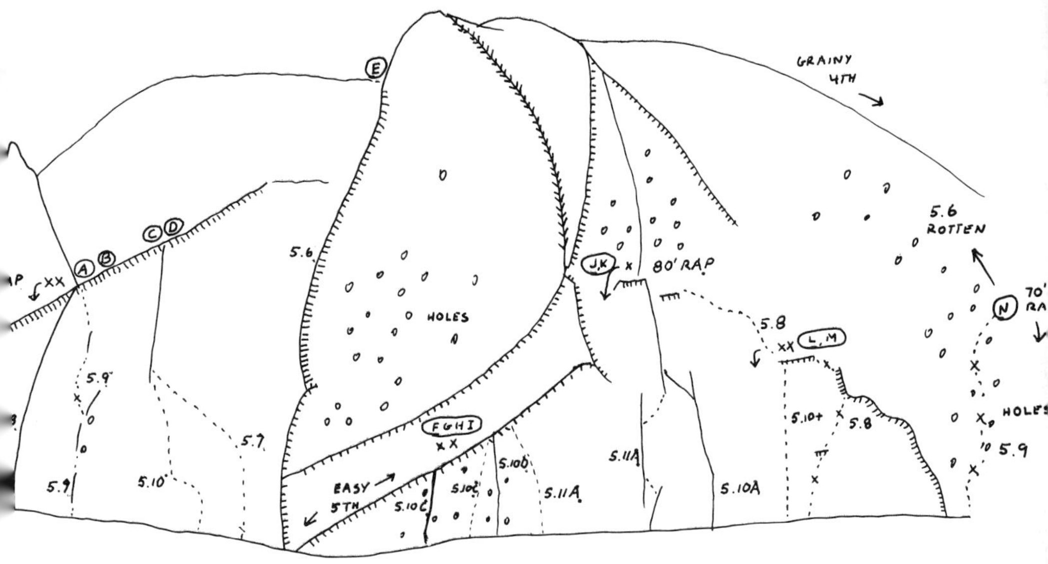

WINDY WALL

The Windy wall is the west face of a large formation northeast of the backside parking area.

- A **Scoot** 5.8 ★★
- B **Holy Smokes** 5.9+ ★
- C **Starting Over** 5.10
- D **Aniphylactic Freakout** 5.7
- E **Coyote Ugly** 5.6
- F **Wild Garlic** 5.10C ★
- G **Stall Wall** 5.10C ★ (TR)
- H **Rubber Gloves and Razor Blades** 5.10D ★
- I **Clean Sweep** 5.11A ★ (TR)
- J **Dr. Detroit** 5.11A ★ serious lead
- K **Dr. Zyme** 5.10A ★★
- L **Allspice** 5.10+ ★ (TR)
- M **Cayenne Pepper** 5.8 ★
- N **Miles From Nowhere** 5.9?

Wavelength 5.11C ★ This is a striking finger crack on the east side of the Windy Wall formation. There is a bolt about a third of the way up though it is usually toproped; approach the top up the grainy south slopes of the rock. Finding an adequate anchor seems to present a problem, though anchoring a rope at the base of the west face and running it over the top works.

WINDY WALL
1 Scoot
2 Holy Smokes
3 Starting Over
4 Aniphylactic Freakout
5 Wild Garlic
6 Rubber Gloves and Razor Blades

RUMP ROCK

A Rumpadoodle 5.10A
B Because It's There 5.9 two bolts
C Stop Smoking Sense 5.9 two bolts
D Mikey Likes It 5.8 1 bolt

Y-BOULDER

A Why Left 5.10C ★ two bolts

B Left Y-Crack 5.9 both starts 5.9, easy above.

C Right Y-Crack 5.8 ★★

D Why Right 5.10B ★★ two bolts

Faith 5.12B ★ Just left and around the corner from Why Left is a steep, small holds face climb.

GROUSE MOUNTAIN

Grouse Mountain is the large round hill about two miles southwest of Buttermilk Country; its summit is about 7500′. There is a fair amount of exposed rock on its flanks, but most of it is dirty or rotten. Nevertheless, this area has some future potential for those climbers willing to make long approaches to short routes. Only two routes are known, both on a buttress called The Claw, located on the southwest side of Grouse Mountain. From the top of these routes it is about a 15 minute walk to the summit of the peak.

To approach The Claw, continue driving past the cattle guard mentioned in the Buttermilk Country text (don't turn right). After 0.4 miles there will be a fork. Either way can be taken as they will rejoin, but the right fork is the better road. After another mile, turn left on a lesser road. This road is very rocky, but most cars should be able to make it another mile farther, ignoring one left turn. Here a stream crossing will prevent all but 4-wheel drive vehicles from driving farther. Continue up the road past the stream crossing, passing along the western slopes of Grouse Mountain until one can see The Claw on the hillside to the left. Drop down and cross another stream, then head up sandy slopes to the base of the rock.

A **The Claw** 5.7 This is a 2-pitch chimney system on the left side of the face.

B **Space Cowboys** 5.10B A long 5.7 pitch leads up to a belay below a crack splitting the overhanging summit headwall, the crux of the route.

BISHOP TUFF

The volcanic tablelands north of the town of Bishop offer a number of possibilities for climbing, mainly bouldering and toproping, although there are a few leadable cracks in some areas. Climbing has gone on in a number of different spots, but this guide will only cover the two most popular (and best) areas, the Chalk Bluffs and the Pink Cliffs. The main advantage of these areas is their easy accessibility during winter; the Chalk Bluffs, facing due south, are climbable even on cold winter days, while the Pink Cliffs, facing east are climbable on winter days that are mild. Both areas would be extremely hot in the summer.

THE CHALK BLUFFS

The Chalk Bluffs are a series of volcanic cliffs from 30-70 feet high and extending for about four miles. They are reached by driving west on Highway 395 from the town of Bishop for about seven miles, then turning north on the Pleasant Valley Road. This road winds through a campground before meeting the Chalk Bluff Road. Turning left will take one to Pleasant Valley Dam and Reservoir, while turning right will take one along the length of the Chalk Bluffs. Toprope problems have been done all along the Chalk Bluffs, but the best problems are the Birdie Cracks and the Catalog Cracks. The Birdie Cracks will be found about 1.3 miles east of the intersection of the Pleasant Valley Road and the Chalk Bluff Road; they are three cracks in an overhanging wall distinguished by an offwidth crack in the center of the wall. The right crack is right of the offwidth, the center crack moves left out of the offwidth a short off the ground, and the left crack slants left, then doglegs right. All of these cracks are in the 5.10+/5.11– range. They have not been led, but potentially could be. Leading them would certainly push them closer to solid 5.11. A thin crack which slants right out of the right Birdie Crack is 5.12.

The Catalog Cracks (named for their appearance in an old Chouinard catalog) will be found about 0.7 mile east of the Birdie Cracks. A faint trail leads to them from a point 0.1 miles farther east along the road. These cracks are shorter and easier than the Birdie Cracks; in the 5.9/5.10– range.

THE PINK CLIFFS

The Pink Cliffs are another volcanic cliff band, about 100 feet high and ⅓ mile long. They offer a number of fine topropes as well as six to eight leadable cracks in the 5.9-5.10 range. Good bouldering is also found nearby. There are potential problems all along the cliff, but the greatest concentration of climbs is near the left end.

To reach the Pink Cliffs, drive north from Bishop on Highway 6. After about 1.5 miles, turn left on Five Bridges Road. This road winds around and passes a cement plant; just past this, turn right on Casa Diablo Road (this point may also be reached by continuing east along the Chalk Bluffs Road from the Pleasant Valley area). Continue on Casa Diablo Road for 6 to 7 miles until the cliffs are visible to the left. Continue driving (seemingly past the cliffs) until a dirt road to the left leads back to the rocks in about 1½ miles. The Casa Diablo Road is rough and rocky, while the unmarked road to the cliff has some sandy spots. Most 2-wheel drive vehicles should be able to make it, but caution is advised.

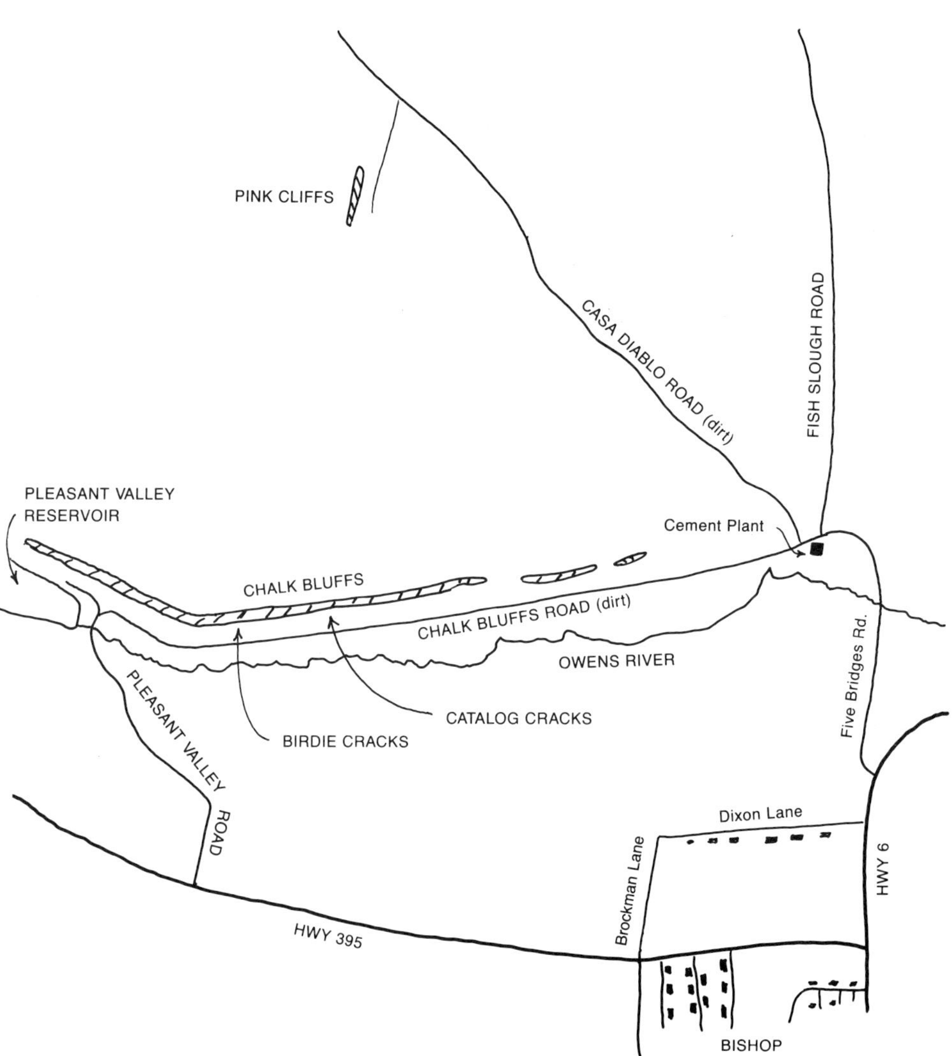
PINK CLIFFS
CASA DIABLO ROAD (dirt)
FISH SLOUGH ROAD
PLEASANT VALLEY
RESERVOIR
Cement Plant
CHALK BLUFFS
CHALK BLUFFS ROAD (dirt)
OWENS RIVER
Five Bridges Rd.
CATALOG CRACKS
BIRDIE CRACKS
PLEASANT VALLEY
ROAD
Dixon Lane
Brockman Lane
HWY 6
HWY 395
BISHOP

SCHEELITE

The Scheelite cliffs are located in Pine Creek Canyon. From Highway 395, 9 miles west of Bishop, turn onto the Pine Creek Road. After 3 miles, the tiny village of Rovana is reached (no services available). Four miles past Rovana there is a dirt pullout on the right at a point where telephone lines cross the road. This is the best parking for the routes Mini-mart through The Rattler. A quarter mile further is a turnout by a group of trees. This is the best parking for PSOM Pinnacle and Elderberry Buttress. One half mile further, several roads lead right, the main one going to the Stratcor Mine storage facilities (no trespassing). Park at the start to one of these roads and walk up the right-most road to reach Pratt's Crack Canyon. For the Cyanide Cliffs, walk up the road partway, then wander up slopes to the left.

The rock is high desert granite of varying quality. One characteristic of these routes is the amount of Mountain Mahogany bushes found on ledges and sometimes, unfortunately, in the middle of pitches. These bushes are often used for belay anchors and rappels, and should be inspected carefully – they are rarely as strong as a pine or oak bush of comparable size. The climbs generally face southeast, making climbing possible year-round, though the climbs within the narrow box canyon containing Pratt's Crack receive no sun in the winter, making them more of a warm weather venture.

CLIFFS BELOW ELDERBERRY BUTTRESS

Mini-mart 5.8 This route climbs up to a left- facing roof and out its right side to the top in two pitches. Descend down and left with one 60′ rappel.

Catholic Boy 5.7 ★ Climb cracks on the left side of the formation leading to a shallow right-facing book and the top. The best descent from this and the following route is to climb straight right (5.3) to a ledge atop Footloose and rappel 70′ into the chimney on the formation's right side.

Eleventh Commandment 5.11A ★★ This follow four bolts 30′ right of Catholic Boy.

Footloose 5.11B ★★ Start in a thin crack just left of a right-facing book. Climb to a bolt, then left to another bolt and back right to a bolt anchor. Rappel, or climb a 5.8 pitch to the top.

PCB Route 5.9 Across the gully from Footloose the route climbs the left side of a broken buttress. The first pitch trends up and left to a ledge with a bush around a corner. Step back right and climb a finger crack to the top. Descend right.

St. Valentine's Day Massacre 5.9 ★ Start at the lower right edge of a slab. Climb up and slightly left past a piton to a blocky belay. The second pitch goes by two bolts, the second having no hanger. Descend right.

Laundromat 5.10D ★ Above and right of St. Valentine's Day Massacre, this route climbs a 3-pitch left- facing book. The first pitch leans sharply left. Rappel Spin Cycle or the gully to the left.

Spin Cycle 5.10C ★ (not shown) This leads 3 pitches up the crack system right of Laundromat.

Beedie Boys 5.9 A1 Wander up the broken buttress above and right of Laundromat for 6 pitches or so, using one or two points of aid only.

Cracks Cross 5.10A ★ This route climbs a chimney to a ledge, then up a crack/groove splitting a smooth wall.

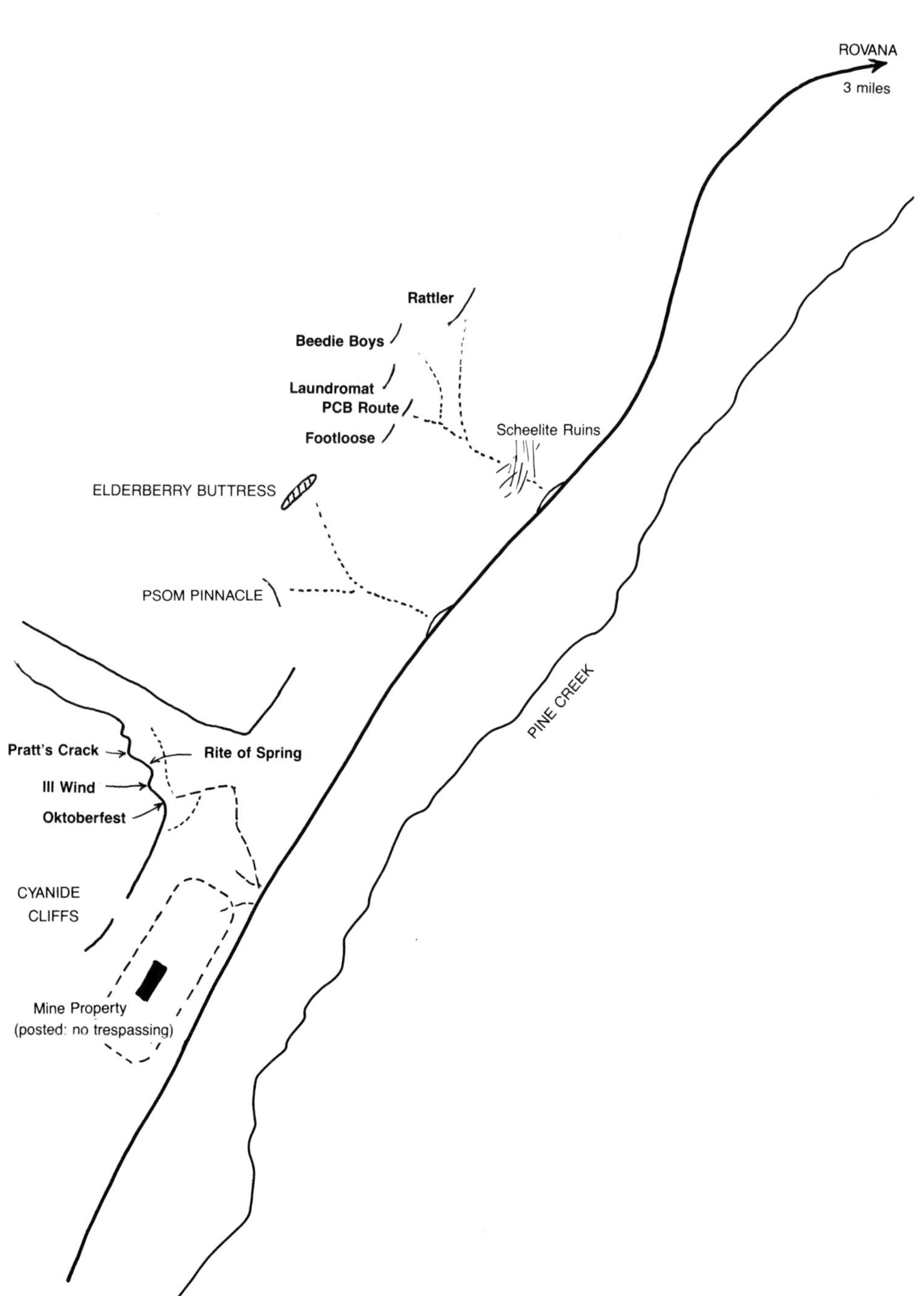
ROVANA
3 miles
Rattler
Beedie Boys
Laundromat
PCB Route
Footloose
Scheelite Ruins
ELDERBERRY BUTTRESS
PSOM PINNACLE
PINE CREEK
Pratt's Crack
Rite of Spring
Ill Wind
Oktoberfest
CYANIDE
CLIFFS
Mine Property
(posted: no trespassing)

Sagebrush Serenade 5.10A ★ Zigzag up cracks and face on the left side of the formation. The first move is the crux. Rappel left; one rope adequate.

The Rattler 5.10B ★ Climb cracks and flakes left of a slanting chimney to an alcove. Tricky moves lead to a belay in a scoop. Continue up and left, then back right to meet the slanting chimney near its top. Rappel right; one rope adequate.

CLIFFS BELOW ELDERBERRY BUTTRESS

1 **Elderberry Buttress – Regular Route**
2 **Mini-mart**
3 **Catholic Boy**
4 **Eleventh Commandment**
5 **Footloose**
6 **PCB Route**
7 **St. Valentine's Day Massacre**
8 **Laundromat**
9 **Beedie Boys**
10 **Cracks Cross**
11 **Sagebrush Serenade**
12 **The Rattler**

ELDERBERRY BUTTRESS AREA

1 **PSOM Pinnacle**
2 **Big Chill**
3 **Elderberry Buttress – Regular Route**
4 **In Dubious Battle**
5 **Joint Effort**
6 **Thin Ice**
7 **Elderberry Buttress approach**

PSOM Pinnacle 5.8 ★ PSOM Pinnacle is a small pillar on a slab distinguished by an orange dike running horizontally through it. There are many variations to this route, but the most obvious is this: Starting about 150′ down canyon (left) from a line dropped from the top of the pinnacle, climb a 5.7 face past a bolt to a ledge. Work up and right on 5.8 cracks to a class 3 area. Higher, traverse right to the pinnacle's left side and climb that to its top. Two 130′ rappels take one to the ground.

Serious but not Desperate 5.10A ★★ (not shown) Starting from a point almost directly below PSOM Pinnacle, climb two bolted pitches to the right side of the pinnacle and follow that to the top.

Big Chill 5.9 Just right of the previous route climb a 5.7 crack and corner to a big ledge. Follow right-slanting cracks and seams past two bolts to a bush belay. Two 2-rope rappels lead to the ground.

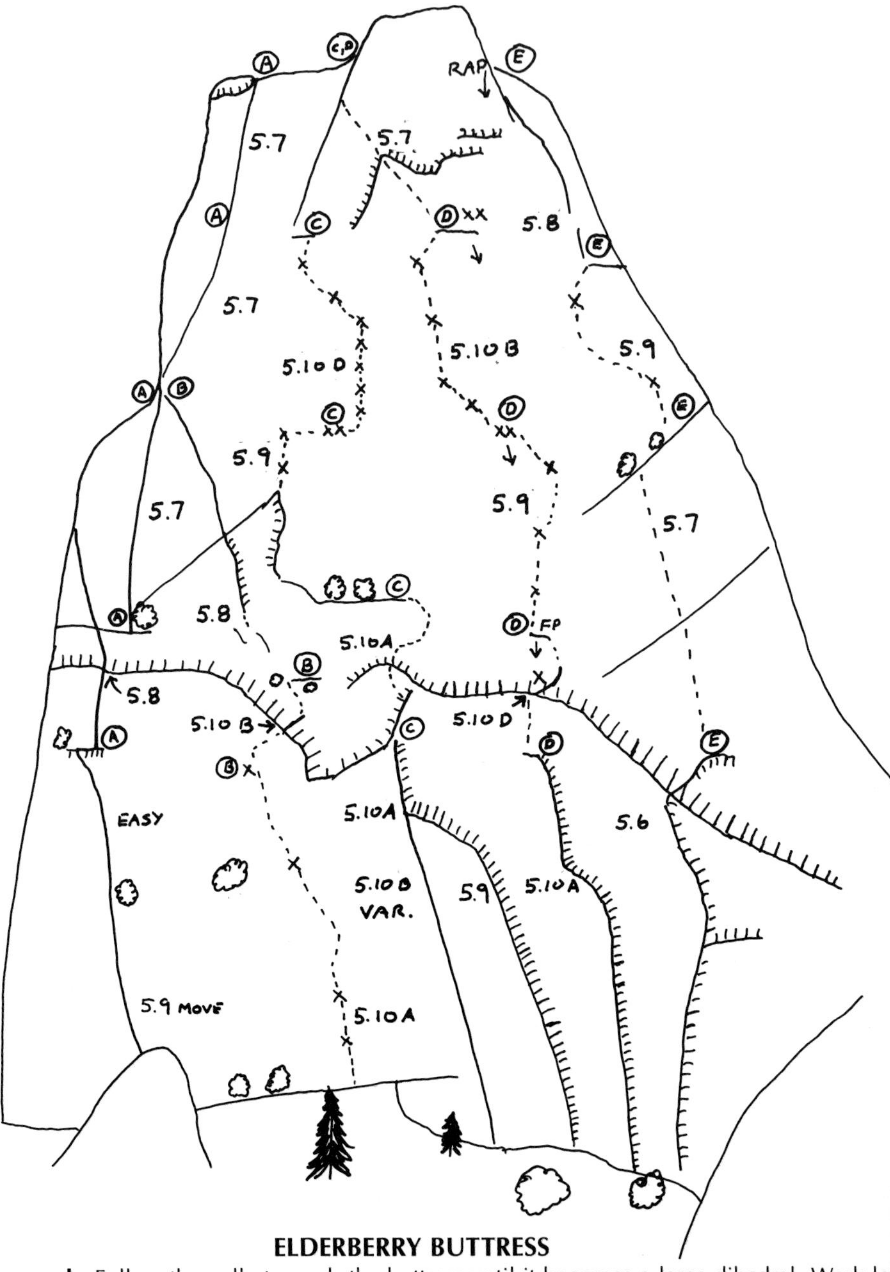

ELDERBERRY BUTTRESS

Approach: Follow the gully towards the buttress until it becomes a large dihedral. Work left on brushy slabs and up about 200 feet until it is possible to climb back into the gully above the dihedral. Be prepared to rope up.

Descent: Four 2-rope rappels lead down Joint Effort, then retrace the approach.

- **A Regular Route** 5.9 ★★
- **B Appolonia** 5.10B ★★
- **C In Dubious Battle** 5.10D ★★
- **D Joint Effort** 5.10D ★★
- **E Thin Ice** 5.9 ★

PRATT'S CRACK BUTTRESS – Left Side

1 Ill Wind
2 Instant Insanity
3 Newlywed Game
4 Keine Route
5 Bwana Dik
6 Armando's Stilletto

PRATT'S CRACK BUTTRESS – Left Side

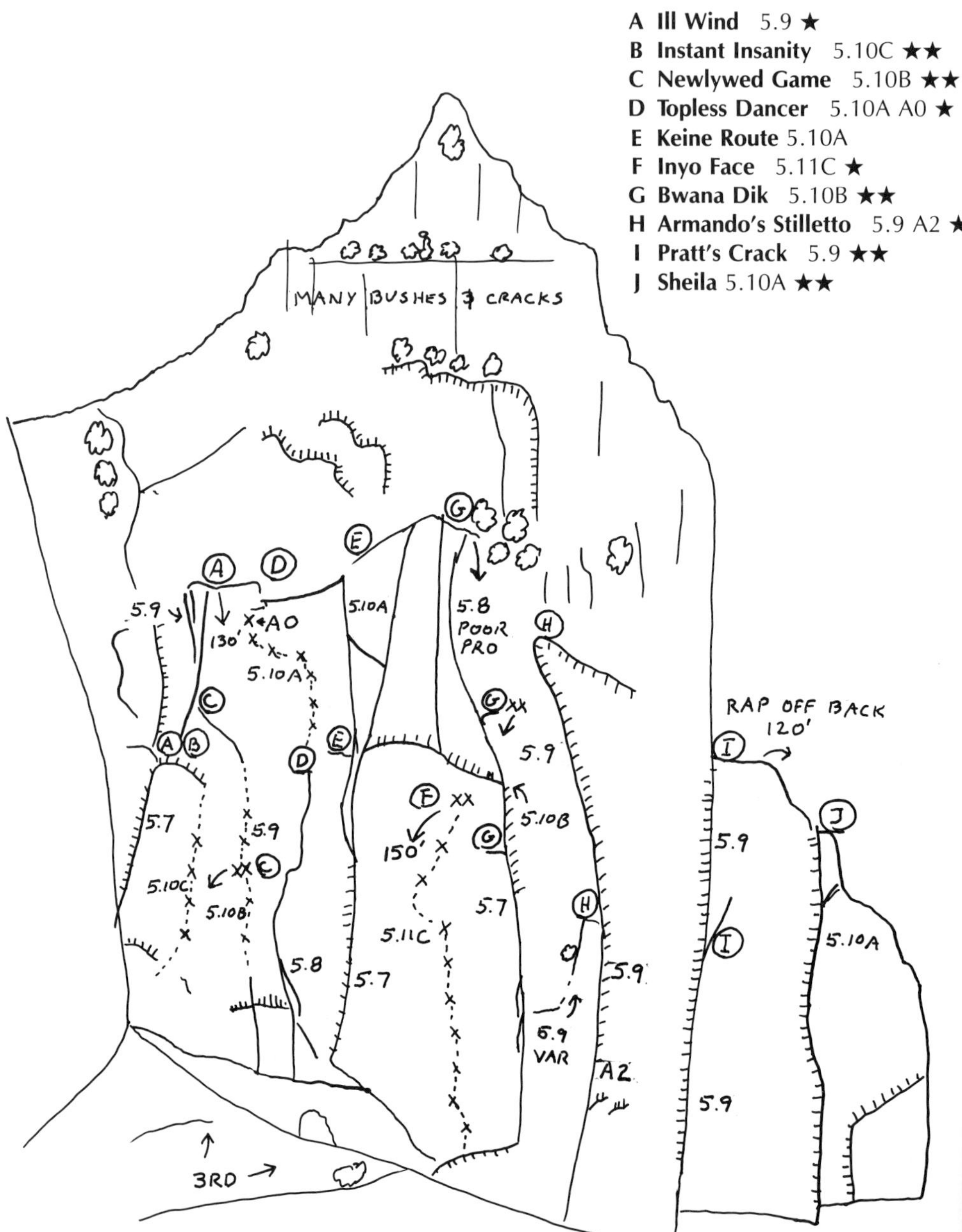

Oktoberfest 5.10B ★ At the left side of the mouth of Pratt's Crack Canyon, near where the approach road narrows to a trail, climb a steep corner just right of an ugly chimney to a roof. Work right under the roof then up easier cracks to the top. Walk off left. Take Friends #1-#3.

Master of the Obscure 5.8 On the wall left of **Ill Wind** are two deep, ugly chimney systems. Climb the right one for two pitches. Rappel 150′.

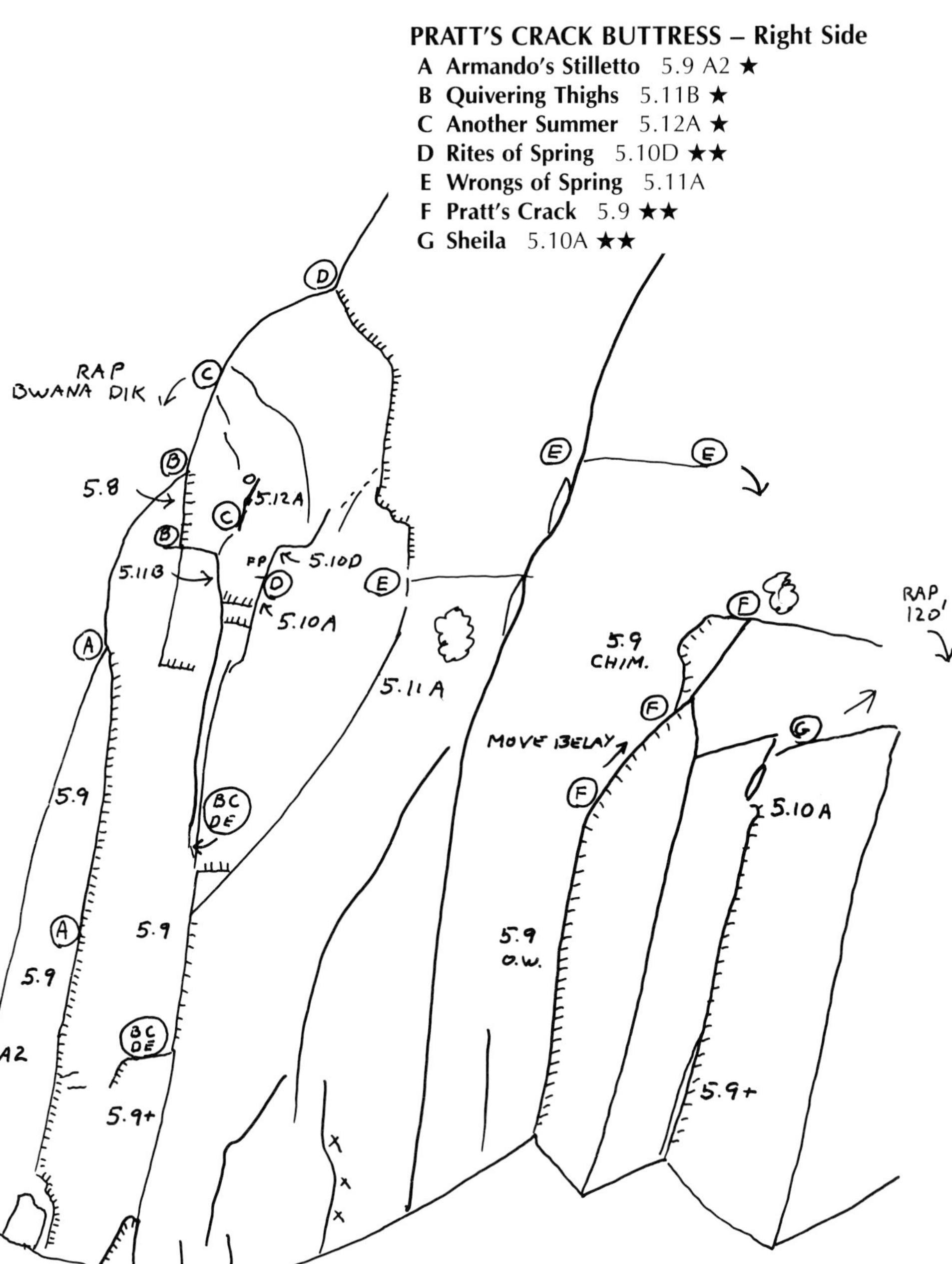

Nice Guys Finish Last 5.10B ★ This route climbs five pitches above the Pratt's Crack rappels. All five pitches are 5.9 or 5.10. Approach via Pratt's, Sheila, or by climbing up the rappels (5.7?). Rappel the route.

Little Pinnacle 5.7 Around the corner to the right of Sheila is an unprotected chimney which leads to the detached summit. There is apparently another route on the back side of the pinnacle that starts from near the base of the Pratt's Crack rappels.

CYANIDE CLIFFS

A Increased Insanity 5.10B Climb cracks on the left side of the formation for two pitches to a large ledge. The third (crux) pitch goes up an open book off the back of the ledge. Downclimb right.

B No Future 5.11A ★ Starting just right of a left-facing book, climb up, then left past bolts and studs and finally back up and right to a ledge with a bush. Downclimb right. Carry tie-offs or keyhole hangers.

C Overhang Bypass 5.8 ★ Climb a 3½″ crack to a belay above a bush and below a roof. Face climb left around the roof.

D Flash or Crash 5.11A ★ Surmount the roof mentioned in the preceding route directly. Carry TCUs.

E Square Meal 5.9 A2 Climb up to a large, square roof and nail out its right side. KBs and horizontals needed.

Star Search 5.11A ★ (not shown) Start on Square Meal then follow double cracks leading to the right lip of the roof. Take TCUs.

F Mystery Novel 5.3 An easy, broken ramp. Rappel Triple Jeopardy.

G Toxic Shock 5.8 Climb loose flakes and cracks on the outer arete of the Mystery Novel ramp. Rappel Triple Jeopardy.

H Triple Jeopardy 5.9 ★ Follow a straight-in crack which turns into triple cracks. Rappel 140′ from a bush at its top.

WHEELER CREST

The Wheeler Crest is a confusing jumble of granite towers and faces on the east side of Wheeler Ridge about 15 miles northwest of Bishop. The routes are well-guarded by strenuous approaches of one to three hours. For this reason, Wheeler Crest has never been a popular climbing area, even though the longest routes in the Bishop vicinity will be found here. Many of the routes listed here are unrepeated, and will probably remain so, even with the publishing of this guide.

When viewed from Highway 395 Wheeler Crest can be divided into three sections. On the left is the Smokestack-Wells Peak section, dominated by the twin towers of the Smokestack and Adam's Rib (also known as the Rabbit Ears), and the larger but less attractive mass of Wells Peak, immediately to their right. Above and right of Wells Peak is Neptune Tower, a wide face with several vertical crack systems. Neptune Tower is the leftmost and highest formation in a band of pinkish-orange crags running down and right; this section is referred to as the Pink Band. Above the right side of the Pink Band is a cluster of grey towers, also running down and right. This is the Grey Band.

Approaches to the routes are all made from dirt roads which originate from the tiny settlement known as Forty Acres, about two miles west of Highway 395 and best reached via Pine Creek Road and North Round Valley Road from the south. Forty Acres can also be reached from Birchim Lane, which runs west off of old Highway 395 (Lower Rock Creek Road) about two miles north of Pine Creek Road.

There are six canyons, or gullies, which one could potentially use to approach the routes. From south to north they will be referred to as Sphinx Canyon, Smokestack Gully, Wells Canyon, Mayfield Canyon, Fifth Canyon, and Sixth Canyon. Far and away, the most commonly used ones by climbers are the Smokestack Gully and Mayfield Canyon. To reach the three southern canyons, drive west on Birchim Lane (this is the northmost street in Forty Acres). The road turns dirt immediately after leaving Round Valley Road. The main dirt road leads to an alfalfa ranch about one mile west of Forty Acres, but the climber should follow a lesser dirt road heading for the mouth of Sphinx Canyon. This road is rocky and gets progressively worse; most 2-wheel drive vehicles will make it about two miles beyond the alfalfa ranch. Continue up the road to reach Sphinx Canyon or walk northwest through the sagebrush to get to the Smokestack Gully or Wells Canyon.

Mayfield Canyon is the approach canyon for most of the routes in the pink and grey bands. It is reached by driving north from Forty Acres on Round Valley Road. The road curves around to the left and heads straight for the crest. One and 1/10 miles after leaving Forty Acres, Round Valley Road turns right; continuing straight towards the crest, the road is now called Ranger Station Road. A locked gate is reached a mile farther on Ranger Station Road, although the road continues on for half a mile or so to a Forest Service storage bunker at Wells Meadow. It is possible to park at the locked gate and approach Mayfield Canyon from there, but a shorter approach can be made by turning right on an unmarked dirt road 0.5 miles past the Ranger Station Road/Round Valley Road junction. Turn left after 0.7 miles, then right again after 0.2 miles. Take another left after 0.7 miles. The road will worsen soon after, forcing one to park. At this point, you are about 250 yards north of the mouth of Mayfield Canyon. About 1/4 mile after entering Mayfield Canyon, the canyon turns to the right. Walking up this section, stay right and above the brush-choked streambed, and faint trails through loose talus may be found. Partway up the canyon, a small pool will be passed; several hundred feet above this, the stream disappears, and it is better to walk in the canyon

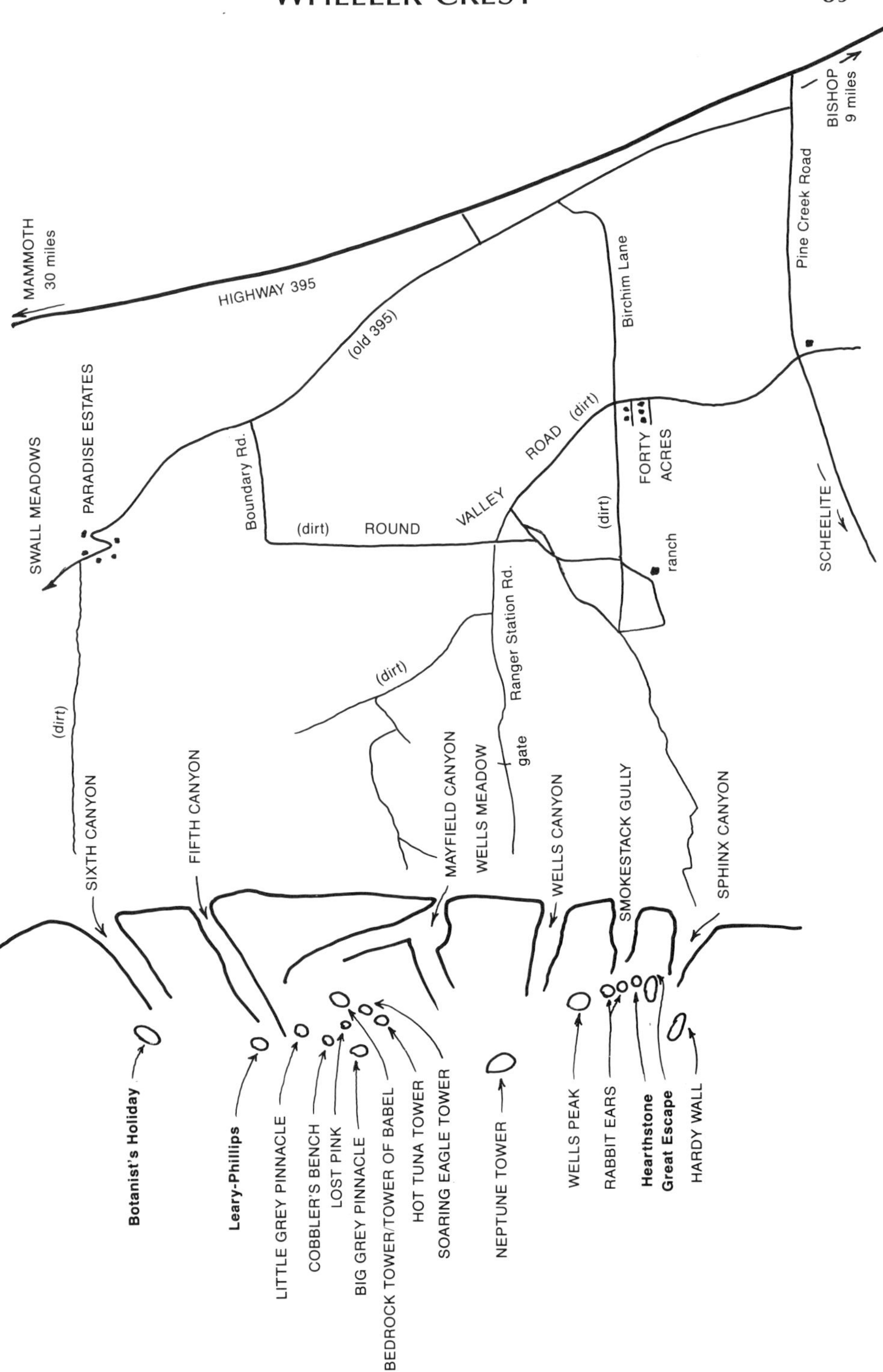
MAMMOTH
30 miles
HIGHWAY 395
BISHOP
9 miles
Pine Creek Road
Birchim Lane
(old 395)
SWALL MEADOWS
PARADISE ESTATES
Boundary Rd.
(dirt) ROUND VALLEY ROAD (dirt)
FORTY ACRES
(dirt)
ranch
SCHEELITE
Ranger Station Rd.
(dirt)
(dirt)
gate
SIXTH CANYON
FIFTH CANYON
MAYFIELD CANYON
WELLS MEADOW
WELLS CANYON
SMOKESTACK GULLY
SPHINX CANYON
Botanist's Holiday
Leary-Phillips
LITTLE GREY PINNACLE
COBBLER'S BENCH
LOST PINK
BIG GREY PINNACLE
BEDROCK TOWER/TOWER OF BABEL
HOT TUNA TOWER
SOARING EAGLE TOWER
NEPTUNE TOWER
WELLS PEAK
RABBIT EARS
Hearthstone
Great Escape
HARDY WALL

bottom itself. Eventually, one will come to the lowest and farthest right formation in the pink band, Bedrock Tower. Walking up and left from here takes one to Tower of Babel, Soaring Eagle Tower, Hot Tuna Tower, and the unnamed towers beyond. Allow one and a half hours to reach Bedrock Tower and two hours to reach Hot Tuna Tower.

To reach the grey band, walk up past Bedrock Tower and Tower of Babel, and cut right below Soaring Eagle Tower. This takes one to a broken, bushy, pyramid-shaped orange formation known as Lost Pink; it has no known routes. To get to Big Grey Pinnacle, walk up and left around Lost Pink. To reach the Cobbler's Bench, go right around Lost Pink. Allow three hours to reach these formations. An alternative approach to the Cobbler's Bench (and probably the best approach to Little Grey Pinnacle) is as follows: after making the right turn in the lower section of Mayfield Canyon, work up and right to reach the outer ridgecrest. It's unpleasant at first, but once on the ridge, the going gets easier. The ridge curves around and hits the main crest right at Little Grey Pinnacle; the Cobbler's Bench is a short distance up and left. Water can usually be found in Mayfield Canyon until mid-May or so.

Fifth and Sixth Canyons each have one known route, and the best approach roads can only be guessed at here. Adventuresome climbers may wish to explore the faint dirt roads which wander through the sage in this area; a 4-wheel drive vehicle could be a big help. Fifth Canyon can certainly be approached from the Mayfield Canyon approach roads, although one can probably get closer by continuing north on the unmarked dirt road ½ mile west of the Round Valley Road/Ranger Station Road junction and finding another road somewhere farther north that would head closer to the mouth of Fifth Canyon. It may also be possible to start from a point about 1.5 miles farther north on Round Valley Road. Sixth Canyon (easily recognizable by the fact that it starts from a highpoint of where the valley floor touches the base of the crest) may be approached the same way as Fifth Canyon, but is probably approached easier from a dirt road running west off Lower Rock Creek Road (old Highway 395) in the vicinity of Paradise Estates, a housing development about five miles north of Birchim Lane.

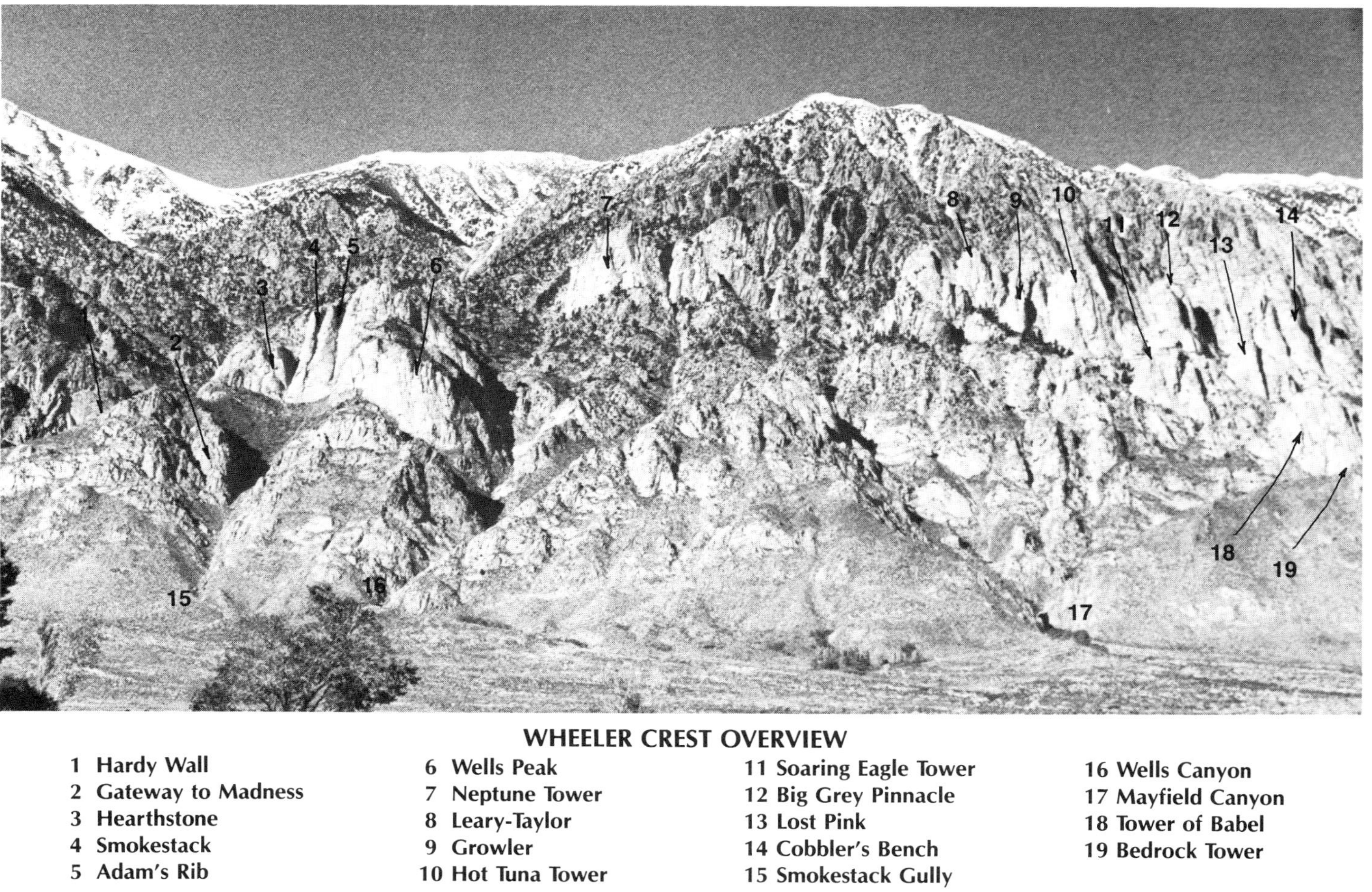

WHEELER CREST OVERVIEW

1 Hardy Wall
2 Gateway to Madness
3 Hearthstone
4 Smokestack
5 Adam's Rib
6 Wells Peak
7 Neptune Tower
8 Leary-Taylor
9 Growler
10 Hot Tuna Tower
11 Soaring Eagle Tower
12 Big Grey Pinnacle
13 Lost Pink
14 Cobbler's Bench
15 Smokestack Gully
16 Wells Canyon
17 Mayfield Canyon
18 Tower of Babel
19 Bedrock Tower

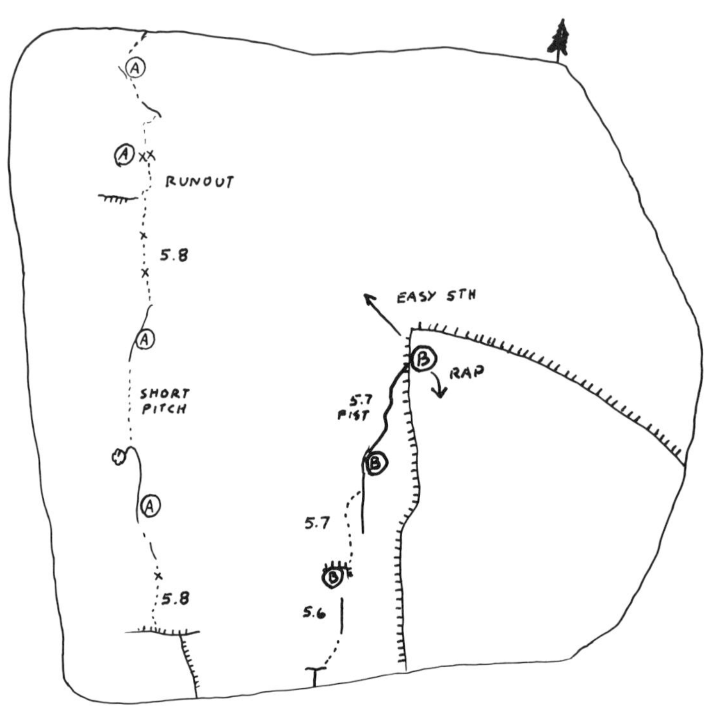

HARDY WALL

This is a slab on the left side of Sphinx Canyon. Allow two hours for the unpleasant approach up the largely trail-less canyon.

Descent: One or two short rappels lead down the right side.

A Fly on a Windshield 5.8 ★ pro: to 3″

B Don't Follow Clay 5.7

The Great Escape 5.10A A2 This route lies on a large formation on the right side of Sphinx Canyon, roughly opposite the Hardy Wall. The first five pitches climb a continuous right-facing dihedral that is right of the center of the face. When the dihedral abruptly ends, face climb up and left to a ledge with a bush. Work up right to a flake, then a few points of aid are used to reach a bolt from which a huge pendulum/rappel is made down and right to broken 4th class rock on the right side of the formation. The bolt should be doubled to make it safer for the follower. A direct finish from the bushy ledge may be possible (bolts would be needed), and this would make it a much better route. To descend, drop off the backside into the gully on the left side of the Smokestack. Partway down this, go right into the gully dropping down along the right side of the Great Escape formation.

Gateway to Madness 5.9 This is a 3-pitch route on the formation halfway up the Smokestack gully, on the left. The route starts with face climbing; the crux is close to the ground. The second pitch is a wide crack on a right-leaning ramp. The 3rd pitch is steep face right of a large roof.

The Hearthstone 5.8 A2 This is the small formation immediately left of the Smokestack. Starting from the base of the Smokestack descent gully, climb up and left on an easy ramp for 200 feet. From its top, a short section of aid leads up a small left-curving arch. Higher on this pitch, another point or two of aid is used to surmount a small roof. A brushy 5.8 pitch leads to easier climbing and the top. Descent: An 80′ rappel leads from the top into the Smokestack descent gully.

SMOKESTACK-ADAM'S RIB (RABBIT EARS)

- **A The Smokestack** 5.9 ★★ pro: to 3½"; many potential belays on this route besides the ones marked
- **B Adam's Rib** IV 5.9 ★ pro: to 3½"
- **C Eve's Wang** IV 5.10B ★★ pro: to 4"; double Friends #1-#2

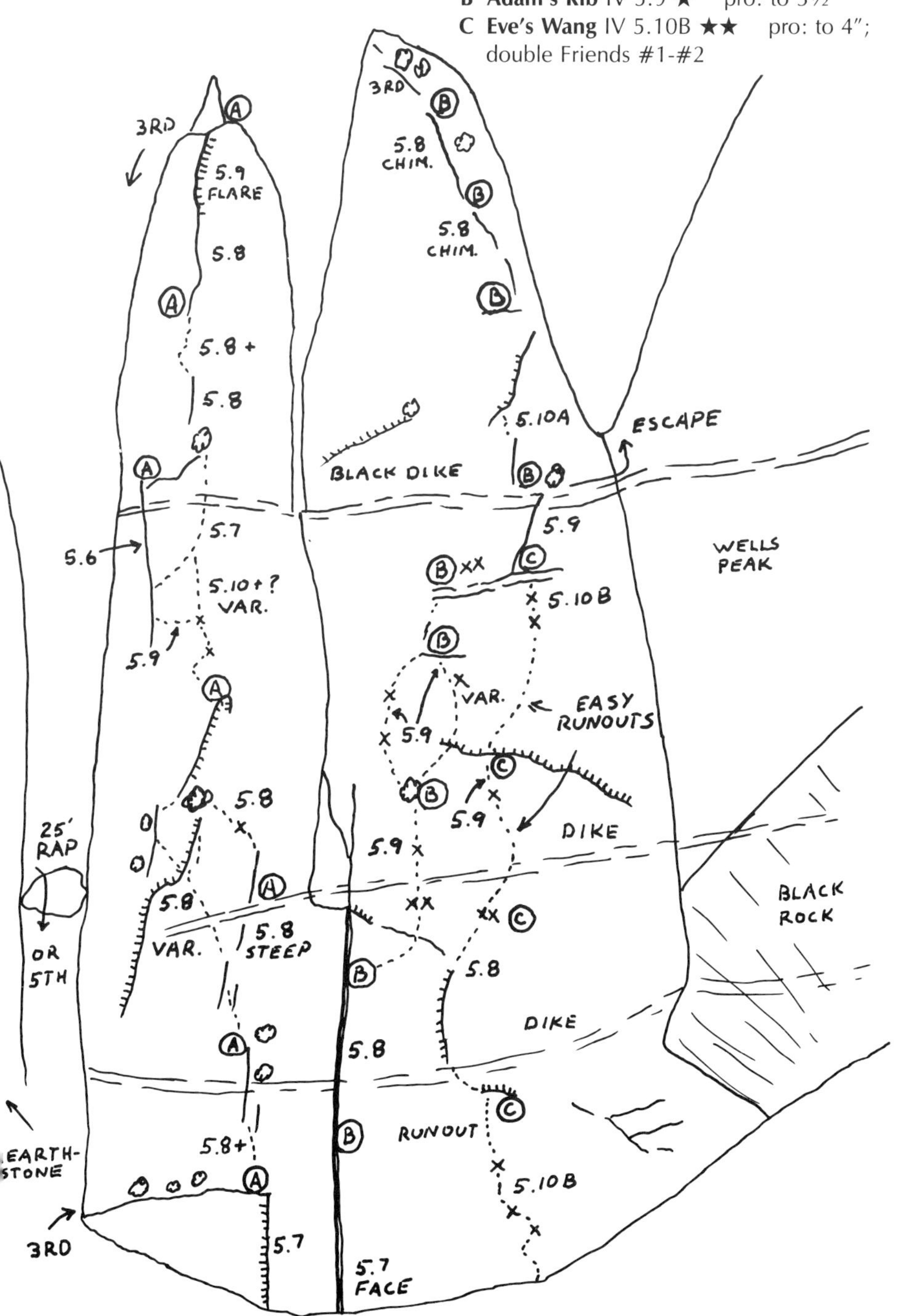

RABBIT EARS – WELLS PEAK
1 Great Escape Formation
2 The Hearthstone
3 The Smokestack
4 Adam's Rib
5 Big Brother
6 Wells Peak – East Face
7 December's Children
8 Wells Peak – North Ridge

WELLS PEAK

Wells Peak is the large mass right of the Rabbit Ears. It is divided into an upper and lower half by a huge class 2-3 ledge of black diorite. Descent from this ledge has been made off its left side with one or two raps, and off its right side with loose class 4-5 downclimbing. To descend from the upper summit, drop into the gully behind Wells Peak, then around its right side.

Big Brother 5.10C Start near the left side of the face and climb up and right through a section of black rock. Pass right of a roof (crux), then work up and right to join the East Face.

East Face 5.8 Start a short distance down and right from Big Brother. Climb up slightly left on slabby rock, passing a bolt near the end of the first pitch. Two pitches of 5.8 cracks lead to the class 2-3 ledge. Continue up the upper half of Wells Peak via the obvious crack/ chimney system near its left side.

December's Children 5.10A ★ This is the first continuous crack system right of the blank center of the lower half of Wells Peak. Three pitches lead up cracks to the left side of a ledge. Start up the left-facing corner on the right side of the ledge, then as progress becomes increasingly difficult, step right around the outside of the corner (5.10A). This soon leads to much easier climbing.

North Ridge 5.9 ★ This climb ascends the right skyline of the upper half of Wells Peak. The crux will be found in the steeper first few pitches. Above, many easier pitches lead up the classic knife-edge ridge. The best approach for this route is up Wells Canyon.

CENTRAL WHEELER CREST

1 Leary-Taylor Route
2 Hot Tuna – Open Book
3 Starkissed
4 Sargasso
5 Soaring Eagle – East Face
6 Twist and Crawl
7 Lost Pink

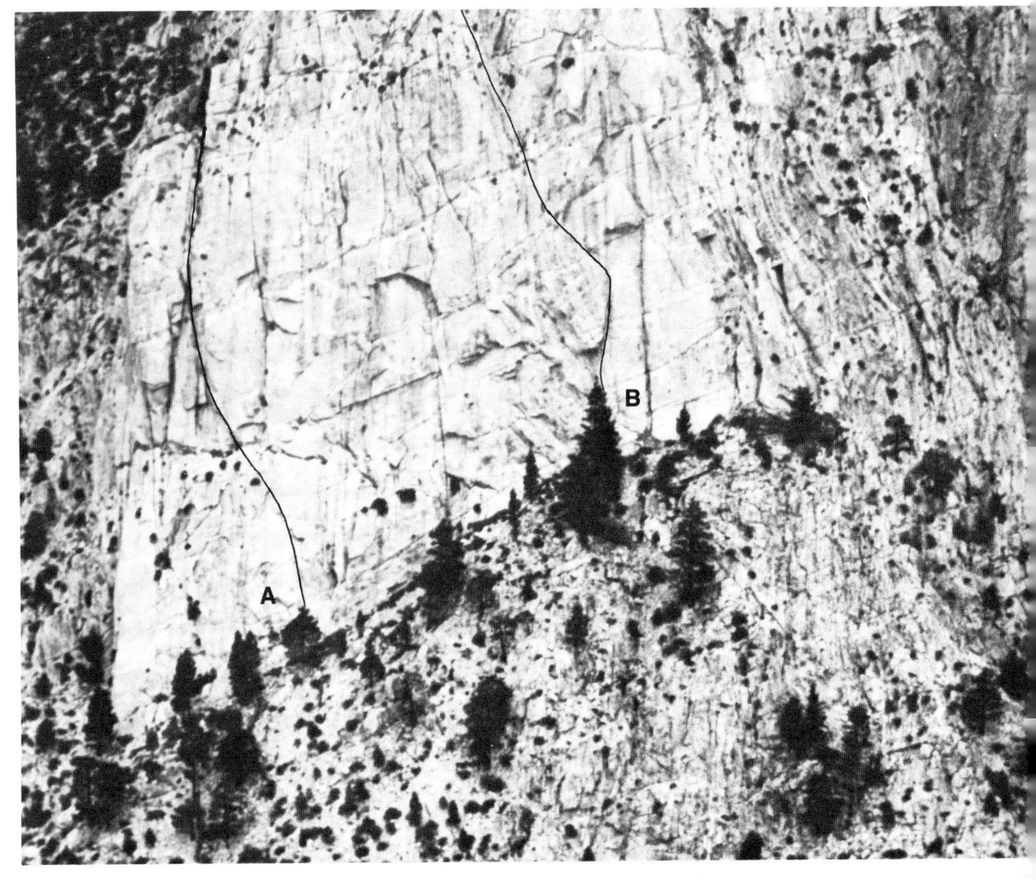

NEPTUNE TOWER

Neptune Tower is best approached via Wells Canyon; allow 3½ hours for this strenuous venture. The two exisiting routes are in the two most obvious systems on the wall. Descend left of the formation.

A Graber-Rowell Route 5.10 ★ The first few pitches of this climb follow a left-curving arch. Higher, work up and left into the leftmost crack system on the wall.

B Stormy Petrel IV 5.8 ★ This is the most obvious line right of the center of the face. There are some bolts in the vicinity of the second or third pitch, where the route tends to the left.

HOT TUNA TOWER

1 Sorry, Charlie
2 Violet Green
3 Open Book
4 Starkissed

Hot Tuna is the largest formation in the central Pink Band. Descents have been made down the second gully left of the tower as well as down the right side. Be prepared to make a short rappel or two.

Open Book Route 5.10B This follows the main system in the center of the formation for about six pitches. At about mid- height, where the book is slightly disconnected, climb up and right in an arching crack, then face climb straight back left to rejoin the main book.

Starkissed 5.9 ★ To the right of the Open Book Route, and starting midway up the face are two similar right-facing books. This route climbs up to and follows the left book, then exits up and right from a point midway up the book. Six pitches.

Sargasso 5.9 This climbs up to and follows the right open book.

Chicken of the Sea 5.5 This climb ascends the right skyline or north ridge of Hot Tuna Tower.

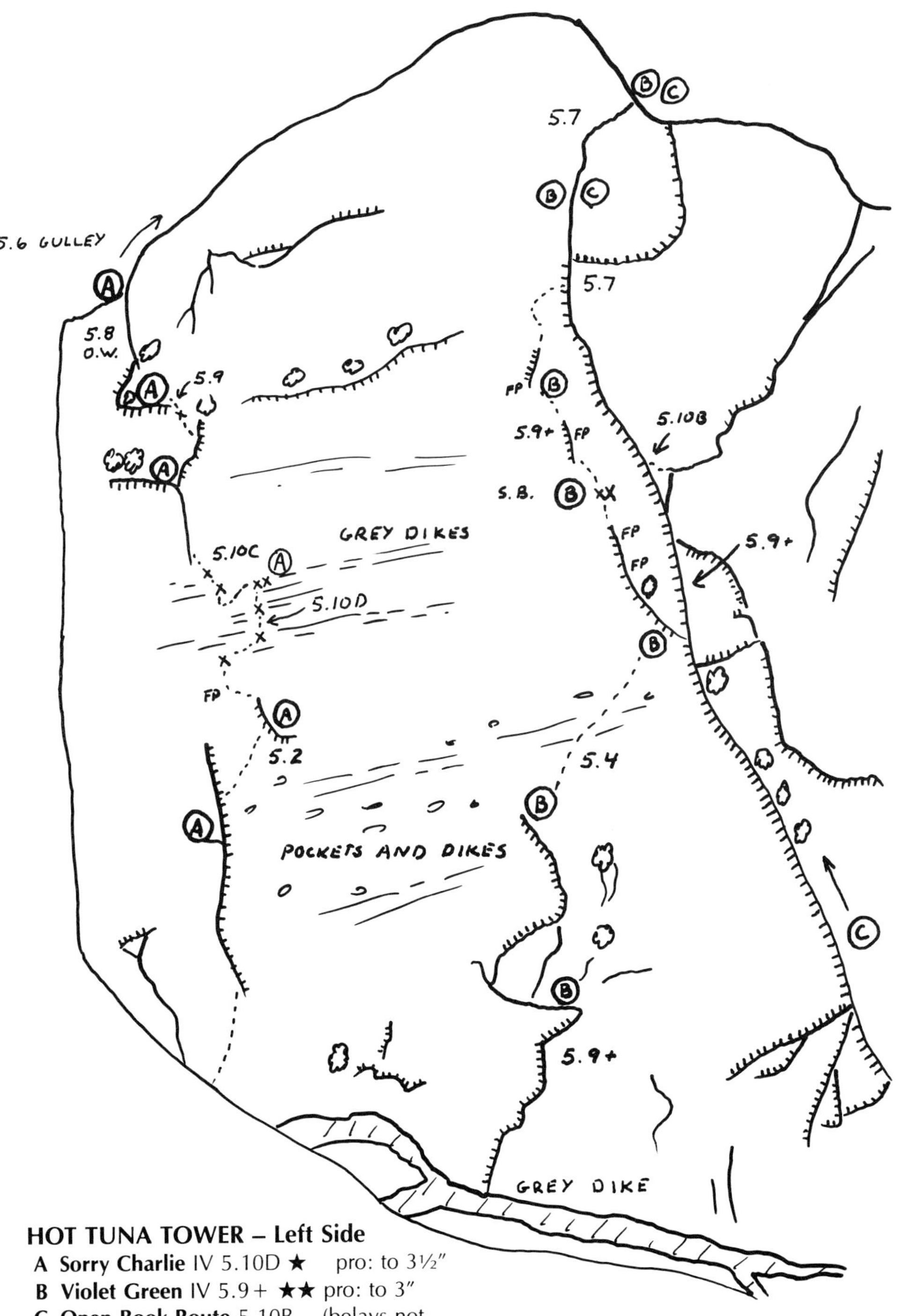

HOT TUNA TOWER – Left Side

A Sorry Charlie IV 5.10D ★ pro: to 3½″
B Violet Green IV 5.9+ ★★ pro: to 3″
C Open Book Route 5.10B (belays not marked)

TOWERS LEFT OF HOT TUNA

A **Leary- Taylor Route** 5.10+ ★ This climb follows the most obvious line on the second tower left of Hot Tuna Tower

B **Growler** 5.9 ★ pro: to 3″; rope drag on 1st and 2nd pitches.

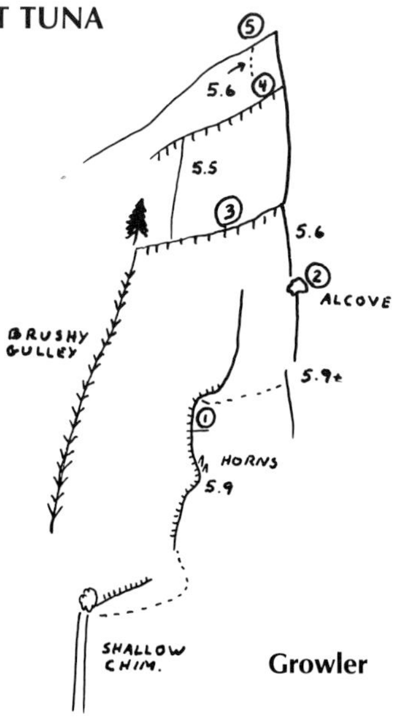

Growler

SOARING EAGLE TOWER

The routes are all on the incredibly featured left side of this formation. Descend left of the tower; this involves a spooky jump or downclimb to get into the gully behind the tower.

Knob Job 5.5? ★ This ascends the knobby left skyline for one or two pitches.

A Chicken Delight 5.6-5.8 ★★ Climb left of the center of the face for three pitches. Many variations are possible in this sea of knobs, plates and buckets. Protection and anchors are sometimes difficult to arrange; take many runners.

B El Pinko 5.9 ★ This climbs more or less straight above a pillar in the center of the face, vaguely following some right-facing books. The crux is on third (last) pitch, in a blanker, lower-angle section.

C John Birch Society 5.9 ★ This starts in the right of two right-facing books down and right of El Pinko. It works through some roofs and tends to the right, passing some bolts. It joins the East Face a short distance from the top.

D East Face Route 5.8 ★ This follows a single crack system for five pitches.

TOWER OF BABEL/BEDROCK TOWER

1 Fault Line
2 Fear Itself
3 The Gambler
4 Fred Flintstone
5 Barney Rubble
6 Hanna-Barbara
7 Yabba-dabba-Doo

When viewed from afar, this appears to be one formation. Actually, it is two, separated by a class 2-3 gully/ledge system running up and right. This gully is the approach for routes on the Tower of Babel, the upper formation. It is also the descent for routes on Bedrock Tower, the lower formation. Descent from the Tower of Babel is down its left side. The topo shows the routes on Bedrock Tower but only the upper pitches of routes on the Tower of Babel in order to match with the photo.

Routes on Tower of Babel

B.S. Special 5.10D ★ Start left of a roof low down and climb up and right on easy ramps. From their end, pass two bolts, then broken climbing leads up to the upper slanting crack of Fault Line.

Fault Line 5.9 ★ Start right of the aforementioned roof and climb up and left on buckets and knobs. Pass a bolt and belay on a good hidden ledge (large Friends needed). Climb to a bolt, then left to a pancake flake. Work up to an obvious bushy right-slanting crack which is followed to its end. Wander up and slightly left to the top.

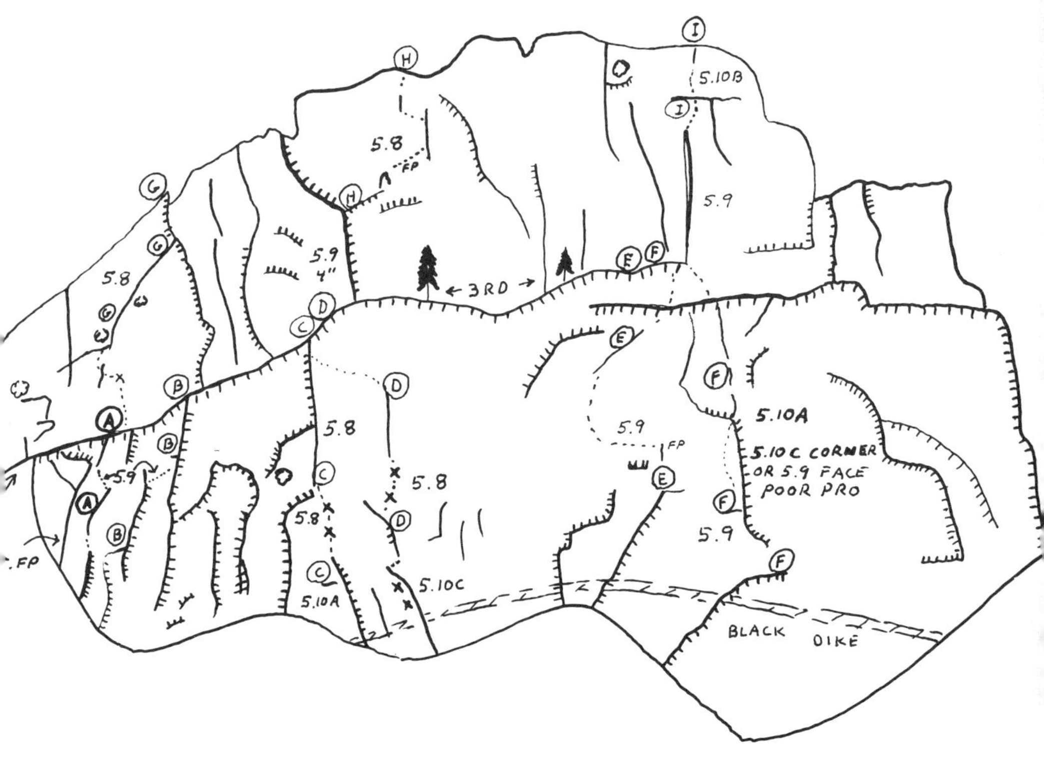

BEDROCK TOWER

- **A Short Street** 5.9
- **B Ocean View Avenue** 5.9
- **C Fred Flintstone** 5.10A ★★ pro: to 3″, esp. ½″ to 1½″
- **D Barney Rubble** 5.10C ★ pro: to 2½″, esp. thin
- **E Hanna-Barbara** 5.9
- **F Yabba-Dabba-Doo** 5.10A or 5.10C ★★ pro: to 2½″, esp. thin

TOWER OF BABEL (Upper pitches)

- **G Fault Line** 5.9 ★
- **H Fear Itself** 5.9 ★ pro: to 4″
- **I The Gambler** 5.10B ★ pro: to 4″

TOWER OF BABEL

The Bastard 5.8 To the right of **Fault Line** is a large dirty right-facing corner. This route wanders up cracks and features to the right of the corner for four or five pitches.

Fear Itself 5.9 ★ The main feature of this route is a large left-facing orange corner starting a pitch up. Below and right of it is a smaller right-facing corner/roof. Start 30 feet right of this and climb to a bush. Traverse left to the corner/roof and cross it, then work up and left to the base of the orange corner. Ascend this for 90 feet to a slanting ledge. Move the belay to the right end of this ledge. Climb a block, then traverse right past a pin to a steep groove. From its top, go left to a crack, then up to the top. Pro: to 4″.

The Gambler 5.10B ★ This climb starts near the end of the class 2-3 gully/ledge system. The first pitch is a long 5.9 chimney. belay above it at a horizontal crack. RP-protected face above leads to the top.

BIG GREY PINNACLE

This large feature has two known routes. Descent is off the back and around the left side of the tower. It is probably also possible to descend around the tower's right side.

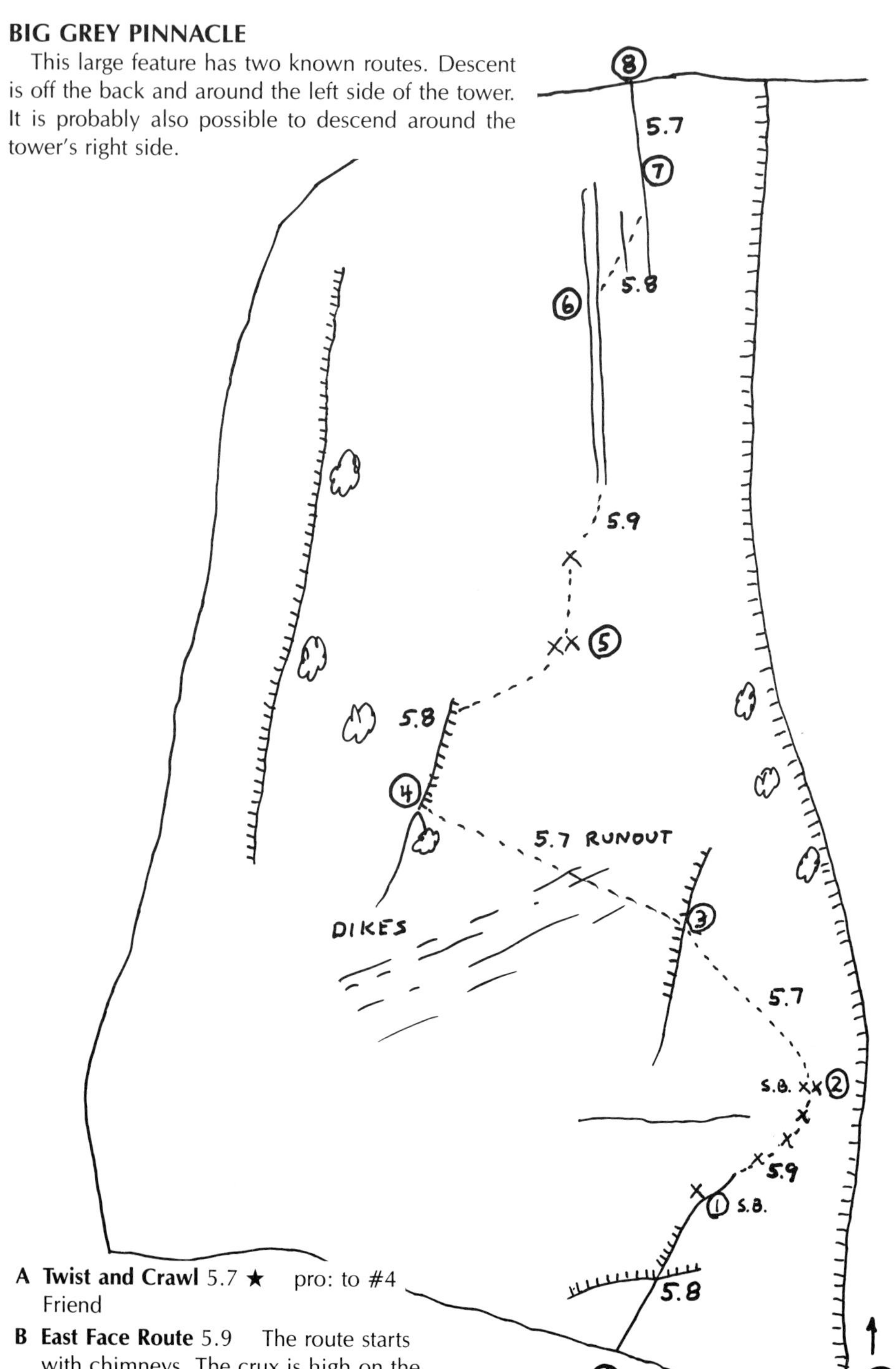

A Twist and Crawl 5.7 ★ pro: to #4 Friend

B East Face Route 5.9 The route starts with chimneys. The crux is high on the route, face climbing right under a roof. Seven pitches or so.

COBBLER'S BENCH

This is the next tower north of Big Grey; it is similar in size and shape. There is one known route, on the right side of the tower. Descent is made to the right.

A Weary Leader 5.10 ★ The route starts with an easy pitch to a ledge. Two pitches lead straight up a crack to a ledge in a horizontal dike. Move left on the dike and follow a corner to a belay on the face to the right. The fifth pitch, the crux, follows a corner, then works right and passes two bolts before moving back left to a finger crack. Two easier pitches follow.

LITTLE GREY PINNACLE

This small tower is down and right from the Cobbler's Bench. Two chimneys drop partway down the face from the summit, giving the tower the appearance of a trident. There is one route.

East Face Route 5.9 This three-pitch route climbs up to the right chimney system. There are two bolts on the first (crux) pitch. Descent was made by downclimbing the left chimney, then rappelling.

Leary-Phillips Route 5.9 This is a four-pitch route in Fifth Canyon. It ascends the most obvious tower on the right side of the canyon, a grey tower with the appearance of a rocket ship. From below, it appears to be one large tower; however, it is really two towers, one below and in front of the other. This route ascends the lower tower only, mainly via face climbing connecting cracks, although no bolts were placed.

Botanist's Holiday 5.7 This route is in Sixth Canyon, on a wall on the right side of the canyon. It climbs a right- facing corner/chimney system for five pitches.

SWALL MEADOWS CRAG

This is a cluster of small outcrops at the north end of Wheeler Crest, plainly visible from Highway 395 near the top of Sherwin Grade. They are approached from dirt roads running northwest from Swall Meadows, a residential area just off Lower Rock Creek Road (old Highway 395). Three routes are known.

A Mr. Green Genes 5.9 Face climbing, following thin RP cracks. Two pitches.

B X-Crack 5.10A?

C S-Crack 5.9?

ROCK CREEK

The Rock Creek Crags are reached by driving south from the tiny village of Tom's Place, located about 25 miles north of Bishop and about 16 miles south of the Mammoth Lakes turnoff on Highway 395. Rock Creek runs north to south, and the routes are all on the west side of the canyon, facing due east, more or less. The road is kept open year-round for access to the ski touring center farther up the canyon, but winter snows usually cover the crags. Also, approaching any of the climbing areas (except Tinytown) involves crossing Rock Creek; this can be a problem in spring, especially after heavy winters. For these reasons, Rock Creek is most climbable from late spring to mid- fall. The rock is grey granite, of High-Sierra quality: some good, some not so good. There is debris on most of the ledges, and small, but sometimes bothersome bushes dot the crags. Nonetheless, a few fine routes will be found in this scenic canyon, as well as an excellent beginners' area, the Iris Slab, which has long been used by the local guiding services.

Driving south from Tom's Place, the first crag reached is Tinytown, 3.8 miles from Highway 395 and seen as a small outcrop high on the hillside to the right.

About 4.1 miles from Highway 395, the entrance to Iris Meadow Campground is reached. The Iris Slab is just across the creek from the campground and up the hill a short distance. Above and to the left of the Iris Slab are nondescript broken crags; The Far Side is the largest of these.

4.4 miles from the highway is a turnoff for Sugar Mountain, a nice-looking outcrop high in a drainage. Sugar Mountain has some of the best rock in Rock Creek as well as the longest approach, about an hour.

After 4.6 miles, the entrance to Big Meadow Campground is reached. The Gong Show area, a wall with several large conspicuous roofs, is approached from here. South of the Gong Show area, the hillside rises to a high point at the top of a talus fan, then drops and rises again in a small tree-filled indentation in the cliff; this is Daknucklehead area. A short distance beyond this and slightly lower on the hillside is a long, broken wall rising up and left. This is Ungracious Wall. Both these areas are best approached from turnouts about 5 miles from 395.

UNGRACIOUS WALL

A **Ungracious and Inconsiderate** 5.10C ★ The first pitch of this route passes four bolts; the second is a short crack leading to a ledge. Rappel with two ropes.

B **Aerobics** 5.9 Climb up to a belay below a triangular roof. The second pitch goes left around the roof and up cracks to the top. Walk off right.

C **Broken Arrow** 5.9 This one-pitch route climbs a crack above a detached flake. Walk off right.

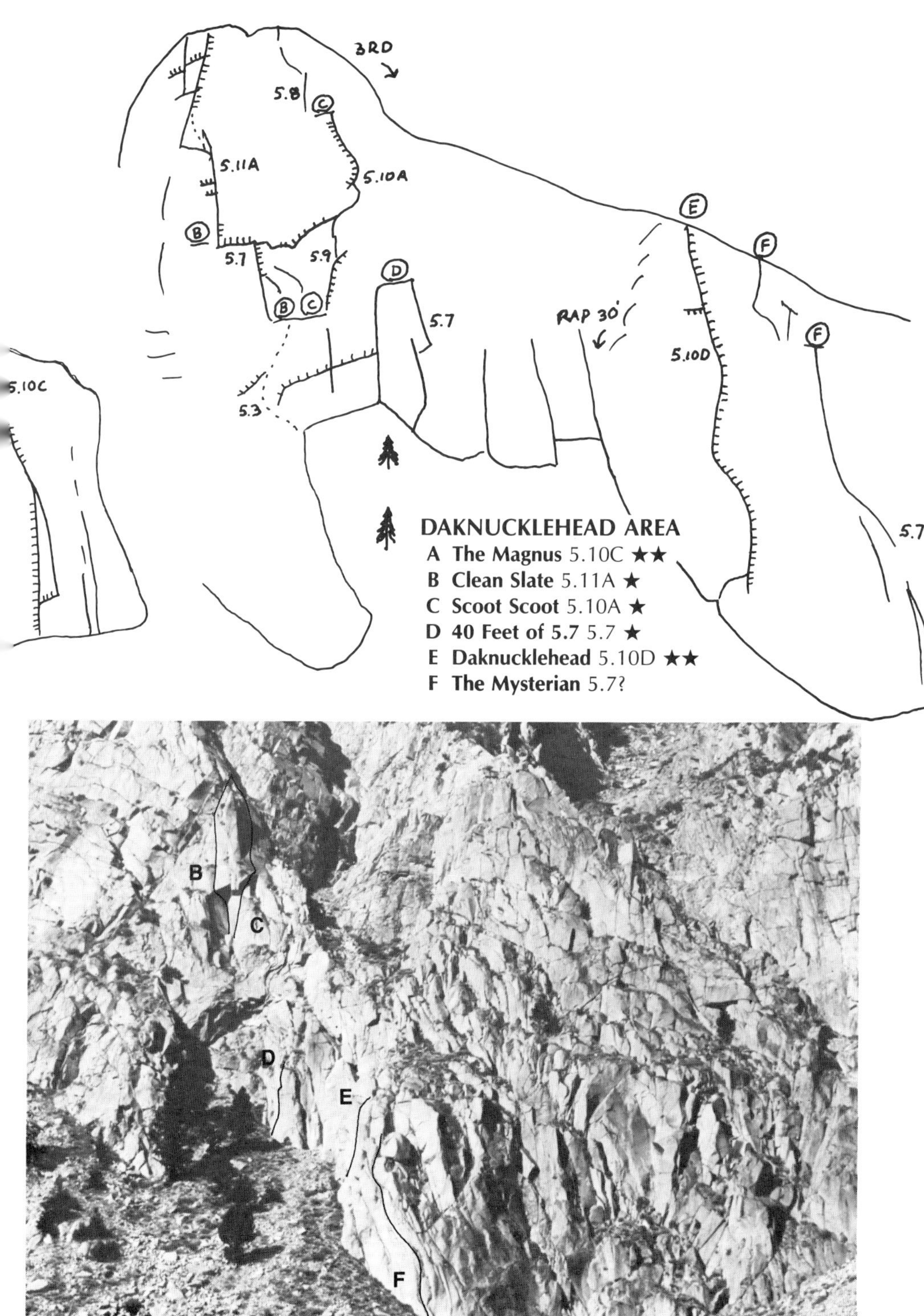
3RD
5.8
5.11A
5.10A
5.7
5.9
5.7
RAP 30'
5.10D
5.10C
5.3
5.7
DAKNUCKLEHEAD AREA
A The Magnus 5.10C ★★
B Clean Slate 5.11A ★
C Scoot Scoot 5.10A ★
D 40 Feet of 5.7 5.7 ★
E Daknucklehead 5.10D ★★
F The Mysterian 5.7?

DAKNUCKLEHEAD AREA
GONG SHOW CLIFF

THE GONG SHOW AREA

Descent: Walk off right. For routes near The Gong Show, one can also rappel The D.M.Z.

Decline of Western Civilization 5.12A ★ (TR) This is a straight-in thin crack on the short steep wall just left of the ramps leading up to The Gong Show.

A **The Gong Show** 5.11C ★ This is a wide crack out a 12′ roof.

B **The D.M.Z.** 5.10A ★ A thin crack.

Social Climber 5.10+ An off-width to the right of The D.M.Z.

Last Exit 5.11A ★ This is a straight- in thin crack which slants up and right to join Overexposure midway up its first pitch.

C **Overexposure** 5.9 ★ This is a left- slanting crack system which passes between two large roofs on the right side of the cliff. The second pitch is a 5.8 wide crack.

D **Brush Up** 5.9 This climbs past several bushes into a chimney behind a giant flake.

E **The Bong Show** 5.10+ (TR) Starting at the same spot as Brush Up, ascend a striking off-width crack which curves right onto the face of a steep slab. It is not known whether this route has been led, or even if it has actually been climbed.

SUGAR MOUNTAIN

A **Roots in the Sky** 5.10C ★★ This is a right-slanting thin crack on a small wall left of the main crag.

Holiday in Cambodia 5.11+ ★ In the gully just right of Roots in the Sky, this climbs a thin hand crack out a five-foot roof. The first ascent party traversed left above the roof, but a direct finish seems obvious and desirable.

Lost Buttress 5.9 This climb is somewhere on the left side of the main formation, following the most obvious cracks near a buttress/arete feature.

B **Chocolate Chips** 5.10B or 5.10D ★★ This is a steep face climb up a wall with many black chickenheads. A roof at the bottom is the crux if one goes directly over it. By turning it on its left side, the upper face (5.10B) becomes the crux. One bolt.

C **Quest for Fire** 5.9+ ★ The left- facing corner to the right of Chocolate Chips.

Goldenlocks 5.10A ★★ Thin double cracks on the short wall right of Quest for Fire.

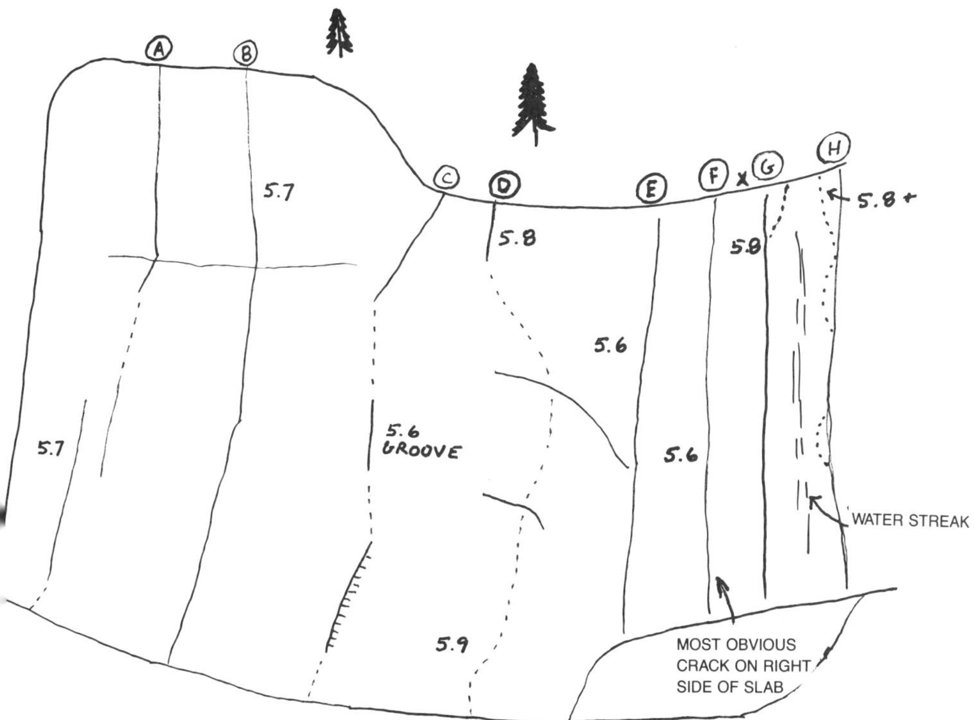

IRIS SLAB

Iris Slab offers fun 50-70-foot routes which can be led or toproped as the mood prevails, as well as the shortest approach in Rock Creek. The routes listed here are not necessarily lines of first ascents but the most obvious separate up-and-down lines on a slab where many variations are obviously possible. The easiest climb up the slab would probably be connecting the lower part of Route 2 with the upper part of Route 3 (5.3 or 5.4).

A Route 1 5.7 good pro
B Route 2 5.7 good pro
C Route 3 5.6 adequate pro
D Route 4 5.9 poor pro
E Route 5 5.6 good pro
F Route 6 5.6 good pro
G Route 7 5.8 adequate pro (with RPs)
H Route 8 5.8+ adequate pro (with RPs)

THE FAR SIDE

This is a formation above and slightly left of the Iris Slab. The two known routes are just right of a bushy left- facing corner. Walk off right.

Bobbing for Poodles 5.10A ★ Starting at the base of a bushy corner, work right into straight-in cracks leading to a roof which is turned on its left.

Aerobics in Hell 5.9 ★ Just right of the previous route, climb cracks that go up and then right around an outside corner.

TINYTOWN

Guano Cracks 5.10A On the right side of the broken south face of this crag, climb cracks leading to double cracks formed by large chockstones in a chimney.

A **Terror of Tinytown** 5.10A ★ This and the following three routes start from the highest ledge running across the east face, best approached from the right, 3rd class. This route starts down and left from the left end of the ledge and follows a thin curving crack above a small roof.

B **Easy Street** 5.7 ★★ This is the shallow corner directly above the left end of the ledge.

C **Voices in the Sky** 5.10A ★ Just right of the preceeding route, climb thin cracks which go over a tiny roof.

Moolar the Llama 5.9 The next crack right of Voices in the Sky.

D **Kiddie Corner** 5.6 This and the following routes are on a small cliff several hundred feet right of Tinytown. This is an obvious right-facing corner.

Alcove Cracks 5.8 Just right of Kiddie Corner is an alcove with cracks on both sides of the roof at its top; the right crack is slightly harder.

MAMMOTH LAKES BASIN

This section covers a number of granite formations around the lakes southwest of the town of Mammoth Lakes. From downtown Mammoth Lakes, follow Highway 203 through town to the second stop light. Drive straight through this light onto Lake Mary Road, which takes you to the Mammoth Lakes Basin. For the first four areas, TJ Lake, Mammoth Crest, Crystal Crag, and Dike Wall, one starts at the parking area at Lake George. This is found by turning left off Lake Mary Road just past Lake Mary, and following the signs to Lake George. For the Secret Stash area, one follows Lake Mary Road to its end at Horseshoe Lake parking area.

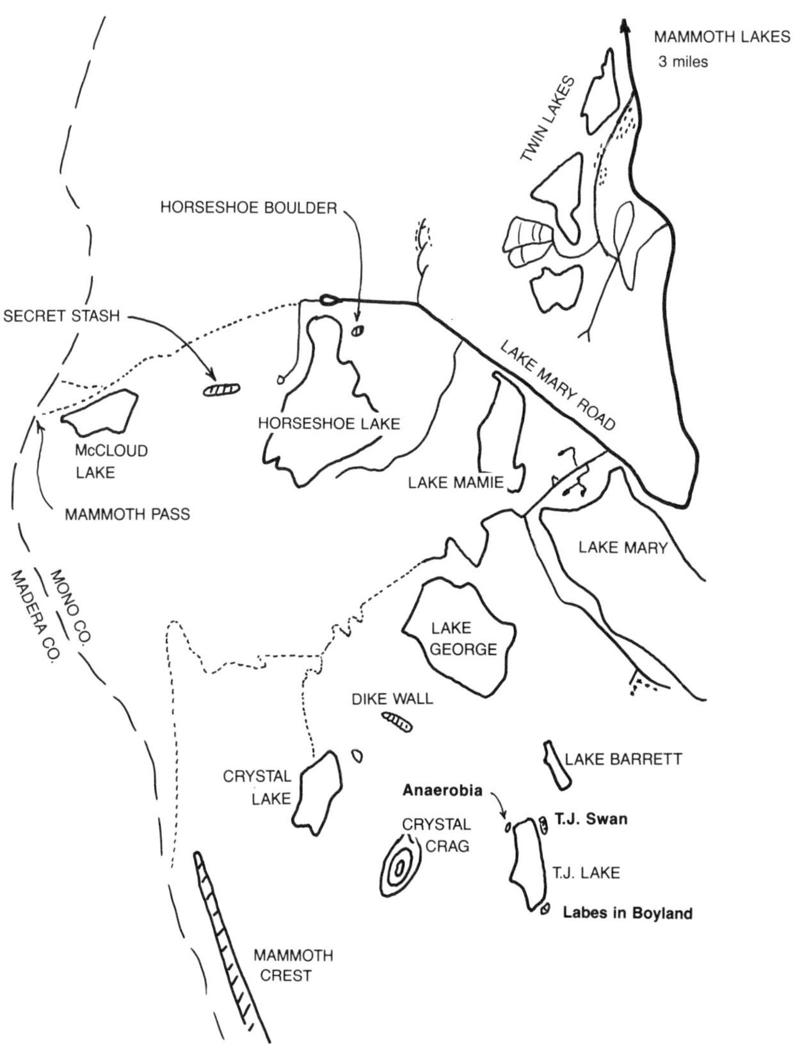

HORSESHOE LAKE AREA

One exceptional high quality boulder with several good problems exists in the woods near the northeast corner of Horseshoe Lake. If you follow the lakeshore left (east) from the parking lot, the Horseshoe Boulder will become barely visible in the woods to the left within 100 yards.

To reach the Secret Stash from the parking lot follow the right (west) lakeshore until encountering a creek flowing into the lake. Follow this upstream until this south facing crag comes into view on the right.

There is also a good beginners area at the southwest end of Horseshoe Lake, reached by walking along the west shore of the lake. A one-bolt face is 5.7 and there are many easier routes nearby in the 30-50 foot range.

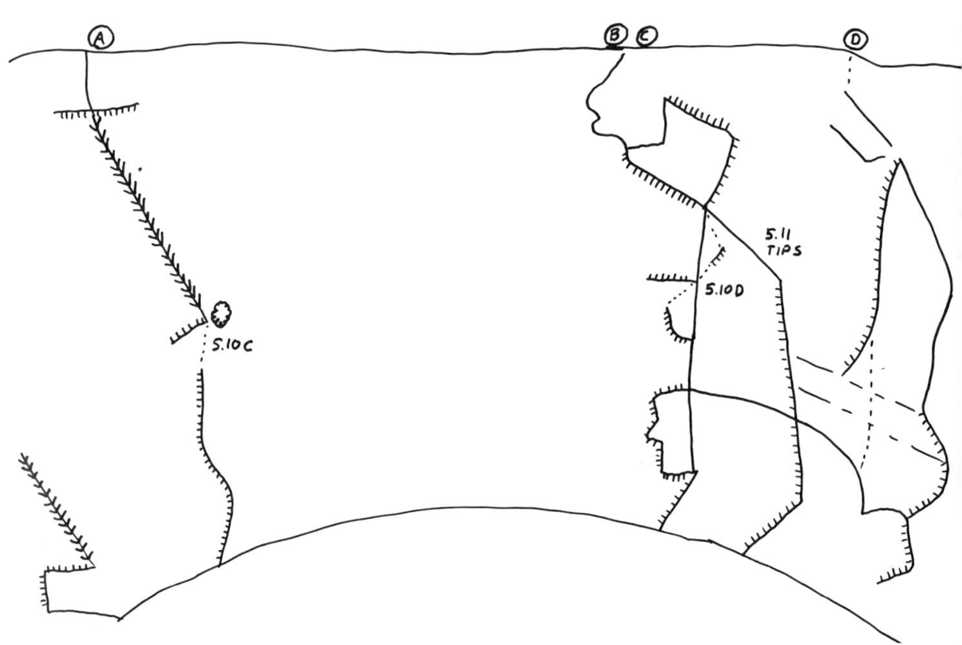

HORSESHOE LAKE – SECRET STASH

A Poop Chute 5.10C
B Mastik Corner 5.10D
C Smooth Move 5.11
D Secret Route 5.??

MAMMOTH CREST

A **Finn-Yager Route** 5.9
B **Buffalo Chips** 5.10C
C **Ski Tracks** 5.9/10
Pigs in Space (right variation) 5.9/10

D **Reaganomics** 5.8/9
Gunboat Diplomacy (left variation) 5.10A This crosses Reagonomics after sharing the second pitch.

Follow the trail to TJ Lake, traverse around the lake and hike up the drainage gully above for about 0.7 miles to the base of Mammoth Crest. Many broken cracks and gullies will be seen. Little information is available about the climbs here. Buffalo Chips (5.10C) is a classic straight-in wide crack with broken 5.8 approach pitch. Ski Tracks (5.9) are a set of steep double cracks that face southeast.

CRYSTAL CRAG AREA

1 East Face Routes (around corner)	**4 North Arete**
2 Northeast Face	**5 North Buttress**
3 Northeast Buttress	**6 Dike Wall**

This broken peaklet dominates the Mammoth Lakes Basin. It is easily approached from Lake George via Crystal Lake. Although not particularly interesting to the modern rock climber, its 10,364-foot summit is well known to local hikers and peakbaggers. The south arete is class 2 and the west face rising above Crystal Lake is class 3. Both the north buttress and the northeast face are class 4; these two routes provide interesting mixed climbing in winter. The following harder routes are also known.

North Arete 5.8 This climb starts in a right-facing book on the very prow of the arete. After a 5.8 pitch, four or five easier pitches lead to the top. There are many variations up to 5.10A left of the upper pitches as well as easier starts to the right.

Northeast Buttress 5.9 This climbs the most obvious corners and ramps to the right of the broken northeast face.

East Face Right 5.9 Climb three pitches to the right of a dihedral rising above a large pine tree.

East Face Left 5.8 This follows the dihedral mentioned in the previous description.

T.J. SWAN AREA

From the parking area at Lake George, a hiking trail will be found traversing around the left (east) end of the lake. Follow this for a short distance to where a marked side trail to T.J. Lake branches off to the left. Where this trail meets T.J. Lake, **Anaerobia** (5.12), a steep thin lieback crack, will be seen on a small formation very close to the right (west) side of the lake. An unmarked trail around the left (east) side of the lake quickly brings you to the T.J. Swan formation, directly across the lake from **Anaerobia.** Continue on this trail to the far (south) end of the lake where a classic square hand traverse boulder will be found. A few minutes hiking uphill from here will bring you to another small crag on which **Labes in Boyland** (5.10C TR), a white dike split by a thin seam, will be found.

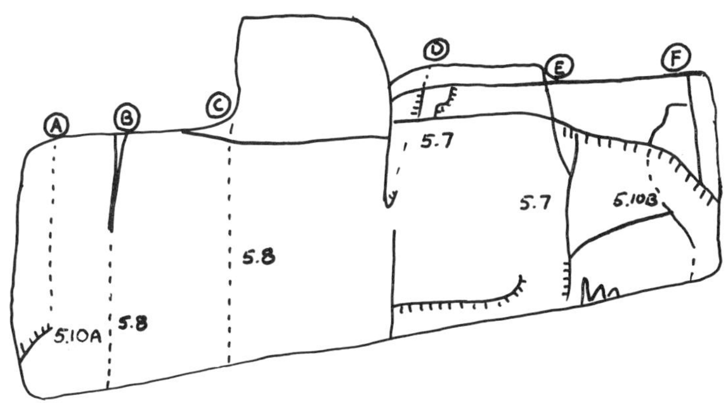

A **Little Archie** 5.10A ★ pro: thin
B **Spinach Patch** 5.8 pro: none
C **G.S. Special** 5.8 ★ (TR)
D **T.J. Swan** 5.7 ★★ pro: to 2″
E **Myers Crack** 5.7 ★★ pro: to 2″
F **905** 5.10B ★ pro: thin

DIKE WALL
1 **Mr. D.N.A.**
2 **Mr. Kamikaze**
3 **Satterfield Corner**
4 **Black Leather**
5 **Dominatrix**

From the Lake George parking area, the Dike Wall can be seen directly across and above Lake George and below Crystal Crag. Follow the hiking trail around the left (east) side of the lake past several summer homes until nearly opposite the parking area. Then hike left up a steep forested slope that turns into a jumble of talus blocks near the wall. All the routes on this excellent steep 70-foot crag may be top roped from bolts or thin to medium-sized stopper cracks.

THE DIKE WALL

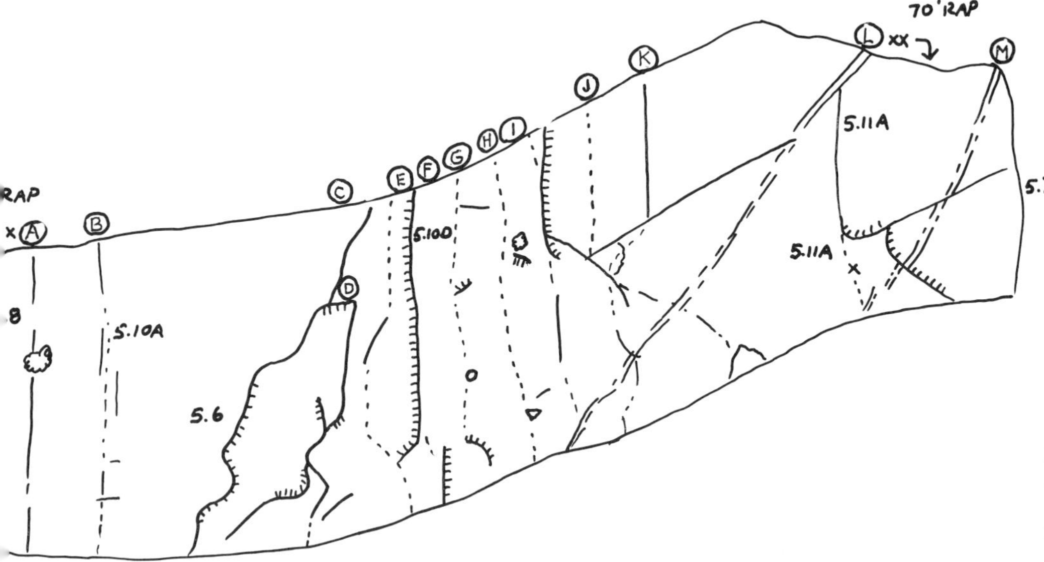

DIKE WALL

- A **Mr. D.N.A.** 5.8 ★ pro: to 2″
- B **Mr. Kamikaze** 5.10A ★ pro: thin to 2″
- C **Satterfield Corner** 5.6
- D **Dichotomy** 5.11C ★ (TR)
- E **Strap-on Tools** 5.11C ★ (TR)
- F **Black Leather** 5.10D ★★ pro: incl. a 6-7″piece
- G **Valley Boys** 5.12A ★ (TR)
- H **Lesbie Friends** 5.11B ★ (TR)
- I **Mammoth Boys** 5.11D ★ (TR)
- J **Going Both Ways** 5.11A ★ (TR)
- K **Double Ender** 5.10C ★ (TR)
- L **Dominatrix** 5.11A ★★ pro: to 2″
- M **Solo Route** 5.7

RAINBOW WALL

This newly-developed crag is west of the Sierra Crest and is approached from Devil's Postpile National Monument, reached by driving over Minaret Summit from Mammoth Lakes. This road is closed in winter, and during peak summer months a mandatory shuttle system runs between the Mammoth Mountain ski lifts and Devil's Postpile. There is a fee for use of the shuttle. It is only permissible to drive into the Monument before 7am or after 5pm, although, once in, you can drive out any time. Climbers are strongly urged to check conditions at the Forest Service Visitor Center at the east end of Mammoth Lakes, on the right as you are coming from Highway 395.

Approach: From the Rainbow Falls trailhead (Red's Meadow Pack Station) hike south to Fish Creek Trail Junction just before reaching Rainbow Falls. Continue south on Fish Creek Trail approximately 1.5 miles to Rainbow Wall on the left side of the trail facing west. There is water year round.

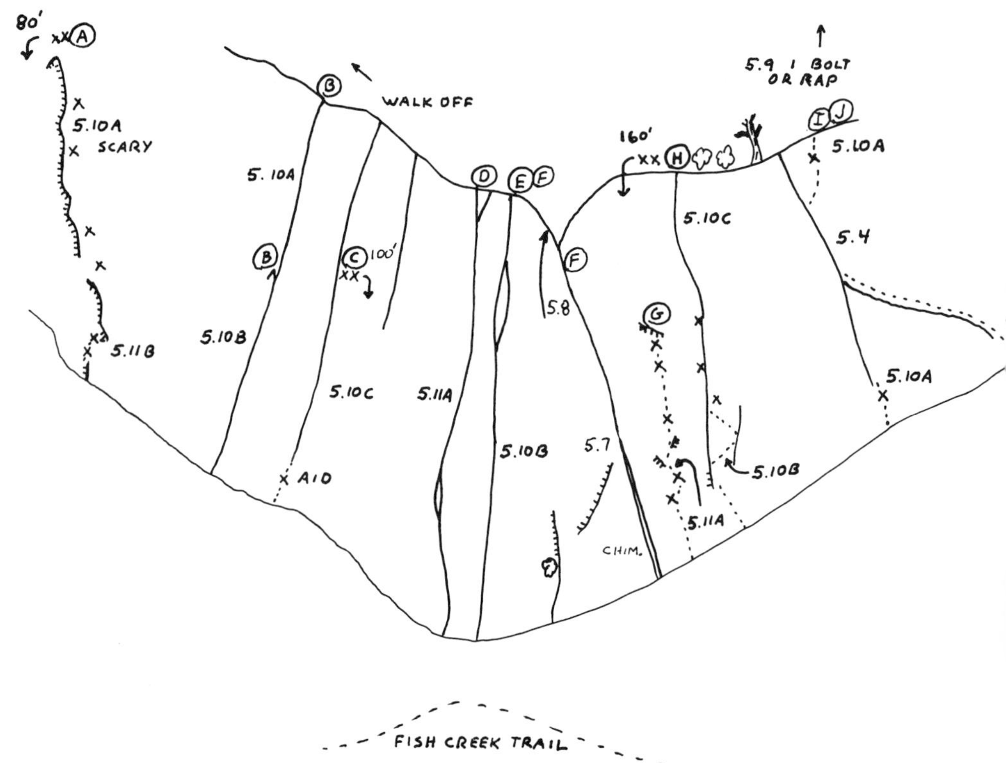

A Guillotine 5.11B ★ loose
B Hall of Brushes 5.10B ★
C Curare 5.10C A1 ★★
D Left Wishbone Crack 5.11A ★★
E Right Wishbone Crack 5.10B ★★
F Mosscular 5.8
G Spectrum 5.11A ★★ unfinished
H Sorry Joe 5.10C poor pro.
I Love Stuck 5.10A
J Love Struck 5.10A

INDIANA SUMMIT NATURAL AREA

To the east of Highway 395 between Mammoth and June Lake lies a wealth of volcanic rock. A number of fine bouldering, toproping, and leadable crags are found in the forests and canyons which crisscross this region. A maze of dirt roads of various quality approach these areas from all directions. Generally, the approaches described here can be done with any 2-wheel-drive vehicle. This area is bordered on the north by the logging camp road or Bald Mountain road, and on the south by the Owens River Road. The roads in this area are identified by a Forest Service numbering system, but only the most prominent roads are posted, with signs being found at intersections. The approaches given are best for those unfamiliar with the area; however, any area may be approached from any other using roads that may not be mentioned here. Refer to the Forest Service map or one below. The starting reference points for these approaches will be the junction of Highways 395 and 203 near Mammoth Lakes, and the junction of Highway 395 and the southern end of the June Lake Loop, hereafter referred to as June Lake Junction.

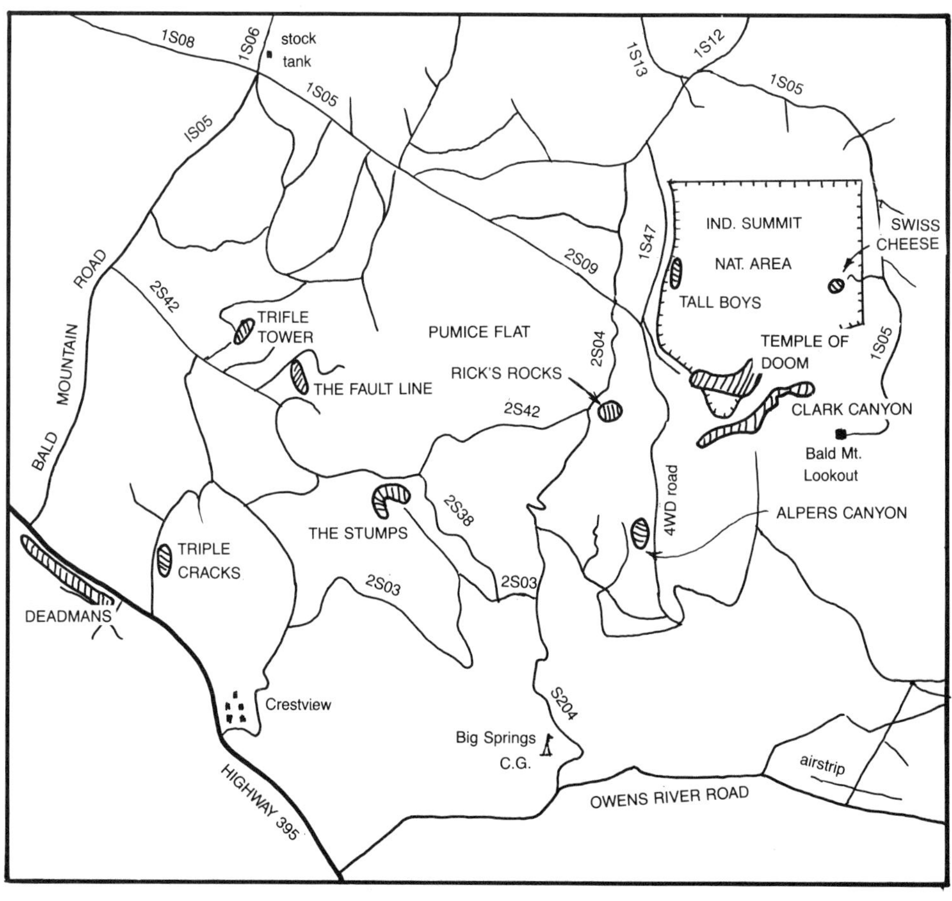

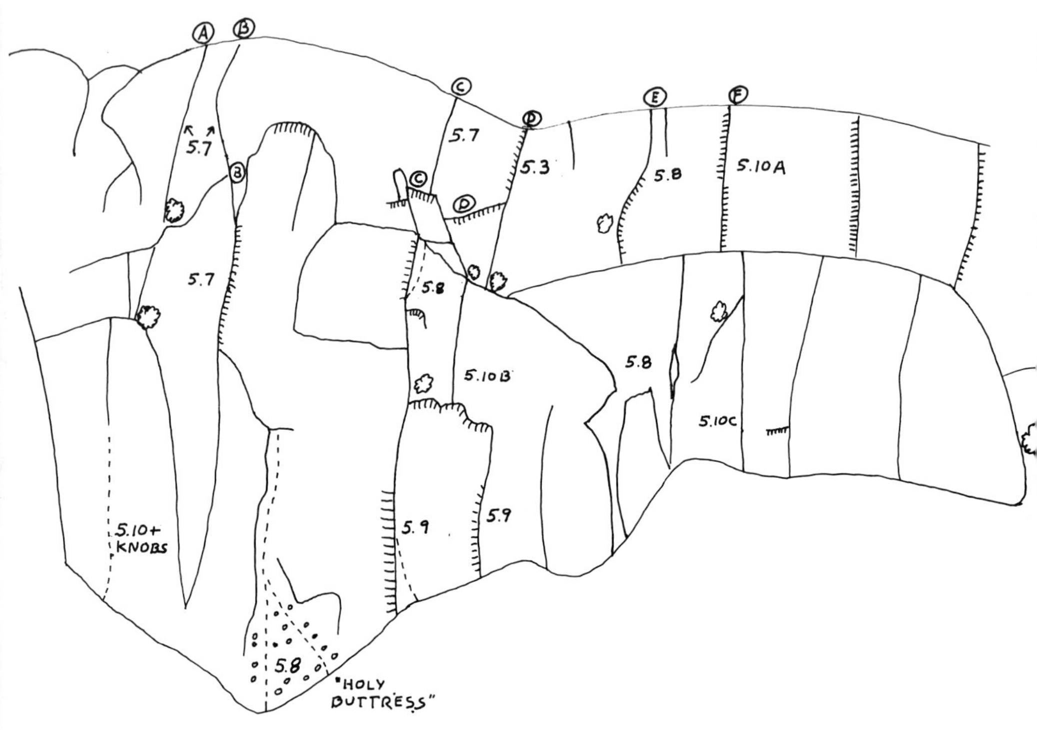

THE STUMPS – Holy Buttress

A Calder's Knobs 5.10+
B Spearhead Arete 5.8 ★★ Pro: to 2½″
C Rat Race 5.9 Pro: to 3″
D Vertebrae 5.10B ★ Pro: to 2½″, many thin
E Dr. Strangelove 5.8
F Slim Pickins 5.10C ★

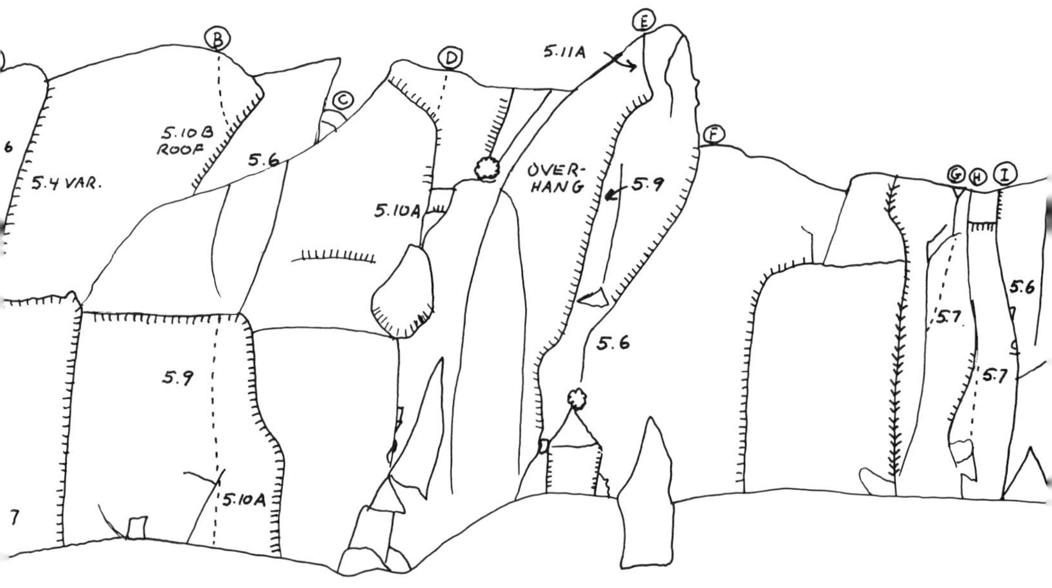

STUMPS – Curly Shuffle Area

- **A Give a Hoot** 5.7
- **B Whoop Whoop Roof** 5.10B
- **C Smiling Faces** 5.10A ★ Pro: thin
- **D H & R Block** 5.10A ★ Pro: to 2½″
- **E Curly Shuffle** 5.11A ★★
- **F Forest Service** 5.6
- **G Corner Market** 5.7
- **H Good 'n Plenty** 5.7 ★
- **I E.Z. Money** 5.6 ★★

ALPERS CANYON

Follow the Stumps approach to Big Springs campground. Follow the Indiana Summit road (2S04) for 2.2 miles and turn right on Alpers Canyon road (unmarked). Take the second prominent left in 0.9 miles and drive 0.6 miles to **Mind Dart** (5.10D), an obvious thin crack in a corner. Two shorter cracks to the right have been done (5.10A). More topropes have been done farther up canyon to the left.

RICK'S ROCKS

From Big Springs campground, follow the Indiana Summit road (2S04) for 3.5 miles to the junction of road 2S42. Park on the right just past this junction. A good bouldering area will be found down a gully to the east (right) of the road.

THE TALL BOYS and THE TEMPLE OF DOOM

From Big Springs campground, follow the Indiana Summit road (2S04) for 4.1 miles and turn right on road 2S09. Drive 0.5 miles to the border of Indiana Summit Natural Area, marked by a sign. For the Temple of Doom boulders drive straight here to a dead end parking area and walk through the woods to the southeast. More bouldering may be found to the northeast. To find the Tall Boys boulders, make a sharp left turn at the "Natural Area" sign and drive 0.5 miles to a small parking area marked by another, smaller, "Natural Area" sign. From here follow a faint road north for 100 yards, then turn right off the road and walk through the woods to the east for 200 yards. Ignore smaller rocks first encountered and walk to 30 and 40-foot steep toprope and boulder faces.

CLARK CANYON

From Big Springs campground follow the Indian Summit road (2S04) for 2.3 miles and turn right onto the Alpers Canyon road. Drive 1.6 miles to the junction of road 1S47. Turn right and drive 0.1 mile to a T junction with a gate on the left. Pass through the gate and drive 1.8 miles to a crossroads in Clark Canyon. One may go straight here to topropes and boulders that are visible ahead and to the left or you can turn right to approach the larger and somewhat decomposed crags upcanyon.

TRIFLE TOWER

From a point 11.2 miles north of the 203/395 junction and 3.7 miles south of June Lake Junction, turn east on Bald Mountain/Logging Camp road (1S05). Follow this for 1.8 miles and turn right on road 2S42 (unmarked). Drive 1.0 miles and turn left on a rough unmarked road that dead-ends in 0.2 miles. The Trifle Tower topropes (both in the 5.11/5.12 range) will be seen right above the road end.

THE FAULT LINE

From the junction of Bald Mountain/Logging Camp road (1S05) and 2S42, follow 2S42 for 1.8 miles and turn left on an unmarked road. Drive 0.2 miles and turn left on a rough road through deep pumice which dead ends in 0.1 miles. The boulders will be seen straight ahead. **Schnieder's Roof** (5.11+) is a classic thin to wide hand crack through a 45° overhang.

THE SWISS CHEESE BOULDER

Follow the Bald Mountain/Logging Camp road (1S05) approximately 10 miles to within 1.5 miles of Bald Mountain Lookout. Half a mile before passing through a gate (usually locked), you will see a sign reading "Locked gate 600 yards." Turn right just past this sign on an unmarked, little-used road and drive 0.5 miles to a dead end parking area. From here walk the left of two gullies that wander off to the south. Shortly, an obvious trail appears on the left side of this gully and is followed for 0.3 miles to the boulder. Two ⅜" eye bolts have been placed for toproping on these excellent overhanging problems, though one may desire a rope on the fifth class downclimb from the summit to reach the bolts, situated right above the overhanging section of the rock.

DEADMAN'S / JUNE LAKE AREAS

Along the corridor of Highway 395 between the Crestview highway maintainance station and the area just north of June Lake Junction lies another extensive network of volcanic bouldering crags. Near the town of June Lake itself, a few short leadable climbs exist on high quality granite. As in the Indiana Summit section, our reference points will be the Highways 203/395 Junction and the June Lake Junction.

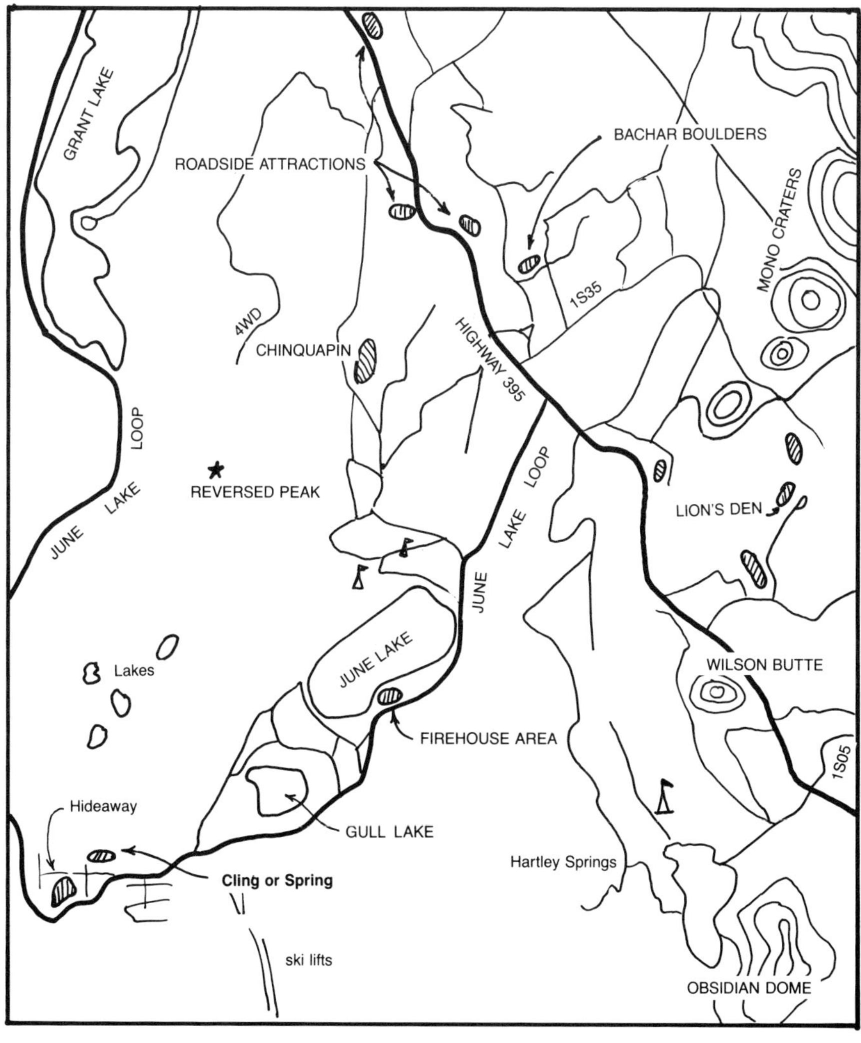

TRIPLE CRACKS

From a point 9.8 miles north of the 203/395 Junction and 5.2 miles south of June Lake Junction, turn east on an unmarked road and drive 0.5 miles. The Triple Cracks will be seen 150 feet from the road, on the right.

DEADMAN'S SUMMIT

To find this highly popular bouldering area, follow Highway 395 0.3 miles north of the Triple Cracks turnoff or 1.1 miles south of the Bald Mountain/Logging Camp road and turn west on an unmarked but well travelled road. Route 395 has a northbound turning lane here. This road quickly splits into three roads. Take the rightmost road for 0.3 miles where a right turn takes you to the easily seen first area. Drive 0.4 miles farther and another right to park at the second area. A third area is another 0.2 miles up the road. All are excellent for toproping or bouldering.

THE LION'S DEN

Follow Route 395 1.5 miles north of Bald Mountain/Logging Camp road or 2.2 miles south of June Lake Junction and turn east onto a dirt road marked by a sign advertising June Lake Village. Take the second left in 0.5 miles and bouldering will be found in 0.3 miles to the left of the road. The Lion's Den itself is found downhill from a dead end loop 0.4 miles farther down the road. **Block and Tackle** (5.11D/.12A) is an excellent thin crack that can be toproped or led. A face route protected by ⅜″ eye bolts to the right is **Bulldog** (5.11C/D). A few easier cracks exist farther right.

THE BACHAR BOULDERS

Immediately north of June Lake Junction turn east on road 1S35. Drive 0.5 miles and go left at a fork. Drive 0.7 miles and turn left at an unmarked road, parking within 0.1 miles. The boulder will be seen on the right.

ROADSIDE ATTRACTIONS

Easily visible because of their proximity to Route 395, the first area is one mile north of June Lake Junction on the east side of the highway. The second area is one mile farther on the same side, and a third small area exists on the west side of the road between the two.

CHINQUAPIN AREA

From June Lake Junction, follow the June Lake Loop west to a sign for "Oh! Ridge" and turn right on the June Lake Beach road. Drive 0.6 miles and turn right on the pole line road which you will follow for 1 mile. Turn left here and in 0.4 miles the boulders will be seen on the right.

JUNE LAKE VILLAGE

From June Lake Junction drive west on the June Lake Loop and turn right at the June Lake Fire Station, parking within a few hundred feet. By walking directly back toward June Lake a small bouldering area will be found containing **Fire, Fire** (5.11D), a 20′ thin finger crack. Five miles west of June Lake Junction and left of a group of private homes, one of which is a geodesic dome, a small, steep, granite outcrop will be seen on the north side of the road. One should take care to avoid private property when approaching this crag. **Cling or Spring** (5.12) is a good crack and face climb left of an old aid bolt ladder. More lead and boulder problems exist around the corner to the right. A little farther down the June Lake Loop, just past the Carson Peak Inn, turn right on the Hideaway Meadows road and follow this as it describes a U-turn through a private neighborhood to the base of a small dome and slab formation. **Three Pops** (5.10B ★) is a steep five-bolt lead problem on the highest face, and there are two bolted 5.7 routes on slabs to the right.

SAGEHEN SUMMIT AREA

This chapter describes the climbing of Dexter canyon, North Canyon, and Granite Basin. All these areas are accessed off Highway 120 East, north of June Lake Junction.

Dexter Canyon is a northeast-southwest running canyon on the north side of the Glass Mountains. Most of the routes are on the northwest side of the canyon, facing southeast. This would make them a potential area for year-round climbing; however, snow blocks the approach roads from the first major storm until April or May. Dexter Canyon offers multi-pitch routes on volcanic rock of generally good quality, but loose rock abounds throughout the area, and most routes have at least one section requiring more than normal caution. Although no one uses a helmet in Dexter Canyon, it couldn't be considered a bad idea.

There are several ways to approach Dexter Canyon, but the best ones all originate from Highway 120. Three roads, the Pilot Springs road (1S17), the Crooked Meadows road (1S04), and the Sagehen Meadows road (1N02) run southeast from Highway 120 at points between 0.6 and 3.4 miles east of the junction of the Logging Camp road and Highway 120. Whichever you take, follow signs for Johnny Meadow. About 3.4 miles after all three roads have met (near Wild Horse Meadow), pass straight through a four-way intersection. Signs here indicate Johnny Meadow to the left and Dexter Creek to the right. Nine tenths of a mile farther a faint road leads to the right where the main road makes a 90° bend to the left. Fifty yards down this faint road is a tiny parking spot and campsite; at this point, the canyon rim is only 5 yards off to the right. This is the best approach for the Vapor Lock area. From the car, walk upcanyon (right) about 200 yards to a descent gully leading down into the canyon. Then walk back downcanyon about 250-300 yards to the first of the routes, Steeplechase. The Clark Kent and Door Into Summer areas are best approached by continuing past the faint road (that leads to the campsite) about a quarter mile to a fork; take the right fork, which ends in another quarter mile or so. At this point you are about 200 yards from the canyon rim. About 200 yards downcanyon (left) is a descent gully leading into the canyon. Walking upcanyon about 150 yards takes one to the first route, Dagwood. Walking downcanyon about a quarter mile leads to the Bowling For Keeps area. The A Dollar Short area lies about midway between the Sandbag and Door into Summer areas, and can be approached by either of the descent gullies. Despite these various approaches, the routes of Dexter Canyon are described as if one is headed downcanyon.

Cantaloupe 5.10B ★ Turn right on the approach road at the four-way intersection, following a sign for Dexter Creek. Park after ¼ mile, walk due south to the rim and descend a gully on the right. This route is on an outcrop on the left, a straight-in crack starting fists and tapering to fingers, finally ending up with face up an arete.

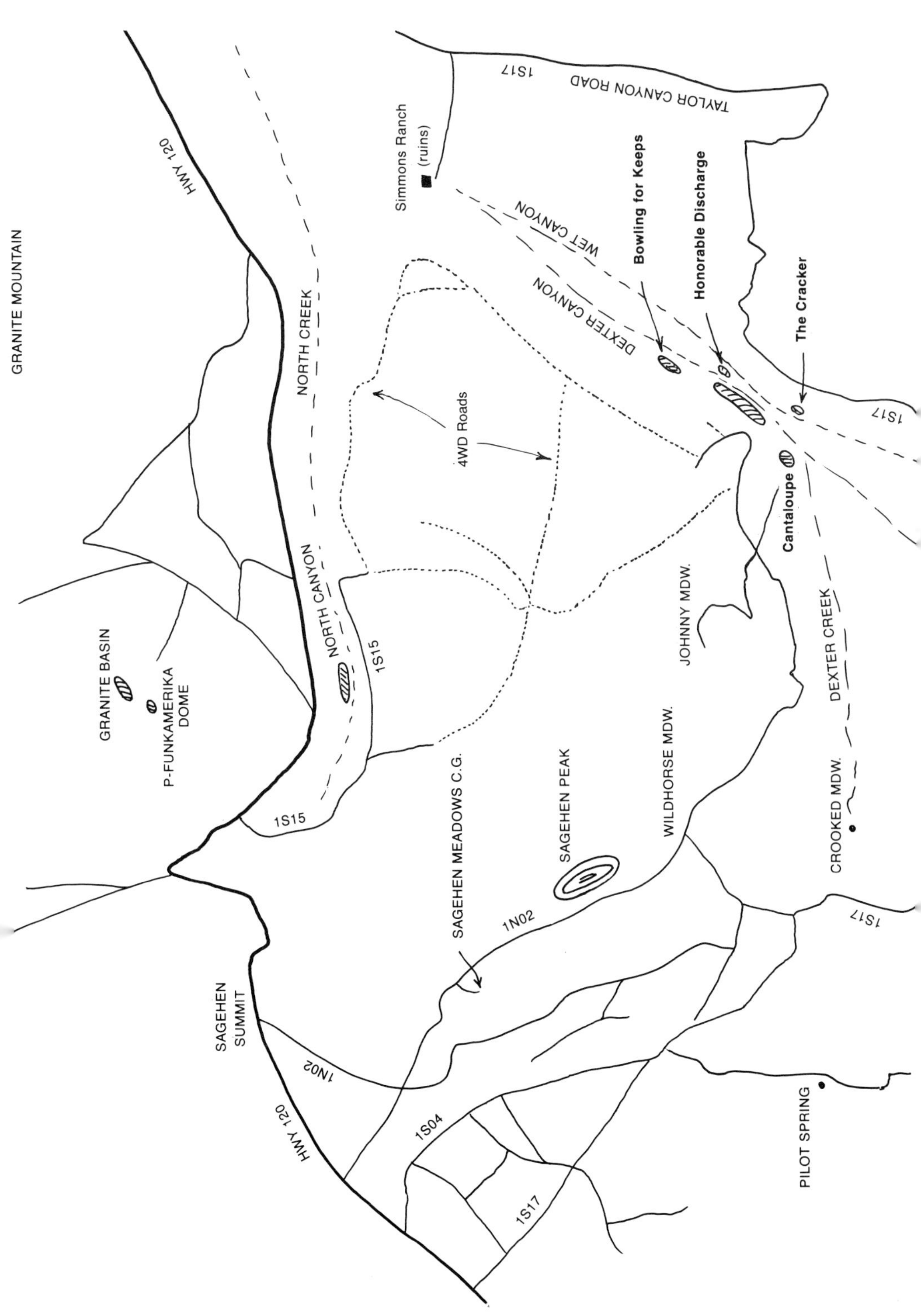
GRANITE MOUNTAIN
HWY 120
NORTH CREEK
NORTH CANYON
Simmons Ranch (ruins)
1S17
TAYLOR CANYON ROAD
WET CANYON
DEXTER CANYON
Bowling for Keeps
Honorable Discharge
The Cracker
Cantaloupe
4WD Roads
1S15
GRANITE BASIN
P-FUNKAMERIKA DOME
JOHNNY MDW.
DEXTER CREEK
WILDHORSE MDW.
SAGEHEN PEAK
SAGEHEN MEADOWS C.G.
CROOKED MDW.
1N02
SAGEHEN SUMMIT
1S04
PILOT SPRING

photo by Gary Sl

VAPOR LOCK AREA

A Steeplechase 5.10A pro: to 3″
B Sandman 5.9 ★ pro: to 4″
C Cell Block 5.10C ★
D Sandbag 5.10A
E Vapor Lock 5.10D ★★ pro: to 4″

photo by Gary Slate

A DOLLAR SHORT AREA

A **A Dollar Short** 5.10B ★★ This follows double cracks (one is offwidth) on the left wall of a giant alcove to a good ledge. A short pitch leads off the left side of the ledge to the top.

B **Road Warrior** 5.10B ★★ Thin crack 100 feet right of A Dollar Short.

C **Lizard Crack** 5.10A The next crack, about 25 feet right of Road Warrior.

D **Shortchanged** 5.9 Right-facing corner 25 feet right of Lizard Crack.

E **Short Stroke** 5.10A ★ Thin hands to offwidth 35 feet right of Shortchanged.

photo by Gary Slate

DOOR INTO SUMMER AREA

A **Fire and Ice** 5.10C ★ Faces left; a thin crack leading to a chimney.
B **Spring Fling** 5.10
C **Door Into Summer** 5.10B ★★ pro: to 3″

CLARK KENT AREA *photo by Gary Slate*

A **Star Beast** 5.10
B **Orphans of the Sky** 5.9
C **Forbidden Planet** 5.9 ★ pro: to 4″
D **B.C.** 5.9 pro: to 4″
E **Clark Kent** 5.10C ★★ pro: to 3½″
F **Tumbleweeds** 5.10B ★
G **Stalactite** 5.10A ★ pro: to 4″
H **Foghorn Leghorn** 5.10C

Grandpa's Challenge 5.11A ★ About a hundred feet right of Foghorn Leghorn, this route starts up a flared chimney, climbs past a thin crux, moves left around a 5.10+ overhang and belays at a bush. The second (5.8) pitch climbs up, angling up and right to the rim.

Yosemite Sam 5.10B ★★ pro: to 4″, incl. several 3-4″. This follows a major left-facing corner that starts on the other side of a giant boulder from the previous route.

Dagwood 5.9 ★★ Starting about 50 feet right of the large boulder mentioned in the previous route description, this follows double cracks on the right wall of a giant left-facing corner in the cliff band. About 100 feet.

BOWLING FOR KEEPS AREA

Gutter Ball 5.11B ★ The crack system on the left side of a blank face which leads to a chimney through a roof about 100′ off the ground.

Bowling for Keeps 5.11A ★★ The crack system on the right side of the blank face. The first pitch (5.10D) leads to a ledge on the right. The crux is face climbing off the ledge following a thin crack and continuing more or less straight up to the top.

Up Your Alley 5.10C ★ 80 feet right of Bowling for Keeps climb thin cracks to a ledge. Continue up a left- facing corner and over a roof. A thin crack in a flare over the roof is the crux.

Honorable Discharge 5.10C ★ This route is on the southeast (opposite) side of the canyon about 250 yards upcanyon from the Bowling for Keeps area. It is a steep thin crack in a small outcrop of rock. The route is about 100 feet long.

NORTH CANYON

North Canyon is a small canyon running east-west and paralleling Highway 120 about ½ mile to the south. To reach North Canyon, turn south on dirt road 1S15. This road is 2.6 miles east of Sagehen Summit and is easy to miss when coming from the west. Follow the dirt road across a tiny creek; it then curves left, paralleling the creek/canyon. A vague parking area is located on the left of the road about 1.5 miles from Highway 120. The canyon rim is 100 feet north of here and the routes are on the opposite side, facing south. This area could feasibly be approached from a point on Highway 120 roughly opposite the west approach road to Granite Basin (1 mile east of road 1S15).

A American Hero 5.11C ★★ This is a 1¼″ crack over a small roof.

B Lamb Chop 5.10A-C ★ Climb to splitter cracks in a slightly overhanging headwall; the left is 5.10A, the right 5.10C.

C Helix 5.10A ★ Starts in a thin crack and higher follows double cracks.

D Ollie North 5.10A ★ Climbs up to and follows a curving crack above a small roof.

E What, Me Worry? 5.10C

The Shredder 5.12B ★★ About 150 feet right of What, Me Worry? is a west-facing wall with this right- facing, right-leaning corner containing a very thin crack. Pro: many thin camming devices.

THE CRACKER AREA

The Cracker, facing northwest, lies on the southeast side of Wet Canyon, which closely parallels Dexter Canyon. It can be seen from the campsite at Dexter Canyon mentioned above, but to approach it you must drive 11.4 miles east of Sagehen Summit on Highway 120 and turn right on Taylor Canyon Road. In 3.6 miles turn left on 1S17, up Taylor Canyon. A large bulldozed turnout will be found in 7.1 miles. Park here. The crag will be seen a few hundred yards down canyon. From right to left, the routes are:

Graham Crackers 5.10A This is a thin to hand crack leading past a shelf.

Tits on a Ritz 5.9 ★ A finger crack.

Shepherd's Crook 5.10D A left-arching system leading to a 3½″ crack.

Two right-facing corners left of Shepherd's Crook have also been toproped (5.11).

GRANITE BASIN

This area is located a few miles north of Highway 120, about midway between Lee Vining and Benton. Coming from the west, turn left onto a dirt road about 3.7 miles east of Sagehen Summit. From the east, take a separate dirt road about 25 miles west of Benton. These two dirt roads merge after 2 miles or so, and a short distance later turn north on another dirt road. This road gets progressively steeper and sandier as it approaches the crag. Be careful about getting stuck in a 2-wheel drive vehicle. See the map on page 131.

Most of the routes are on one large formation, with a few climbs on a smaller dome to the left. The rock is a high desert granite, with quality ranging from poor to excellent. Most of the routes face south, making climbing possible year-round, though mid- summer may be brutally hot, and in mid-winter the approach roads may get enough snow to make them impassible.

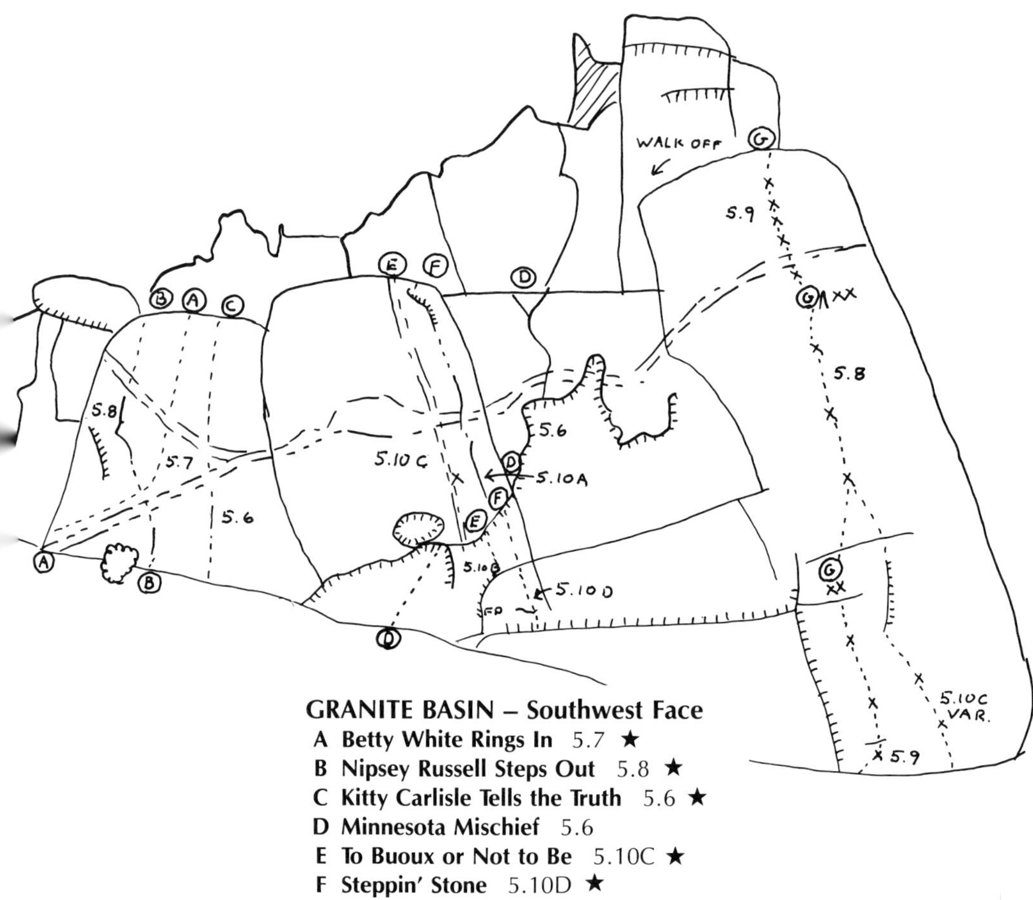

GRANITE BASIN – Southwest Face

- **A Betty White Rings In** 5.7 ★
- **B Nipsey Russell Steps Out** 5.8 ★
- **C Kitty Carlisle Tells the Truth** 5.6 ★
- **D Minnesota Mischief** 5.6
- **E To Buoux or Not to Be** 5.10C ★
- **F Steppin' Stone** 5.10D ★
- **G Hair Raiser Buttress** 5.9 ★★

Spuds Gurgling Cock Holster 5.10D ★ This is a steep bolted face to the left of To Buoux or Not to Be.

GRANITE BASIN – Southwest Face
1 Betty White Rings In
2 Nipsey Russell Steps Out
3 Kitty Carlisle Tells the Truth
4 To Buoux or Not to Be
5 Steppin' Stone
6 Hair Raiser Buttress

GRANITE BASIN – Southeast Face (Left)

- A **Hair Raiser Buttress** 5.9 ★★
- B **Clevenger Route** 5.9 ★
- C **All Along the Watchtower** 5.10– ★★
- D **Firefall** 5.9 ★★
- E **The Wanderer** 5.6 or 5.9 or 5.10
- F **Grunt Mountain** 5.9
- G **Deadline** 5.7

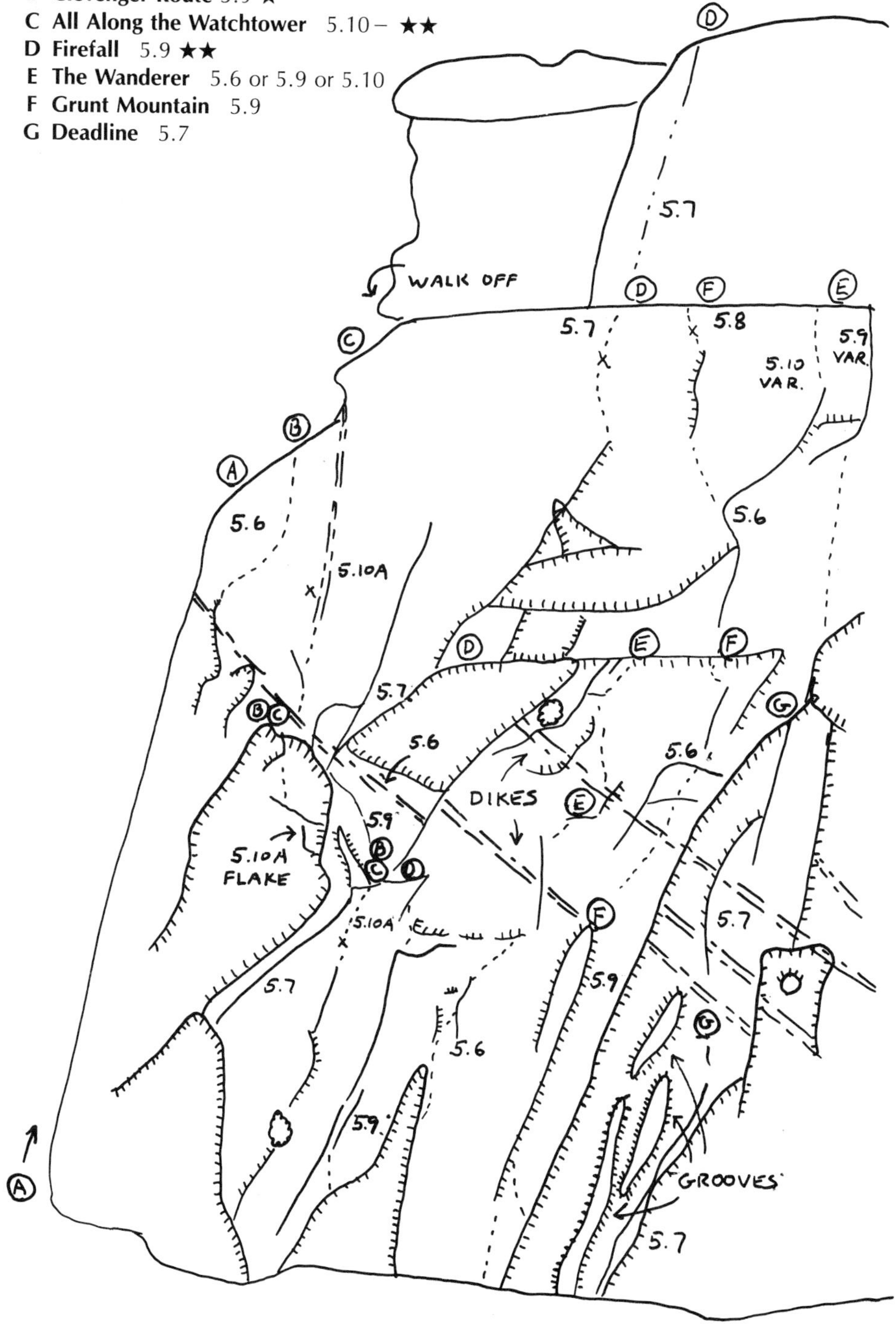

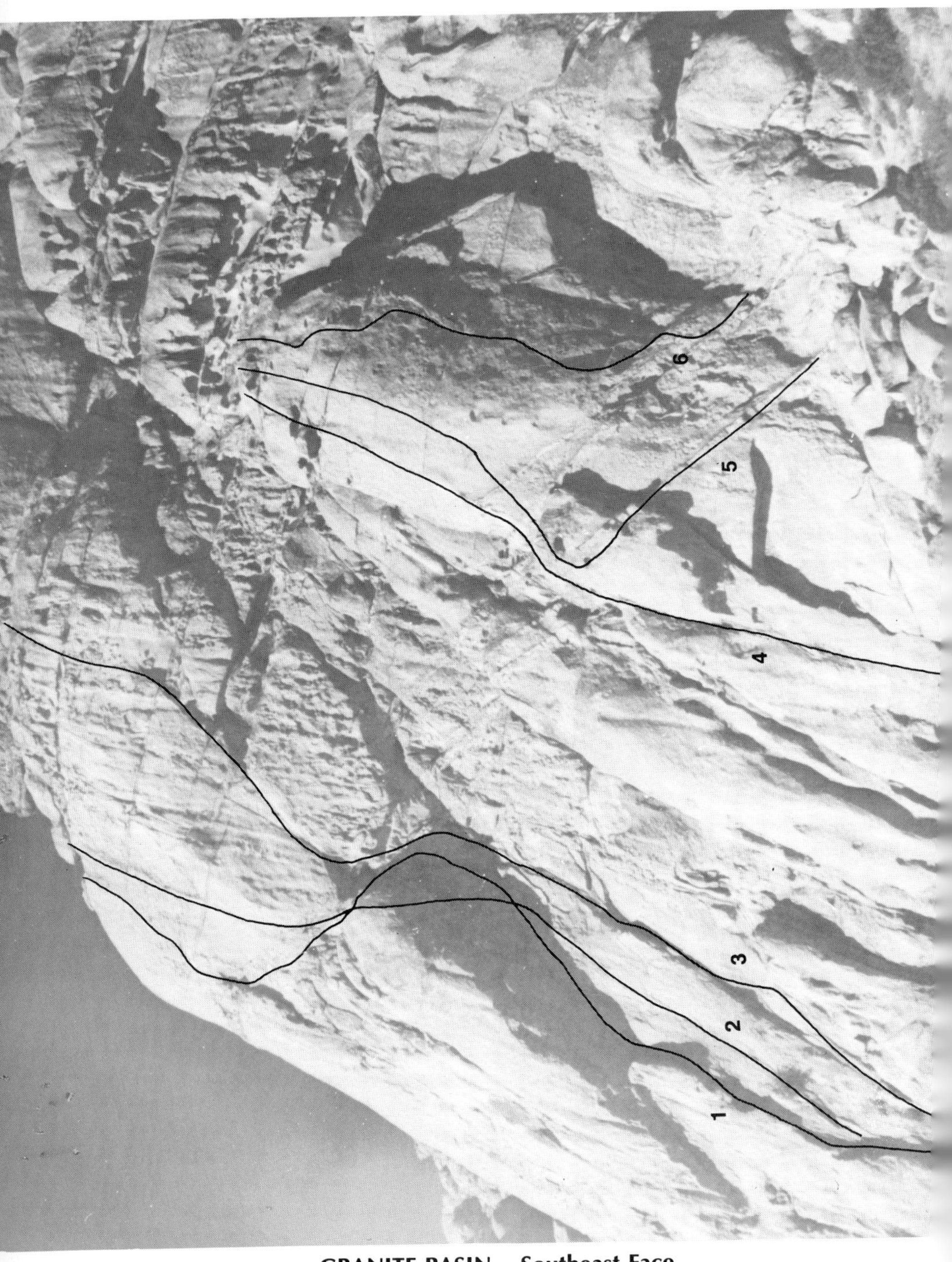

GRANITE BASIN – Southeast Face

1 Clevenger Route
2 All Along the Watchtower
3 Firefall
4 Grape Nuts
5 Frosted Flakes
6 Never Mind the Bollocks

GRANITE BASIN – Southeast Face (Lower Right Side)

- A **Deadline** 5.7
- B **Grape Nuts** 5.9 ★
- C **Frosted Flakes** 5.8
- D **Never Mind the Bollocks** 5.9
- E **Post Nasal Drip** 5.9 ★
- F **Archie Andrews** 5.7? ★
- G **The Tube** 5.9

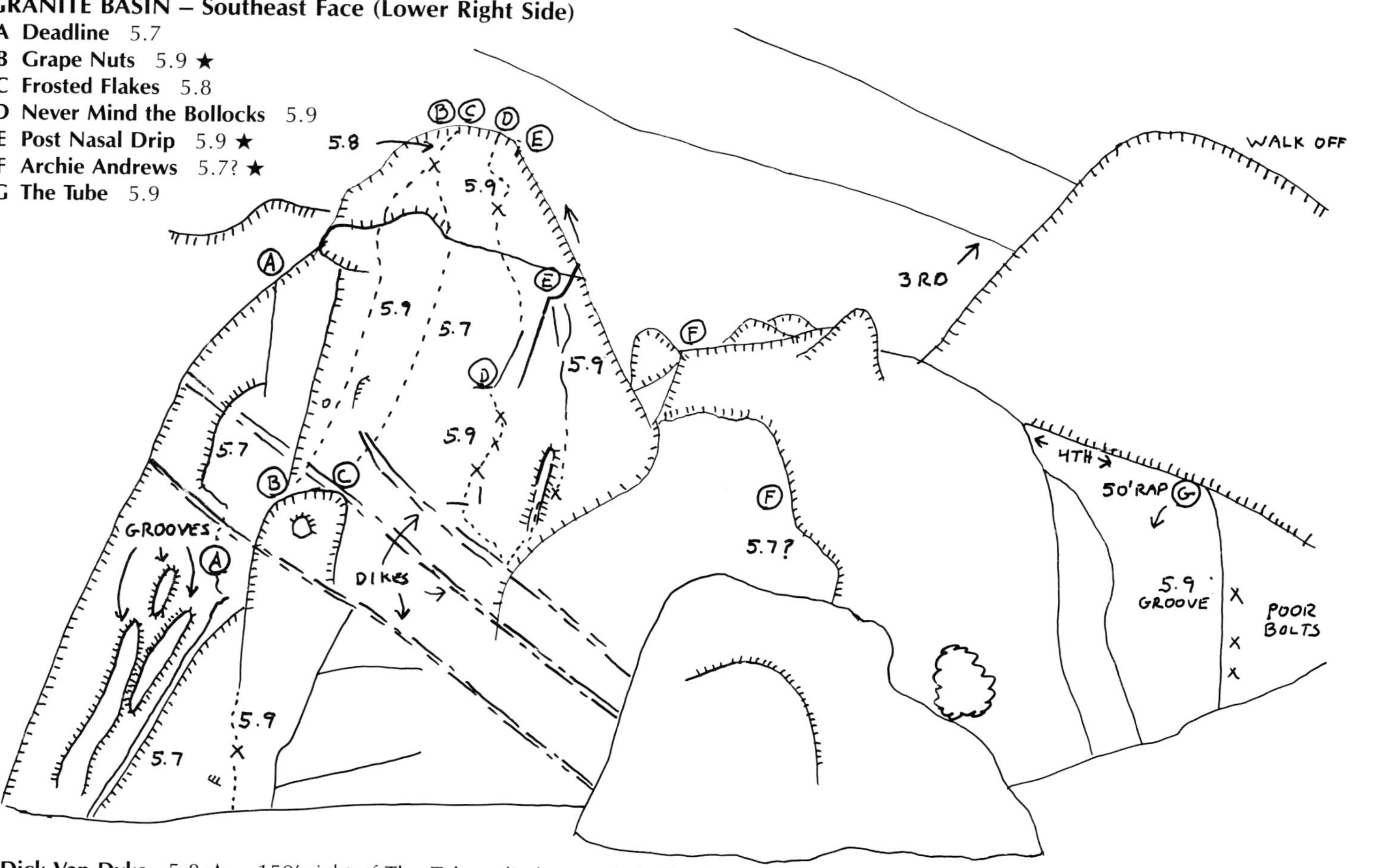

Dick Van Dyke 5.8 ★ 150′ right of The Tube, climb a vertical dike for one pitch.

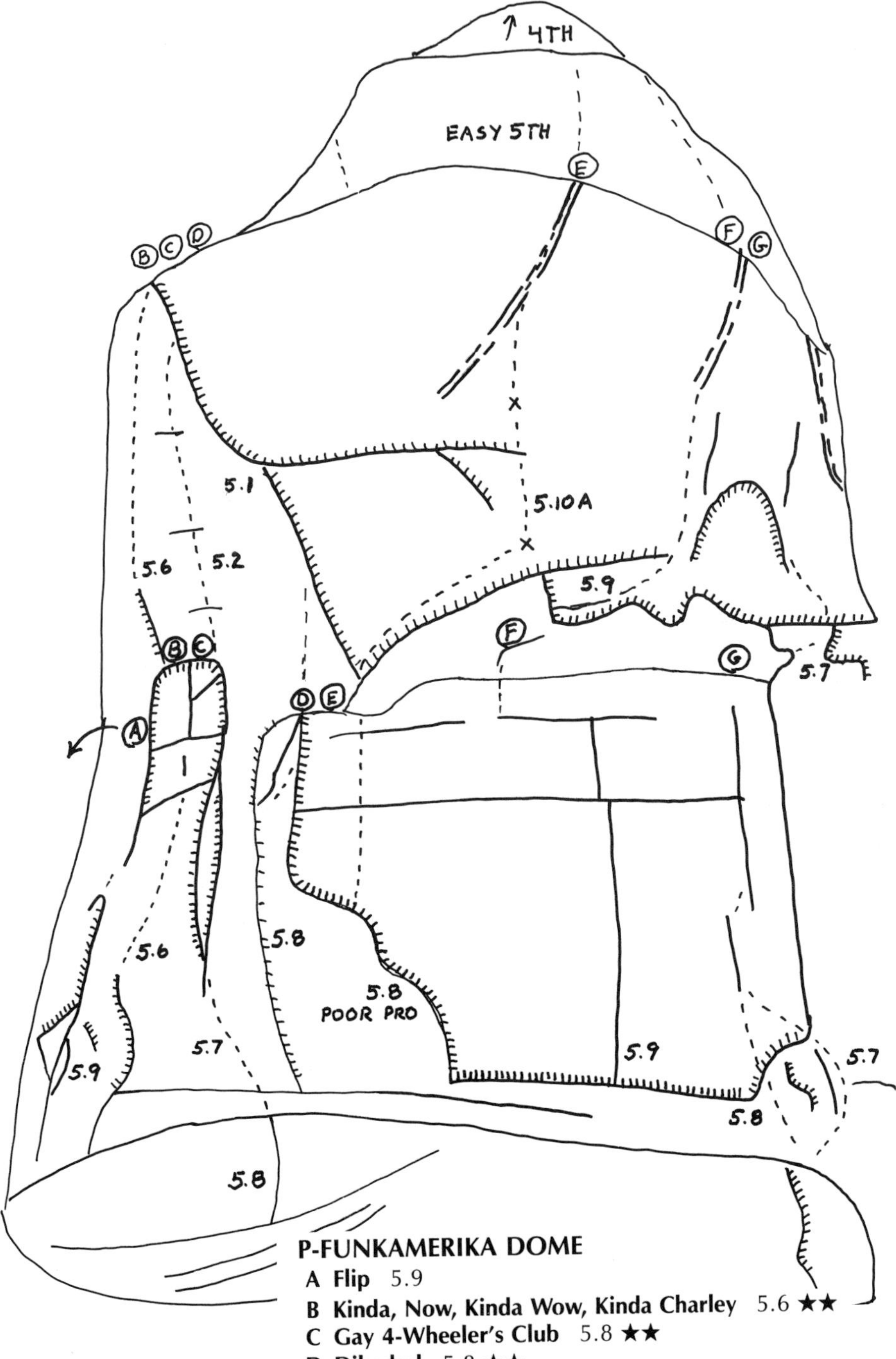

P-FUNKAMERIKA DOME

- **A Flip** 5.9
- **B Kinda, Now, Kinda Wow, Kinda Charley** 5.6 ★★
- **C Gay 4-Wheeler's Club** 5.8 ★★
- **D Dihedral** 5.8 ★★
- **E The Upstairs Lounge** 5.10A ★
- **F P-Funk of Amerika** 5.9 ★★
- **G Wild Eyrie** 5.7 or 5.8 ★

P-FUNKAMERIKA DOME

1 **Kinda Now, Kinda Wow, Kinda Charley**
2 **Gay 4-Wheeler's Club**
3 **Dihedral**
4 **Upstairs Lounge**
5 **P-Funk of Amerika**

Prepare to Qualify 5.11A ★ Up an left from P-Funk Amerika Dome and on a slightly separate formation, this route goes out a roof crack formed by a striking, overhanging flake.

BENTON CRAGS

The Benton Crags are a group of west- facing rocks on the west side of the Benton Range. The rock is high-desert granite of varying quality, and climbing is possible most of the year, though in winter snow may block the approach roads. They are approached from the Benton Crossing Road, a circuitous road (partially paved) that leads east from Highway 395 to Highway 120 about 6 miles west of the town of Benton.

From the Mammoth Lakes area the west end of the Benton Crossing Road is located about 6 miles south of the 395/203 junction and is marked by a small green church and signs for Whitmore Hot Springs. The crags come into view on the right in about 20 miles. Make a sharp east turn onto road #3S50 and after a half mile turn left onto another dirt road leading towards the plainly-visible crags. At a point 1.2 miles past this turn a small dirt turnout on the right is used for parking, just below the left side of Locals Only Rock.

From Bishop and points north it is easiest to reach the north end of the Benton Crossing Road, located 6 miles west of Highway 6 and the town of Benton. Six miles south on the Benton Crossing Road from Highway 120 is found the dirt road #3S50. Turn east here and follow the approach described above.

DOUBLE DOME

The first five routes are on the north side of the rock; the last route is on the south side.

Double Trouble 5.9 This is the left of two distinct cracks on the left side of the north face.

Double Dealing 5.10A The right crack, which turns into a dike near the top.

Pachyderm 5.8 To the right of the preceeding routes, and separated by a ridge of rock is this obvious crack.

Brontosaurus 5.4 An obvious wide white dike.

A Pinch is All it Takes 5.8 This climb follows a thin white dike and flake.

No Grain, No Gain 5.11A On the south side of the rock, climb a right-facing corner left of a dike, then continue past three bolts to the top.

CLOCK ROCK

Quartz Digital 5.8 This is a foot-wide, right- leaning white dike on the west face.

9 to 5 5.9 This route starts near the right side of the south face. Climb up and left on a small arete. Step over a bulge and follow thin cracks and face past a piton to the top.

Waste of Time 5.5 This route starts just right of 9 to 5 and wanders up ramps and ledges to the top.

PETROCLIFF

Several cracks from 5.6 to 5.8 will be found on a wide short cliff ½ mile west of the parking area, left of the approach road.

Psycho Killer
Junk Food
Crocodile Rock

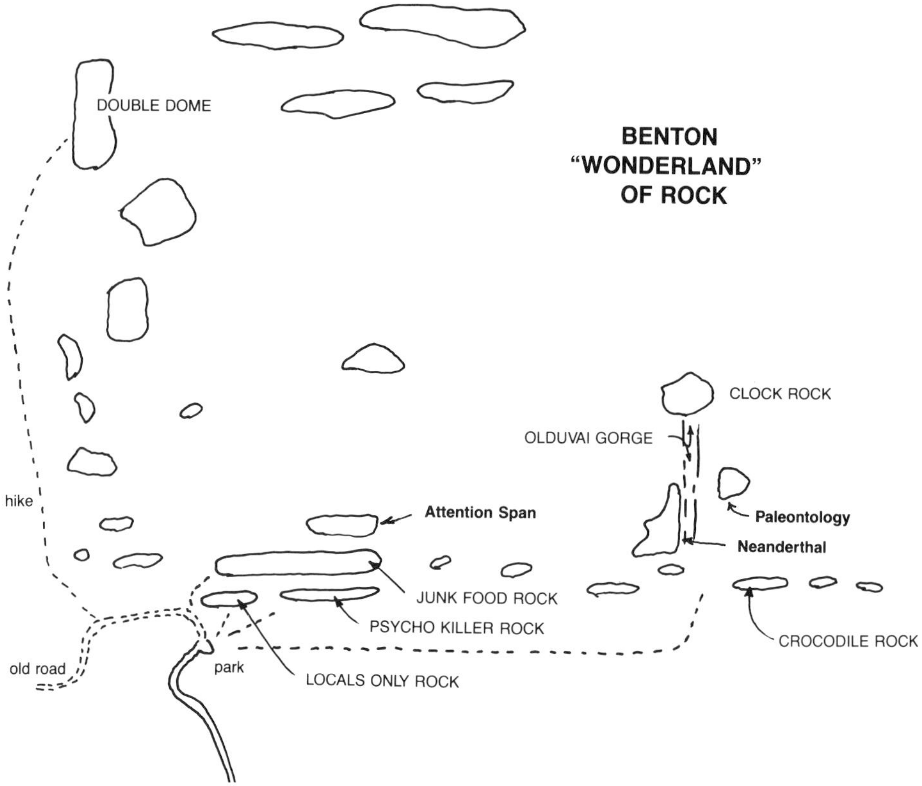

BENTON "WONDERLAND" OF ROCK
DOUBLE DOME
CLOCK ROCK
OLDUVAI GORGE
Paleontology
Neanderthal
Attention Span
hike
JUNK FOOD ROCK
PSYCHO KILLER ROCK
CROCODILE ROCK
old road
park
LOCALS ONLY ROCK

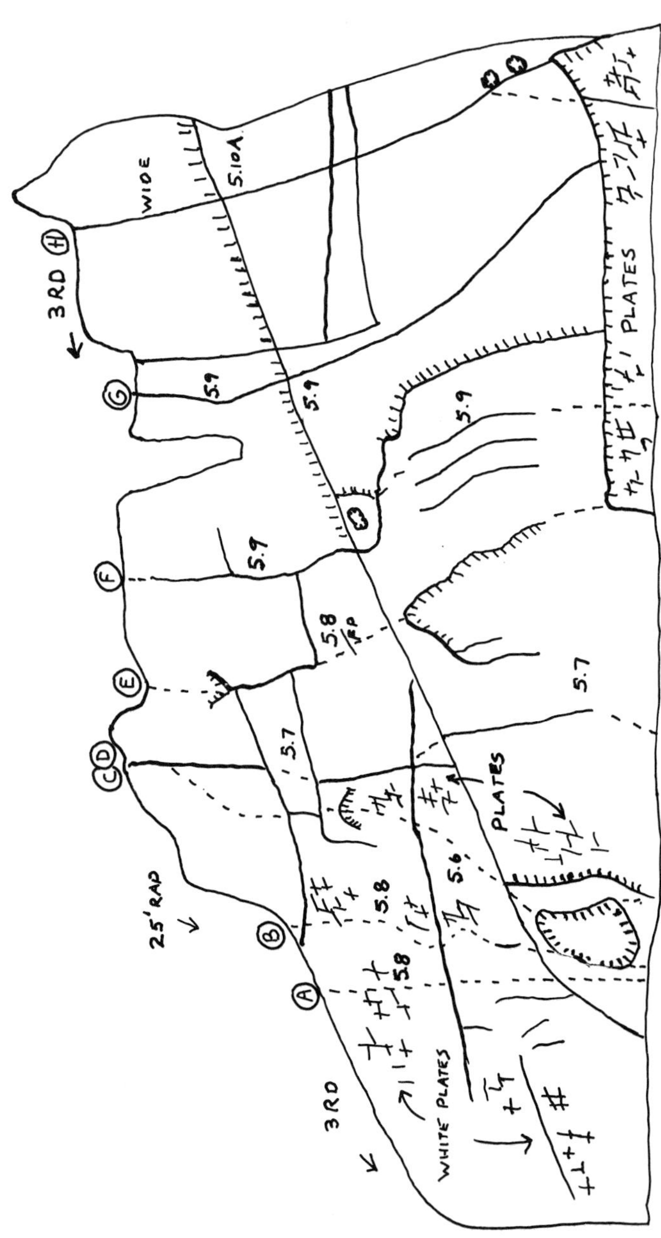

LOCALS ONLY ROCK – West Face

A The Tube 5.8 ★
B Pipeline 5.8 ★
C Locals Only 5.6
D Get Lost 5.7 ★★
E No Trespassing 5.8 ★
F Surfin' Safari 5.9 ★★
G Tough Muffin 5.9 ★
H Low Cal 5.10A

PSYCHO KILLER ROCK – West Face

- **A Jimmy Jones** 5.9
- **B Caligula** 5.9 ★
- **C Psycho Killer** 5.10A ★★
- **D Psycho Chicken** 5.8
- **E Mayhem** 5.9
- **F Hillside Strangler** 5.4 ★

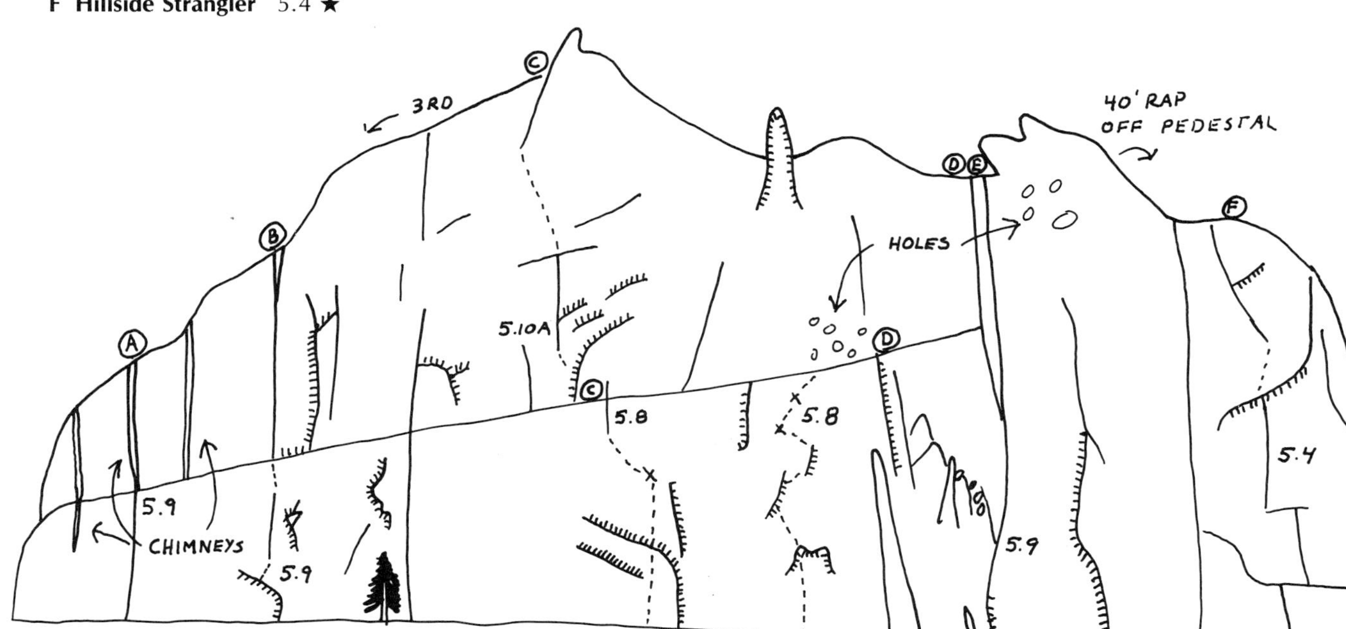

JUNK FOOD ROCK – West Face (Left Side)

- A **M.D.R.** 5.5
- B **Scrambled Eggs** 5.8
- C **Bit O' Honey** 5.10B ★
- D **Post Toasties** 5.7 ★★
- E **Wheaties** 5.6 ★
- F **High Weed Glutin** 5.10A ★
- G **Granola Crunch** 5.10A ★
- H **Frosted Flakes** 5.10A ★

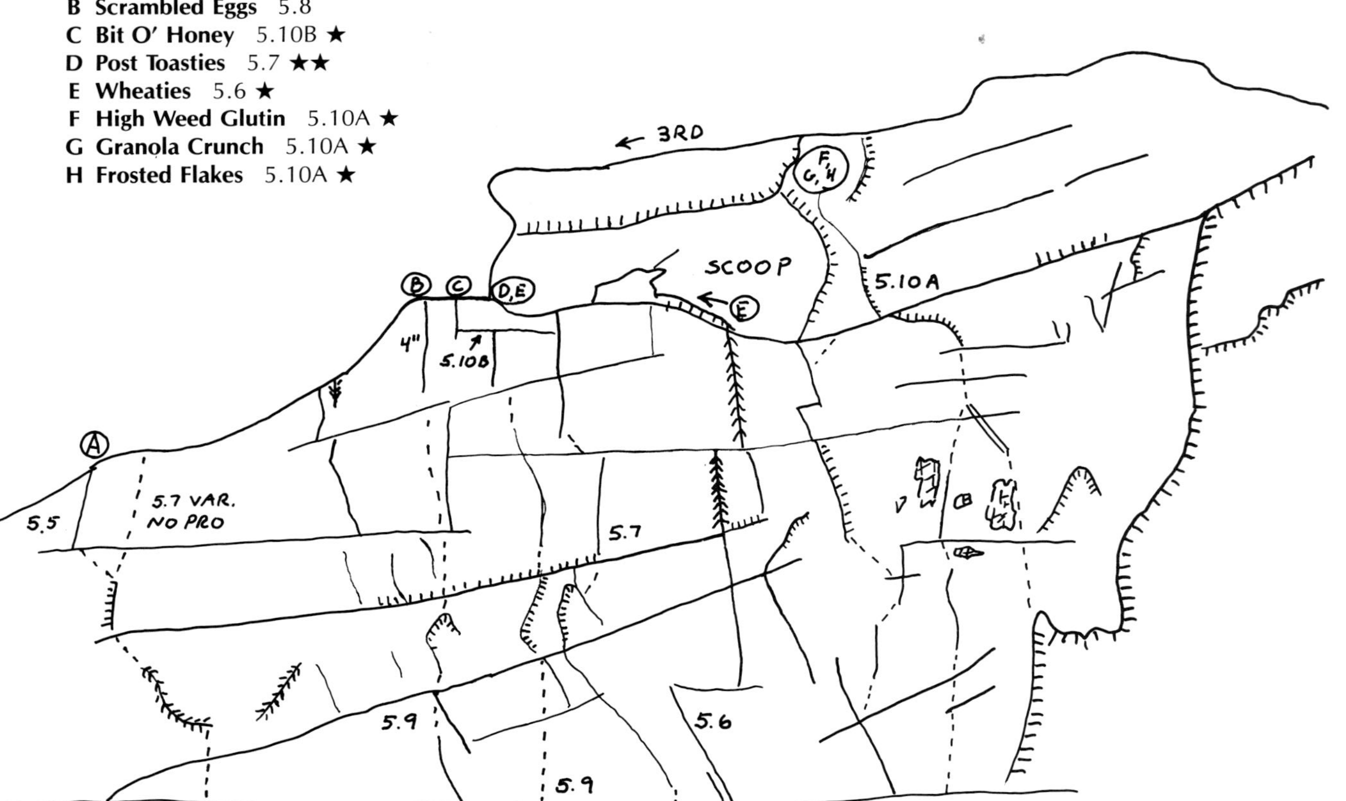

JUNK FOOD ROCK – West Face (Right Side)

A Pops 5.8
B Kix 5.5
C Twinkie Defense 5.8
D Wheateena 5.7
E Grape Nuts 5.8
F Cream of Wheat 5.8 ★★
G Hearts, Moons, Clovers 5.8
H Magically Delicious 5.9
I Lucky Charms 5.8 ★

Amber Waves 5.8 This follows a grainy crack on the right side of the Lucky Charms buttress.

Attention Span 5.9 Follow a hand crack through a tiny roof on the south face of a formation directly behind the right side of Junk Food Rock.

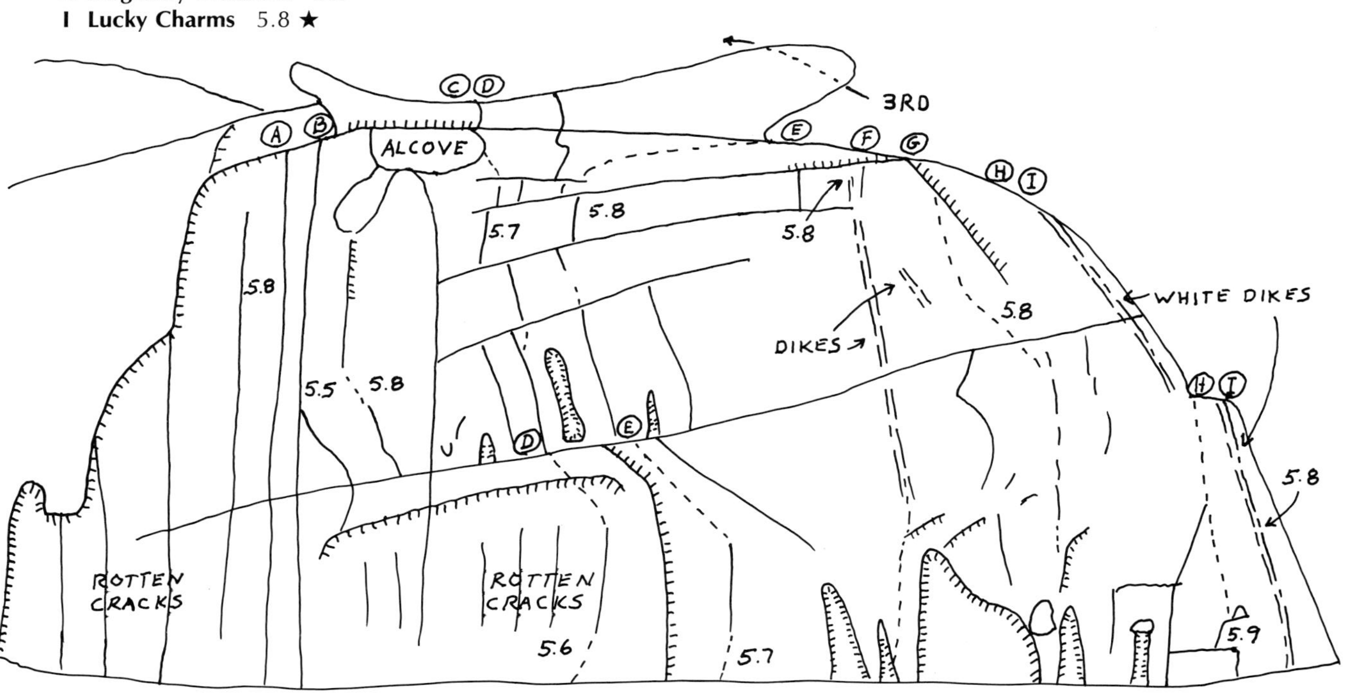

CROCODILE ROCK – West Face

A Slither 5.10A
B Poacher 5.10D ★
C Challenger 5.10C ★★
D Competitive Edge 5.10A ★
E King Snake Flakes 5.10C ★★
F Lizard 5.4

Running Scared 5.10B Just right of King Snake Flakes, climb a thin crack, then left to a giant knob. Higher, work up and right under a small arch, then up loose rock to the top. Poor pro.

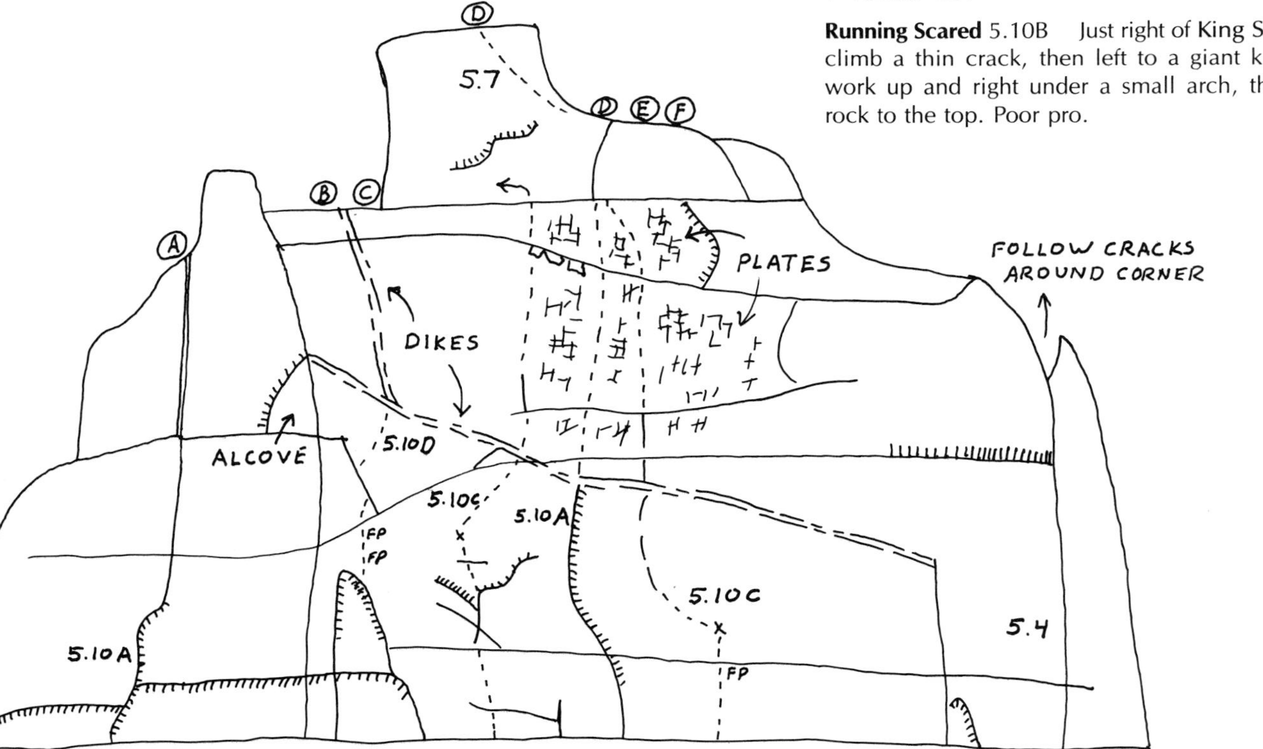

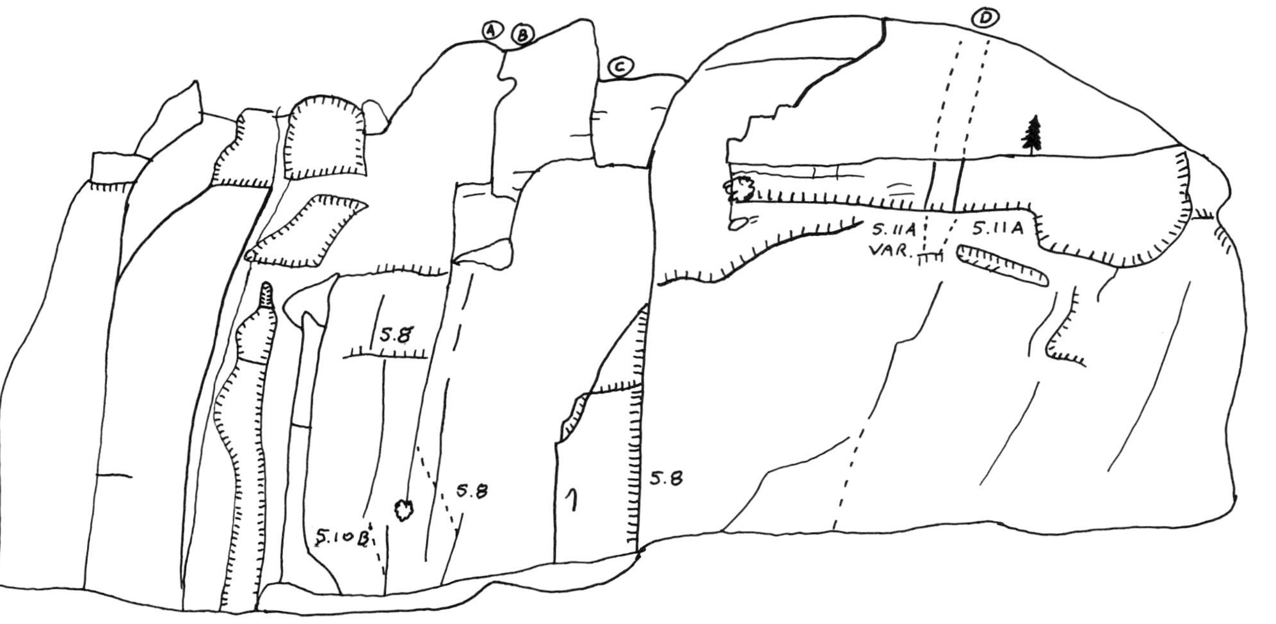

OLDUVAI GORGE
South Face

A **Neanderthal** 5.10B ★
B **Dr. Leaky** 5.8
C **Lucy** 5.8
D **Australopithicus** 5.11A ★★

Topropes: Directly across the gully from the Neanderthal Cliff are two short, steep toprope walls with excellent rock.
Paleontology 5.6 Follow a shallow crack that splits the west face of a small formation near the top of the gorge.

ICE CLIMBING

The East Sierra has perhaps the best winter ice climbing in California. Lee Vining Canyon has long been known to contain excellent steep icefalls to challenge the expert. Lesser known but equally high quality routes are found in the June Lake area. Overall, the routes in Lee Vining Canyon are more difficult due to their steeper average angle. Some routes in June Lake, however, have some excellent steeper sections that any climber will find stimulating. Both areas usually form up soon after the first major snowfall of the winter, but an unusually dry winter may make for poor ice climbing; the volume and quality of ice varies widely from year to year. Local climbers or climbing shops can provide the most up-to-date information on the routes.

LEE VINING

To approach the climbs in Lee Vining Canyon, turn west from Route 395 onto Route 120 south of the town of Lee Vining. Drive for several miles until a sign for the California Edison gernerating station marks a paved left turn. Turn left here and make an immediate right to continue driving up the canyon, eventually reaching the power station and the end of the road. Park here and sign out at a register located a short distance beyond. Recent climbing activity and conditions are usually documented here. From the register continue up Lee Vining Creek for about 300 yards before crossing the creek to the north side. After about a quarter mile, recross the creek and continue up the narrow canyon for about twenty minutes. The climbs will appear on the wall to the left.

Only the heaviest snowfall years make skis with climbing skins a practical necessity for the approach. Because of the blocky talus found on parts of the approach, snowshoes are generally more useful. If there hasn't been any recent snowfall, a trail will probably be broken, making the approach easier. Allow about an hour for the approach from the power station to the climbs.

There are three main icefalls in the canyon. The middle one has the greatest volume of ice and is the only one that forms in a dry year. The left fall usually forms two columns at the base and is both the most difficult and tallest. It may be done in two pitches but most people break it into three. Five different routes may be done here. Fixed rock anchors will be found at the top. The middle fall is one long pitch and has three possible routes. Take tie off slings for the anchors. Two one-pitch routes can be done on the right fall; slings are required for anchors. Ice screws are needed for protection on all routes. Directly across the canyon from the middle fall is some lower angle ice that is good for beginners or practice soloing. Many other falls form in very good ice years, however, but these are seldom seen and quite difficult.

JUNE LAKE

The ice climbing at June Lake is better for beginner or intermediate ice climbers though some difficult climbing may be found. To approach the climbs, turn off Highway 395 onto the June Lake Loop and follow the road through the town to the winter snow closure at the Edison power station complex. The first area is straight down the snow-covered road and on the left. Several short mixed rock and ice variations may be led or top roped. To set up a top rope, climb a narrow snow gully to the right of the climbs.

The main route, called Horsetail Falls, may be approached by walking through the power station and finding the old wooden pentstock tram track which follows the Agnew Lake Creek drainage. Hike up this for half a mile and cut left (south) to this 200- foot climb. It averages 55° with some steeper sections. A more difficult route will be found by cutting right (north) from the pentstock at about the same place and hiking up through the forest. A 225-foot icefall will be found that averages 65°, with one section of 85°.

Another area, Dream Mountain, can be found by parking a quarter mile before the power station and walking straight west through the trees for a minute. A short 20-foot wall exists here with many steep variations for soloing or top roping.

FIRST ASCENTS

Alabama Hills
KRUGERRANDS: Dave Kruger, et al
ROCKY TOP: Gary Slate, Dennis Jensen
BODACIOUS: G. Slate, D. Jensen
SOUTHERN GIRLS: G. Slate, D. Jensen
RADAR RODEOS: G. Slate, D. Jensen
BLOCKADE RUNNER: D. Kruger FFA: Marty Hornick
SEGREGATION: unknown
SWEET HOME ALABAMA: unknown
DARK TOWER: G. Slate, D. Jensen
SWEET HOME ARIZONA: Mike Lawson, Bobbi Bensman

WHITNEY PORTAL

Bastille Buttress
BASTILLE ROUTE: Fred Beckey, Eric Bjørnstad

Candlelight Buttress
EAT YOUR GREENS: Steve Plunkett, Errett Allen
PRO BOWLERS TOUR: S. Plunkett, E. Allen
TWO LANE BLACKTOP: S. Plunkett, E. Allen, Gary Slate
FAMOUS AUTHORS: Alan Bartlett, E. Allen
BO BO'S BONANZA: G. Slate, E. Allen
STRESS MANAGEMENT: Alex Schmauss, Charlie Johnson
NO PIE ALA MODE: Darrell Hensel, Kevin Powell
NERVOUS HABITS: Alex Schmauss, Charlie Johnson (9/87)
MOE'S LIQUORS: Bob Finn, E. Allen
MR. GREEN JEANS: Kevin Powell, Darrell Hensel (9/85)
DINTY MOORE: Dave Scott, Colin Chambers (9/85)
MULLIGAN STEW: Kevin Powell, D. Hensel (9/85)

Whitney Portal Buttress
ORIGINAL ROUTE: Fred Beckey, Pat Callis (5/67)
SARTORIS: Alan Bartlett, Dave Black, Steve Eddy (7/76)
WONDERWALL: A. Bartlett Jack Roberts (6/79)
CLOUDS: A. Bartlett, Bob Harrington (11/83)
NIMBUS: Gary Slate, Errett Allen (4/87)

Moonstone Buttress
MOONCHILD: G. Slate, D. Jensen, John Aughinbaugh
TYCHO: G. Slate, E. Allen (4/87)
VENUS: G. Slate D. Jensen
PLEIADES: G. Slate, E. Allen (5/87)
CORPUS CHRISTI BUTTRESS: A. Bartlett, G. Slate, Fred Beckey (4/84)

El Segundo Buttress
ORIGINAL ROUTE: Fred Beckey, Mike Heath (3/71), FFA: Dean Hobbs, Will Crljenko (2/ 77)
TOO LOOSE TO TREK: Jack Roberts, Alan Roberts, Mark Menge (10/78)
BRAINSTORM: A. Bartlett, Bob Harrington (5/78)

Premier Buttress
PREMIER ROUTE: Fred Beckey, Brian Goechel (11/68), FFA: unknown
THE PHOENIX: Don Reid, A. Bartlett (3/77)

Solstice Celebration
TOOTH DECAY: A. Bartlett, D. Jensen (5/87)
BARN DANCE: A. Bartlett, D. Jensen (5/87)
SOLSTICE CELEBRATION: G. Slate, E. Allen (12/86)

Roadwork Wall:
OUT ON A LIMB: E. Allen, A. Bartlett, Steve Plunkett (2/87)
MADE IN THE SHADE: Alex Schmauss, Charlie Johnson (3/87)
CERRO GORDO: G. Slate, A. Bartlett, James Wilson (4/87)
MANZANAR: A. Bartlett, Steve Plunkett, E. Allen (2/87)
MOJAVE: G. Slate, Tony Puppo
ASPHALT JUNGLE: E. Allen, Chris Lindell
SIERRA WAVE: A. Bartlett, G. Slate, Kim Walker (4/87)
SHERWIN GRADE: A. Bartlett, Katie Wilkinson (5/87)
ROADWORK: Kevin Calder, E. Allen
SO MUCH BAGGAGE: Darrell Hensel, Kevin Powell, Margie Floyd, Dave Evans, Paula Phillips, Rob Raker (9/86)
MOONSHADOW: Darrell Hensel, Kevin Powell (9/86)
RTE. 395: Marty Lewis, S. Plunkett, E. Allen
HUEVOS POQUITOS Ron Overholtz, Jim Endo, Eric Hein
CARTAGO: Marty Lewis, E. Allen
EASY BLACK MAMA: R. Overholtz, E. Hein
SPEEDTRAP: Kevin Calder, E. Allen
SKIDMARK: K. Calder, E. Allen
SOFT SHOULDER: K. Calder, E. Allen
ROADKILL: K. Calder

El Gaucho
INFIDELS: G. Slate, A. Bartlett, Kim Walker (4/87)
CINCO DIEZ SI: G. Slate, E. Allen
GAY CABALLERO: Jim May, Steve Plunkett, E. Allen
PUPPY WOOF: Chris Lindell, Kymm Lindell
OMERS ROUTE: Scott Cole, G. Slate, E. Allen
ROOM FOR IMPROVEMENT: R. Overholtz, E. Hein
EL DIABLO: Darrell Hensel, Colin Chanbers
EL GAUCHO: D. Hensel, K. Powell, Dane Scott (9/85)
EL BOLO: G. Slate, E. Allen
CUBAN SLIDE: A. Bartlett, G. Slate, E. Allen (11/86)
CARA DE ORO: G. Slate, A. Bartlett, John Aughinbaugh (3/87)
FRIGIDAIRE: G. Slate, J. Aughinbaugh
DELERIOUS: G. Slate, J. Aughinbaugh
WAY BENT: A. Bartlett, Robert Davis (5/87)

Dynamic Duo:
DYNAMIC DUO: G. Slate, J. Aughinbaugh
STAGE FRIGHT: G. Slate, A. Bartlett (3/87)
STEEL DRIVIN' MAN: G. Slate, A. Bartlett, Tony Puppo
STINKFOOT: G. Slate, J. Aughinbaugh
STEEL DRIVIN' BLUES: Slate, Joe Rousek
TANGO TOWER: A. Bartlett, J. Aughinbaugh (8/87)

The Whale

BONY FINGERS: G. Slate, J. Aughinbaugh, (direct start) G. Slate, Jeff White, Leona Mukai
BARNACLE BILL: Dennis Jensen, G. Slate, Sandy Redman
APLOMB: Rob Muir, Tony Condon
DANCING ON THE EDGE: Urmas Franosch, G. Slate
FAMOUS POTATOES: G. Slate, J. Aughinbaugh

Pool Hall Wall

CORNER POCKET: A. Bartlett, S. Plunkett, E. Allen (2/87)
BLACKBALL: A. Bartlett, Kevin Calder (12/86)
BLUEBALLS: S. Plunkett, E. Allen (12/86)
SNOOKER: A. Bartlett, S. Plunkett, E. Allen (2/87)
MARVIN GARDENS: A. Bartlett, Tony Puppo (4/87)
CRACK ADDICT: Kevin Calder, A. Bartlett (12/86)
PORTALEDGE: Joe Rousek, J. Aughinbaugh

South Lake Area

CHIMNEY CRICKET: A. Bartlett, J. Aughinbaugh (10/86)
ORANGE PEEL: A. Bartlett, J. Aughinbaugh (10/86)
DERILICTS DELIGHT: A. Bartlett, Rick Wheeler (9/79)
TWO FINGERS: A. Bartlett, Robb Dellinger (9/79)
PEACH JAM: A. Bartlett, Rick Wheeler (9/79)
BRITISH CHIMNEY: Bill St. Jean, Tom Fox, Rod Pashley
STRAWBERRY JAM: unknown
BILLY'S PILLAR-LEFT: Bill St. Jean, Rick Wheeler
BILLY'S PILLAR-RIGHT: Bill St. Jean, Roger Breedlove
THIN MAN: A. Bartlett, Tony Puppo (5/78)
STEMS AND SEEDS: A. Bartlett, T. Puppo (5/78)
WILD ROSE: Kevin Leary (5/78)
BOB-BOB-A-RAMP: T. Puppo, Paul Brown
BOBCRACK: Kevin Leary, Bob Harrington (5/78)
SPIRAL STAIRCASE: unknown
SLOT MACHINE: A. Bartlett, Allan Pietrasanta (10/85)
STRONGER THAN DIRT: A. Bartlett, A. Pietrasanta (5/85)
BLOCKHEAD: A. Bartlett, Bob Bartlett, Shari Schubot (7/85)
FLAKED OUT: James Wilson, Bill St. Jean
THE SHYSTER: Dean Hobbs, Alan Roberts (1982)

Cardinal Pinnacle

V-8 CRACK: Dean Hobbs (1974), FFA: Mike Graber, Mike Farrell, Rick Wheeler (1976)
WILD KINGDOM: D. Hobbs, Andy Selters
MARLON PERKINS: Kevin Leary, Rick Thomas
CRACK OF NO HOPE: Doug Robinson, Jay Jenson
ROMANCING THE STONE: D. Hobbs, Russ McClean, FFA: D. Hobbs, Steve Mankenberg
CARDINAL SIN: Tony Puppo, Paul Brown
I HEARD IT THROUGH THE GRAPEVINE: Mike Pope, Bobbi Bensman
TAN, DON'T BURN: Joe Rousek, Tony Puppo
THE PROW: Gordon Wiltsie, Jay Jenson, FFA: (pitch 3) Dale Bard
REACH FOR THE SKY: D. Hobbs, A. Bartlett
PLIGHT OF PARTED LOVERS: Gary Slate, Rick Thomas
SHADOWS IN THE RAIN: G. Slate, Rick Thomas
ARTICHOKE: FA unknown, FFA: Kevin Leary, Joe Rousek
REDLINE: G. Slate, D. Hobbs, Jeff White
CUCUMBERS: Doug Robinson, Dennis Hennek
RED BUSH: D. Hobbs, FFA: unknown
WHERE EAGLES DARE: D. Hobbs, T. Puppo

REGULAR ROUTE: D. Robinson, Lester Robertson, Curt Foote (1969)
DAG STYLE: Dag Kolsrud, Hank Levine ('81)
NO BOZOS: Bob Harrington, A. Bartlett
AGRARIAN REFORM: D. Hobbs, Richard Cilley
GLASS HOUSES: D. Hobbs, A. Roberts
STONES THROW: T. Puppo, Alan Roberts

Little Egypt
DOG DAY AFTERNOON: Dag Kolsrud (tr 1981), Claude Fiddler (lead 1986)
EXPRESSO: Kevin Leary (tr 1977), Vern Clevenger (lead 1986)
HIEROGLYPHICS: D. Hobbs, T. Puppo (1982)
FLIGHT: D. Hobbs, A. Roberts
CLASSIC CRACK: A. Bartlett, Bill St. Jean, Robb Dellinger (5/77)
THE GUTTER: D. Hobbs, A. Roberts
4 THOSE ABOUT 2 ROCK: Dale Bard
ROSETTA STONE: A. Bartlett, B. Harrington, T. Puppo (4/84)
CANNIBAL: K. Leary, J. Rousek (1977)
DECAF: K. Leary, B. Harrington (5/84)
PYRAMID POWER: A. Bartlett, Katie Wilkinson (4/85)
KING TUTS TOMB: Rick Thomas, et al
JAMMING WITH JANE: D. Hobbs, Jane Sievert
CARAVANS: A. Bartlett, D. Hobbs, T. Puppo, Janet Wilts, Lidija Painkiher (3/85)
ARABESQUE: D. Hobbs, Grant Hiskes, Scott Cole
LAST ROUTE: unknown
COFFEE BEAN: A. Bartlett, Dave Field (10/85)
ROUTE IN EXILE: D. Hobbs, et al
EXPLODING CRYSTAL GALAXY: B. Harrington, A. Bartlett (5/84)
EASY WAY OUT: D. Hobbs, et al
DEATH IN THE AFTERNOON: Richard Cilley, et al

The Buttermilks
SCOOT: Rick Wheeler, et al(1977)
HOLY SMOKES: Alan Bartlett, John Aughinbaugh, Bobbi Bensman (1/86)
ANAPHYLACTIC FREAKOUT: Grant Hiskes, Bob Finn, Ken Yager
WILD GARLIC: Grant Hiskes, Ken Yager
STALL WALL: Grant Hiskes, Ken Yager
RUBBER GLOVES AND RAZOR BLADES: Grant Hiskes, Ken Yager
CLEAN SWEEP: Grant Hiskes, Ken Yager
DR. DETROIT: G. Hiskes, K. Yager
ZYME: G. Hiskes, K. Yager
ALLSPICE: G. Hiskes, K. Yager
CAYENNE PEPPER: Marylyne Weisner, G. Hiskes, K. Yager
MILES FROM NOWHERE: Gary Slate (solo)
WAVELENGTH: Dale Bard (tr), Doug Nidever (lead)
MORTICIA: G. Hiskes, et al
THE TEMPEST: G. Hiskes et al
PUGSLY: G. Hiskes et al
UNCLE FESTER: G. Hiskes, et al
LISA'S CRAC K: G. Hiskes et al
SPITOON: E. Allen, Jim Yost
BUTTERMILK PANCAKES: G. Hiskes, K. Yager, Marylyn Weisner
GRANOLA: A. Bartlett, Katie Wilkenson (2/85)
DUNE: A. Bartlett, John Aughinbaugh (2/86)
FREEDOM OF CHOICE: G. Hiskes, Dean Hobbs
MY BEACH, MY WAVE: D. Hobbs, Rick Ackerman
WEEKEND WARRIORS: unknown

MIRACLES OF MODERN SCIENCE: D. Hobbs, Rick Ackerman
WIDE BERTH: D. Hobbs, R. Ackerman
SEAN'S TOPROPE: Sean Plunkett
REGULAR ROUTE: unknown
EXTREME LEVINE MEETS GODZILLA: D. Hobbs, Andy Selters,
VERTICAL SMILES: D. Hobbs, Alan Roberts
WAY COOL TANKS: Gary Slate, Sean Plunkett
ARMADILLO CRACK: Doug Robinson, et al
DAYDREAM: unknown
DEAN'S DREAM: Paul Neil, Hank Levine
MACHO HOMO: Bill Russell, Sean Plunkett
ROBBINS CRACK: unknown
SLAB DIRECT: D. Hobbs
SLAB, REGULAR ROUTE: Dave Sharp, Tex Mock
BEARFIGHT: unknown
GREAT BUTTERMILK CRACK: Tom Herbert, Tony Puppo
NO FAT CHICKS: J. Aughinbaugh, Shane Laidlaw
HOT MAPLE SYRUP: G. Slate, Sean Plunkett
RUMPADOODLE: James Wilson (1977)
BECAUSE IT'S THERE: A. Bartlett, Katie Wilkenson (10/87)
STOP SMOKING SENSE: Kevin Calder, Marty Lewis
MIKEY LIKES IT: J. Wilson, Bill St. Jean (1977)
FAITH: Tom Herbert (12/87)
WHY LEFT: T. Herbert, J. Aughinbaugh, Shelley Presson (11/87)
WHY RIGHT: J. Aughinbaugh, Shane Laidlaw (10/87)
THE CLAW: Bill Denton, Dave Sharp (1969)
SPACE COWBOYS: Hobbs, Andy Selters (1983)

Wheeler Crest
FLY ON A WINDSHIELD: Randy Jewett, Eddie Joe (9/81)
DON'T FOLLOW CLAY: R. Jewett, Clay Cutter, Steve Beard (7/83)
GREAT ESCAPE: A. Bartlett, Kim Walker (3/78)
GATEWAY TO MADNESS: Dean Hobbs, Dan Chitty
HEARTHSTONE: A. Bartlett, Allan Pietrasanta (6/82)
SMOKESTACK: Doug Robinson, Galen Rowell
ADAM'S RIB: D. Robinson, G. Rowell, Chuck Kroeger
EVE'S WANG: Bob Harrington, D. Hobbs, Randy Jewett
BIG BROTHER: A. Bartlett, Allan Pietrasanta (1/84)
WELLS PEAK, EAST FACE: A. Bartlett, Fred Beckey, Jack Roberts (2/74)
DECEMBER'S CHILDREN: A. Bartlett, James Wilson (12/77)
NORTH RIDGE: John Fischer, Jay Jensen
GRABER-ROWELL RTE. : Mike Graber, Galen Rowell (12/79)
STORMY PETREL: Fred Beckey, Bryce Simon, John Feder (5/82)
LEARY-TAYLOR RTE. : Kevin Leary, Bill Taylor
GROWLER: K. Leary, Bob Harrington, Joe Rousek (5/78)
SORRY CHARLIE: A. Bartlett, Bob Harrington, Will Crijenko (5/78)
VIOLET GREEN: Bob Harrington, James Wilson (6/78)
OPEN BOOK: Galen Rowell, David Belden (2/76) FFA: A. Bartlett, B. Harrington (4/78)
STARKISSED: J. Wilson, Kim Walker, Paul Brown (6/78)
SARGASSO: A. Bartlett, Tony Puppo (4/78)
CHICKEN OF THE SEA: Galen Rowell, Chris Vandiver
KNOB JOB: B. Harrington, W. Crljenko (1978)
CHICKEN DELIGHT: R. Wheeler, J. Wilson (1978)
EL PINKO: A. Bartlett, Bob Bartlett, Dave Field (5/81)
JOHN BIRCH SOCIETY: R. Wheeler, Bill St. Jean

EAST FACE RTE. : G. Rowell, Chris Vandiver
B.S. SPECIAL: Mike Strassman, Bobbi Bensman
FAULT LINE: A. Bartlett, Randy Jewett (1/86)
BASTARD: Allan Pietrasanta, Bill St. Jean
FEAR ITSELF: A. Bartlett, Tony Puppo (6/82)
THE GAMBLER : A. Bartlett, T. Puppo (1/86)
SHORT STREET: A. Bartlett, Bob Bartlett (10/83)
OCEAN VIEW AVENUE: A. Bartlett, Bob Bartlett (10/83)
FRED FLINTSTONE: J. Wilson, T. Puppo (4/80)
BARNEY RUBBLE : A. Bartlett, Bill St. Jean (4/80)
HANNA-BARBARA: A. Bartlett, Will Crijenko (4/80)
YABBA-DABBA-DOO: A. Bartlett, T. Puppo, Ron Overholtz (4/80)
TWIST AND CRAWL: J. Wilson, B. Harrington
BIG GRAY, EAST FACE: Galen Rowell, David Belden (11/75)
WEARY LEADER: R. Wheeler, Kevin Leary (5/78)
LITTLE GRAY, EAST FACE: A. Bartlett, Bill St. Jean (4/80)
LEARY-PHILLIPS ROUTE: K. Leary, Dennis Phillips
BOTANIST'S HOLIDAY: B. Harrington, W. Crljenko (12/78)
MR. GREEN GENES: A. Bartlett, A. Pietrasanta, Dave Field (10/83)
X-CRACK: Art Hanon, K. Leary
S-CRACK: Art Hanon, K. Leary

Scheelite (Pine Creek Canyon)
INCREASED INSANITY: A. Bartlett, J. Aughinbaugh
NO FUTURE: A. Bartlett, J. Aughinbaugh
OVERHANG BYPASS: A. Bartlett, Mark Herndon (11/86)
FLASH OR CRASH: Tom Herbert, A. Bartlett, Alan Roberts
SQUARE MEAL: Dean Hobbs, et al (1974)
STAR SEARCH: Tom Herbert, A. Roberts, A. Bartlett
MYSTERY NOVEL: unknown
TOXIC SHOCK: A. Bartlett, M. Herndon (11/86)
TRIPLE JEOPARDY: D. Hobbs, et al(1979)
OKTOBERFEST: A. Bartlett, et al(10/85)
MASTER OF THE OBSCURE: D. Hobbs, Dan Chitty
ILL WIND: A. Bartlett, Bob Bartlett, Randy Jewett (9/84)
INSTANT INSANITY: A. Bartlett, Shari Schubot (6/85)
NEWLYWED GAME: Dave Field, Gail Wilts, Alan Bartlett (10/85)
TOPLESS DANCER: Alan Bartlett, Randy Jewett (5/85)
KEINE ROUTE: Helmut Keine, et al(1972)
INYO FACE: Bob Harrington (1986)
BWANNA DIK: unknown, FFA: A. Bartlett, T. Puppo, R. Overholtz (12/78)
ARMANDO'S STILLETTO: unknown
QUIVERING THIGHS: A. Bartlett, R. Wheeler, FFA: B. Harrington
ANOTHER SUMMER: B. Harrington, D. Bard
RITE OF SPRING: K. Leary, B. Taylor
WRONGS OF SPRING: J. Wilson, B. Harrington
PRATT'S CRACK: Chuck Pratt, Bob Swift
SHIELA: Joe Herbst, Jay Jensen
LITTLE PINNACLE: Smoke Blanchard
NICE GUYS FINISH LAST: D. Hobbs, Andy Selters
PSOM PINNACLE: John Fischer et al
PSOM PINNACLE DIRECT: B. Harrington, A. Bartlett, B. Bartlett, H. Levine (5/84)
BIG CHILL: A. Bartlett, Shari Schubot (10/84)
ELDERBERRY BUTTRESS REGULAR ROUTE: Doug Robinson, Lester Robertson
APPOLONIA: T. Puppo, A. Bartlett (9/84)

IN DUBIOUS BATTLE: A. Bartlett, J. Wilson, Paul Brown (11/77)
JOINT EFFORT: R. Wheeler, Mike Graber, A. Bartlett (10/77)
THIN ICE: A. Bartlett, R. Wheeler, J. Wilson (1/77)
MINI-MART: A. Bartlett. Bob Bartlett (1/84)
CATHOLIC BOY: A. Bartlett, T. Puppo, K. Wilkenson (3/84)
ELEVENTH COMMANDMENT: A. Bartlett, Gail Wilts (9/87)
FOOTLOOSE: Gary Slate, A. Bartlett (11/86)
PCB ROUTE: G. Slate, A. Bartlett (11/86)
ST. VALENTINES DAY MASSACRE: A. Bartlett, T. Puppo Katie Wilkenson (2/84)
LAUNDROMAT: A. Bartlett, Paul Brown, FFA: G. Slate, Errett Allen
SPIN CYCLE: E. Allen, G. Slate (10/86)
BEEDIE BOYS: A. Pietrasanta, John Fischer, Gordon Wiltsie
CRACKS CROSS: Gordon Wiltsie, Jay Jensen
SAGEBRUSH SERANADE: A. Bartlett, Shane Laidlaw (9/87)
THE RATTLER: A. Bartlett, J. Aughinbaugh, S. Laidlaw (8/87)

Rock Creek
UNGRACIOUS AND INCONSIDERATE: Joe Rousek, Jim Stimson
AEROBICS: Alan Bartlett, Robb Dellinger
BROKEN ARROW: A. Bartlett, R. Dellinger
THE MAGNUS: Mike Strassman, Scott Ayers
CLEAN SLATE: M. Strassman, Alex Schmauss
SCOOT SCOOT: M. Strassman, S. Ayers
40 FEET OF 5. 7: M. Strassman, S. Ayers
DAKNUCKLEHEAD: M. Strassman, Paul Linaweaver
DECLINE OF WESTERN CIVILIZATION: Richard Cilley
THE GONG SHOW: Kevin Leary, Art Hanon
THE D.M.Z.: Jim Stimson, et al
SOCIAL CLIMBER: Richard Cilley
LAST EXIT: Dale Bard, Tony Puppo
OVEREXPOSURE: unknown
BRUSH UP: A. Bartlett, T. Puppo
THE BONG SHOW: unknown
ROOTS IN THE SKY: Dean Hobbs, Alan Roberts
HOLIDAY IN CAMBODIA: R. Cilley, D. Hobbs
LOST BUTTRESS: A. Roberts, D. Hobbs
CHOCOLATE CHIPS: D. Hobbs, A. Roberts, Gary Slate
QUEST FOR FIRE: A. Roberts, D. Hobbs
GOLDEN LOCKS: D. Hobbs, A. Roberts
BOBBING FOR POODLES: D. Hobbs, A. Roberts
AEROBICS IN HELL: ZD. Hobbs, A. Roberts
IRIS SLAB ROUTES: unknown
GUANO C RACKS: A. Bartlett, Ron Overholtz
TERROR OF TINYTOWN: A. Bartlett, R. Overholtz
EASY STREET: A. Roberts, Joe Rousek
VOICES IN THE SKY: J. Rousek, A. Roberts
MOOLAR THE LLAMA J. Rousek, A. Roberts
KIDDIE CORNER: A. Roberts, J. Rousek
ALCOVE CRACKS: R. Overholtz, A. Bartlett

Mammoth Lakes Area
ANAEROBIA: Kevin Leary
LITTLE ARCHIE: Gary Slate
SPINACH PATCH: G. Slate
G. S. SPECIAL: G. Slate

T. J. SWAN: unknown
MYER'S CRACK: unknown
905: G. Slate
BUFFALO CHIPS: Chuck Cochrane, Bob Finn
SKI CRACKS: Ken Yager, Bob Finn
REAGANOMICS: Scott Cole, Bob, the scuba diving instructor
GUNBOAT DIPLOMACY: S. Cole, Chuck Satterfield

Crystal Crag
NORTH ARETE: unknown
NORTHEAST BUTTRESS: Vern Clevenger, Bill Dougherty
EAST FACE RIGHT: V. Clevenger, Galen Rowell
EAST FACE LEFT: Greg Donaldson, Chuck Calef

The Dike Wall
MR. KAMAKAZE:
MR. DNA:
SATTERFIELD CORNER: Chuck Satterfield
DICHOTOMY: Urmas Franosch
STRAP ON TOOLS: Urmas Franosch
BLACK LEATHER: Urmas Franosch, Errett Allen
VALLEY BOYS: Dmitri Barton, Roland Arsons
LESBIE FRIENDS: Urmas Franosch
MAMMOTH BOYS: Scott Burke
GOING BOTH WAYS: Urmas Franosch
DOUBLE ENDER: Urmas Franosch, E. Allen
DOMINATRIX: Urmas Franosch, Scott Cole
NO ERECTION NEEDED: Urmas Franosch, Scott Cole

Rainbow Wall
GUILLOTINE: Dennis Jensen, Alex Schmauss
HALL OF BRUSHES: Alex Schmauss, Charlie Johnson
CURARIE: Joe Rousek, Tony Puppo
LEFT WISHBONE: Alex Schmauss, Charlie Johnson
RIGHT WISHBONE: Alex Schmauss, Charlie Johnson
MOSSCULAR: Joe Rousek, Tony Puppo
SPECTRUM: Dennis Jensen, John Aughinbaugh
SORRY JOE: D. Jensen, J. Aughinbaugh
LOVE STUCK: D. Jensen, J. Aughinbaugh
LOVE STRUCK: J. Rousek, Anne Mullier

The Stumps
ORANGE ZIGZAG: Grant Hiskes, Ken Yager, Marylyn Wiesner, Errett Allen
KNUCKLE NUTZ: G. Hiskes, K. Yager, M. Wiesner
ROLL UM EASY: E. Allen, G. Yager, K. Yager, M. Wiesner
FREE BURNING: G. Hiskes, K. Yager, M. Wiesner
CALDERS KNOBS: Kevin Calder et al
SPEARHEAD ARETE: G. Hiskes, K. Yager
RAT RACE: K. Yager, G. Hiskes
VERTABRAE: K. Yager, Dave Schultz
DR. STRANGELOVE: K. Yager, G. Hiskes
SLIM PICKENS: K. Yager, G. Hiskes
GIVE A HOOT: Marylyn Wiesner, Errett Allen
SMILING FACES: G. Hiskes, Sean Plunkett, E. Allen
WHOOP-WHOOP-ROOF: Neil Newcomb, Bill Tretheway, Dan Robbins
H&R BLOCK: G. Hiskes, K. Yager

CURLY SHUFFLE: K. Yager, G. Hiskes, Sean Plunkett
FOREST SERVICE: unknown
CORNER MARKET: unknown
GOOD & PLENTY: K. Yager, E. Allen
E.Z. MONEY: K. Yager, E. Allen

Deadmans/Natural Areas
BLOCK AND TACKLE; Dale Bard
BULLDOG: John Bachar
GOLDILOCKS: Grant Hiskes, Ken Yager
HANSEL AND GRETEL; G. Hiskes, K. Yager

June Lake Area
THREE POPS: Rick Mosher et al
CLING OR SPRING: Doug Nidever
FIRE FIRE: D. Nidever

Granite Basin Area
PREPARE TO QUALIFY; M. Strassman, Scott Ayers
FLIP: M. Strassman
KINDA NOW. . .: M. Strassman, P. Linaweaver
GAY 4-WHEELERS CLUB: M. Strassman, P. Linaweaver
DIHEDRAL: unknown
UPSTAIRS LOUNGE: M. Strassman, Alex Schmauss
P-FUNK AMERIKA: Mike Strassman, Paul Linaweaver
WILD EYRIE: M. Strassman, Chris Lindell
BETTY WHITE. . .: unknown
NIPSY RUSSELL. . .: M. Strassman, P. Linaweaver
KITTY CARLISLE. . .: unknown
SPUDS GURGLING COCK HOLSTER: M. Strassman John Sherman
MINNESOTTA MISCHIEF: M. Strassman, Dan McConnel
TO BUOUX OR NOT TO BE: M. Strassman, Scott Ayers
STEPPIN'STONE: M. Strassman, Chris Bishop
HAIR RAISER BUTTRESS; Vern Clevenger, Tom Higgins
CLEVENGER ROUTE: Vern Clevenger, Dennis Hennek, Galen Rowell
ALL ALONG THE WATCHTOWER: M. Strassman, A. Schmauss, Tim Noonan
FIREFALL: unknown
THE WANDERER: unknown
GRUNT MOUNTAIN: M. Strassman, S. Ayers
DEADLINE: unknown
GRAPE NUTS: M. Strassman, Craig Broderick
FROSTED FLAKES: M. Strassman, Wendy Borgerd
NEVER MIND THE BOLLOCKS: Alan Bartlett, M. Strassman
POST NASAL DRIP: M. Strassman, Chris Lindell
ARCHIE ANDREWS: unknown
THE TUBE: Chris Lindell
DICK VAN DYKE: Mike Strassman, Wendy, Scott Ayers

North Canyon Area
AMERICAN HERO: Vern Clevenger, Lydija Painkiher, Grant Hiskes, Urmas Franosch, Gary Slate
LAMB CHOP: Ken Yager, Grant Hiskes
HELIX: Gary Slate, Errett Allen
OLLIE NORTH: Grant Hiskes, Ken Yager
WHAT-ME-WORRY?: G. Slate, Alan Bartlett
THE SHREDDER: Lydija Painkiher, Vern Clevenger

Dexter Canyon Area

STEEPLECHASE: Gary Slate, Errett Allen (4/85)
SANDMAN: Fred Feldman, E. Allen (4/85)
CELL BLOCK: E. Allen, Scott Cole (5/85)
SANDBAG: Ken Yager, E. Allen (8/84)
VAPOR LOCK: K. Yager, E. Allen (4/85)
A DOLLAR SHORT: G. Slate, E. Allen
LIZARD CRACK: G. Slate, E. Allen (5/85)
ROAD WARRIOR: G. Slate Jeff White
SHORT CHANGED: G. Slate, E. Allen (5/85)
SHORT STROKE: Scott Cole, Fred Feldman, E. Allen (4/85)
SPRING FLING: Ken Yager, Grant Hiskes
DOOR INTO SUMMER: E. Allen S. Cole, F. Feldman (4/85)
FIRE AND ICE: S. Cole, G. Hiskes, F. Feldman, E. Allen (4/85)
STAR BEAST: F. Feldman, E. Allen (4/85)
ORPHANS OF THE SKY: Fred Feldman, E. Allen (4/85)
FORBIDDEN PLANET: Gary Slate, E. Allen
B.C.: F. Feldman, E. Allen (4/85)
CLARK KENT: Ken Yager, E. Allen (10/84), Variation: K. Yager, Grant Hiskes
TUMBLEWEEDS: K. Yager, E. Allen (10/85)
STALACTITE: G. Slate, E. Allen
FOGHORN LEGHORN: K. Yager, Marylyn Weisner, E. Allen (5/85)
GRANDPA'S CHALLENGE: Dave Yerian, E. Allen
YOSEMITE SAM: K. Yager, E. Allen (10/84)
DAGWOOD: K. Yager, E. Allen (10/84)
GUTTER BALL: K. Yager, Al Swanson (8/87)
BOWLING FOR KEEPS: Dave Schultz, K. Yager, G. Slate
UP YOUR ALLEY: K. Yager, E. Allen (6/85)
CANTALOUPE: G. Slate, Dave Schultz, K. Yager
HONORABLE DISCHARGE: K. Yager, Marylyn Weisner (10/85)

Benton Crags

THE TUBE: Jon-Mark Baker, Sean Plunkett
PIPELINE: Sean Plunkett, Errett Allen, Scott Cole (5/83)
LOCALS ONLY: S. Cole, E. Allen, Stan VonMarbod (5/83)
GET LOST: E. Allen, S. Cole, Stan VonMarbod (5/83)
NO TRESSPASSING: E. Allen, Steve Kabala (6/83)
SURFIN' SAFARI: S. Cole E. Allen, S. VonMarbod (5/83)
TOUGH MUFFIN: S. Cole, E. Allen (6/83)
LOW CALORIE: Ken Yager, E. Allen
JIMMY JONES: Fred Feldman, E. Allen
CALIGULA: F. Feldman, E. Allen
PSYCHO KILLER: Kevin Calder, Marty Lewis
HILLSIDE STRANGLER: Jim Yost, E. Allen (6/83)
PSYCHO CHICKEN: unfinished
MDR: Grant Hiskes
SCRAMBLED EGGS: Jim Yost, Errett Allen (11/83)
BIT-O-HONEY: Marty Lewis, Kevin Calder, E. Allen
POST TOASTIES: Scott Cole (6/83)
WHEATIES: S. Cole (6/83)
HIGH WEED GLUTTIN: Bob Finn, Scott Burke (6/83)
GRANOLA CRUNCH: S. Burk, Bob McLaughlin (6/83)
FROSTED FLAKES: E. Allen, S. Cole, S. Burke (6/83)
POPS: E. Allen, Stan VonMarbod (6/83)
KIKS: E. Allen, Stan VonMarbod (6/83)

CREAM OF WHEAT: Fred Feldman, E. Allen (7/83)
MAGICALLY DELICIOUS: S. Cole, Connie, E. Allen (6/83)
LUCKY CHARMS: E. Allen, S. Cole (5/83)
GRAPE NUTZ: Mark Yingst, E. Allen
WHEATEENA: M. Yingst, E. Allen
ATTENTION SPAN: Fred Feldman, Marylyn Wiesner, Ken Yager, E. Allen (6/83)
NEANDERTHAL: S. Cole, E. Allen Sean Plunkett (6/83)
DR. LEAKY: S. Cole, E. Allen, Jim Yost (6/83)
LUCY: Fred Feldman, S. Cole (6/83)
AUSTRALOPITHICUS: S. Cole (6/83), variation: Roland Arsons, Dave Griffth (1987)
SLITHER: Fred Feldman, E. Allen
POACHER: Steve Snyder, Kevin Calder (1/86)
CHALLENGER: S. Snyder, K. Calder, E. Allen (1/86)
COMPETITIVE EDGE: Grant Hiskes, Ken Yager, Sean Plunkett
KING SNAKE FLAKES: E. Allen, Ken Yager (10/83)
RUNNING SCARED: Tom Herbert, Alan Bartlett (10/87)
LIZARD: F. Feldman, E. Allen

APPENDIX

Phone List
For any Emergency, dial 911
Area code for all the following numbers is (619)
Mono County Sheriff: Bridgeport, 932-7549
Mammoth Lakes, 934-6058
Inyo County Sheriff: Bishop, 872-7361
Independence, 878-2441
Lone Pine, 876-5606

Guide Services
Alpine Expeditions
Box 1751
Bishop, CA 93514
phone: 873-5617

Palisade School Of Mountaineering
Box 694
Bishop, CA 93514
phone: 873-5037

Shops
MAMMOTH LAKES

Mammoth Sporting Goods
Sierra Centre Mall
Mammoth Lakes, CA 93546
phone: 934-3239

Wheeler and Wilson Sports
Main Street – Village Center West
Mammoth Lakes, CA 93546
phone: 934-3773

BISHOP
Wheeler and Wilson Sports
206 N. Main Street
Bishop, CA
phone: 873-7520

Buttermilk Mountain Works
2333 A N. Sierra Hwy. (Rt 395)
Bishop, CA 93514
(619) 872-1946

Campgrounds

Areas that are not listed have no convenient developed campgrounds.

ALABAMA HILLS/WHITNEY PORTAL AREAS
Lone Pine Campground (fee required)
Whitney Portal C.G. (fee required)

UPPER BISHOP CREEK
Big Trees C.G. (fee required)
Bishop Park C.G. (fee required)
Forks C.G. (fee required)
Four Jeffery C.G. (fee required)
Mountain Glen C.G. (no fee)
North Lake C.G. (fee required)
Sabrina C.G. (no fee)
Table Mountain C.G. (no fee)
Willow C.G. (no fee)

ROCK CREEK
Rock Creek
Big Meadow C.G. (fee required)
East Fork C.G. (fee required)
French Camp C.G. (fee required)
Holiday C.G. (fee required)
Iris Meadow C.G. (fee required)
Lower Rock Creek C.G. (no fee)
Mosquito Flat C.G. (fee required)
Mosquito Flat Trailhead C.G. (no fee)
Palisade C.G. (fee required)
Pine Creek C.G. (fee required)
Rock Creek Lake C.G. (fee required)

SAGEHEN SUMMIT AREA
Sagehen Meadows C.G. (no fee)

MAMMOTH LAKES VILLAGE
Pine Glen C.G. (fee required)
Shady Rest C.G. (fee required)
Sherwin Creek C.G. (fee required)

MAMMOTH LAKES BASIN
Coldwater C.G. (fee required)
Horseshoe Lake C.G. (fee required)
Lake George C.G. (fee req)
Lake Mary C.G. (fee required)
Pine City C.G. (fee required)
Twin Lakes C.G. (fee required)

REDS MEADOW (Rainbow Wall)
Agnew Meadows C.G. (fee required)
Minaret Falls C.G. (fee required)
Pumice Flat C.G. (fee required)
Reds Meadow C.G. (fee required)
Soda Springs C.G. (fee required)

DEADMANS/NATURAL AREAS
Big Springs C.G. (no fee)
Deadman C.G. (no fee)
Glass Creek C.G. (no fee)
Hartley Springs C.G. (no fee)

JUNE LAKE LOOP
Aerie Crag C.G. (fee required)
Gull Lake C.G. (fee required)
June Lake C.G. (fee required)
Oh! Ridge C.G.(fee required)
Reversed Creek C.G. (fee required)
Silver Lake C.G. (fee required)

INDEX

INDEX

INDEX